Media Freedom
and
Accountability

Recent Titles in
Contributions to the Study of Mass Media and Communications

MEDIA FREEDOM
AND
ACCOUNTABILITY

Edited by

Everette E. Dennis,
Donald M. Gillmor,
and
Theodore L. Glasser

Contributions to the Study of Mass Media
and Communications, Number 14

GREENWOOD PRESS
New York • Westport, Connecticut • London

Library of Congress Cataloging-in-Publication Data

Media freedom and accountability / edited by Everette E. Dennis,
   Donald M. Gillmor, and Theodore L. Glasser.
      p.   cm.—(Contributions to the study of mass media and
   communications, ISSN 0732–4456 ; no. 14)
      Bibliography: p.
      Includes index.
      ISBN 0–313–26727–8 (lib. bdg. : alk. paper)
      1. Mass media—Social aspects—United States.   2. Mass media—
United States—Moral and ethical aspects.   3. Freedom of the press—
United States.   I. Dennis, Everette E.   II. Gillmor, Donald M.
III. Glasser, Theodore Lewis.   IV. Series.
HN90.M3M42   1989
302.23′0973—dc20   89–2148

British Library Cataloguing in Publication Data is available.

Library of Congress Catalog Card Number: 89–2148
ISBN: 0–313–26727–8
ISSN: 0732–4456

First published in 1989

Greenwood Press, Inc.
88 Post Road West, Westport, Connecticut 06881

Printed in the United States of America

∞™

The paper used in this book complies with the
Permanent Paper Standard issued by the National
Information Standards Organization (Z39.48–1984).

10 9 8 7 6 5 4 3 2 1

CONTENTS

INTRODUCTION

Everette E. Dennis and Donald M. Gillmor

Whether, when, and to what extent people should be able to talk back to the mass media is an unresolved question in American life. To some, the franchise of freedom of expression means that people can speak about or criticize any institution—including the press—anytime they choose to do so. Others ask whether that is really so, whether there is any meaningful forum where citizens can make their views about the media known to a large enough audience to make a difference.

While the issue of public comment on the media, sometimes called "the accountability factor" or, simply, feedback, is long-standing, the sense of urgency about it is not. During the 40 plus years since World War II, the mass media have become more central and more powerful than ever before in human history. Their role in public and consumer life is profound, and their ability to help and harm is generally regarded as powerful indeed. It was not always so. There was a time when editors pooh-poohed the alleged power of their editorial voice and when scholars who studied media influence and impact minimized their effects. Now that is less often the case. Media organizations ranging from editors' and broadcasters' groups to corporate owners and researchers across many fields are paying heed to media power and influence. A flurry of studies of media credibility in the 1980s, in the aftermath of the Grenada crisis, put the public view of the press right up there on the public agenda with confidence in Congress, the Supreme Court, big business, and other institutions.

Until recently, those concerned with "talking back" to the media included a few critics, public-spirited citizens and organizational spokespersons. Now that has changed, as programs such as ABC's "Viewpoint" and other efforts often make media feedback the focus of their concern. National studies of some scope and even advertising campaigns by media companies reflect on the public's attitudes toward the media and its confidence in the people who bring news, entertainment, and opinion through print and broadcast outlets.

Still, the discussion of media accountability—which always encounters the freedom guaranteed by the First Amendment, seconded in state constitutions, and ensured in many laws, court decisions, and other official commentary—remains in a conceptual muddle. Although in the United States there are a few ombudsmen at news organizations, one state press council, and a number of fair trial-free press councils, the formal mechanisms for public feedback and criticism are few in number and generally feeble in their effect.

The support for forms of accountability that do not do damage to freedom of the press, however, is substantial. Whether one is interviewing the chief executive officers of major companies or looking at poll data about the press, it is clear that both numbers and noise are on the side of some appropriate approach to public comment and formal feedback.

With that recognition in mind and with deep concern for freedom from censorship, we, the directors of two new institutions—the Gannett Center for Media Studies at Columbia University and the Silha Center for the Study of Media Ethics and Law at the University of Minnesota—conferred and agreed to sponsor a joint inquiry to examine the problems of media freedom and accountability, both at a public forum ("Media Freedom and Accountability," held April 4, 1986, at the Gannett Center) and in a subsequent book. This volume is a partial result of that inquiry as we asked how people talk back to the media, what works, what doesn't, and what's possible.

In our search for a framework, Theodore Glasser of the University of Minnesota offered an initial model that was later refined through discussion. What we tried to do was scope out the various forms of media accountability, ranging from those activities that actually exist to those that are only potential. In this process we identified several arenas for discussion. They include the marketplace model, the self-regulatory model, the voluntary model, the fiduciary model, and the legal model. Finally, we also wanted to look at our American experience from an international perspective, asking whether there were examples from abroad that would have any pertinence to the American scene, given the particulars of our First Amendment system of freedom of expression.

To some, accountability is found only in the marketplace. In this system the marketplace of ideas exists within the economic marketplace. People will reward and punish the media and their workers by buying, subscribing, listening, or viewing (or not doing the same); such open forums as letters to the editor columns, radio and television call-in and talk shows, as well as heart-to-heart (and head-to-head) talks with media leaders will serve as social safety valves for the people.

Others argue that self-regulation within the media is an effective means of accountability. People who are incompetent or unethical or unprofessional will be fired or put on notice with a reprimand. Codes of ethics, internal systems of corrections, and other practices will be self-correcting in such a system as long as there is some means of enforcement. Ombudsmen hired by media organizations to facilitate public complaints constitute another form of self-regulation.

Those who believe that internal regulation will not satisfy the public or correct the problems that the public sees argue for press councils, even though the first major experiment of this kind in the United States lived only a short while and has little prospect of being revived. Still, state press councils have been tried. Issues involving prejudicial publicity have led to cooperative committees—fair trial-free press councils in many states that encourage good practice by those in the press, bar, and bench. Citizen groups such as Action for Children's Television and Accuracy in Media are other examples of voluntary feedback mechanisms for the media.

Within broadcasting and other such broadband technologies there is a tradition of government regulation and control, which is found under the fiduciary model. The Federal Communications Commission, Federal Trade Commission, and various state public utility and cable commissions have stood for a system of regulated accountability. In the 1970s and 1980s, however, a deregulatory mood in the country and in official Washington significantly altered government regulation and weakened any hope the fiduciary model might have had. Newspaper and other print media rarely come under this model, with the rare exception of those involved in joint operating agreements, which exist under an exemption to the antitrust laws and thus have a kind of accountability that is usually unknown in print.

If the marketplace is the court of first resort, litigation is the court of last resort. It is here where angry and aggrieved people talk back to the media through their lawyers. The increased number of libel suits are an indication that this form of accountability is drawing more converts. Libel suits, of course, are only one of the many forms of legal action that bring members of the public into conflict with the press.

Finally, what, if anything, can be learned from other countries, other societies? Is our system so idiosyncratic that "nothing like it ever was," or are there ideas and concepts at work in other countries that ought to command our attention and consideration? The international connection, in the form of a look at the British Press Council, is found in this volume.

In fourteen chapters some of the great issues and problems involved in the media freedom and accountability debate are examined here. Donald M. Gillmor asks whether the media can truly be free and accountable by drawing on key media leaders and commentators. John C. Merrill, a professor of journalism and philosophy, argues in favor of the marketplace model, but is challenged by A. H. Raskin, formerly of *The New York Times*, who finds fault with the commercial media today. Clifford Christians, communications professor and ethics scholar, looks at self-regulation with particular attention to the underlying purposes of codes of ethics. His analysis, in turn, is assessed by Richard P. Cunningham, former newspaper editor and National News Council executive. Alfred Balk, who once edited the *Columbia Journalism Review* and is now with *World Press Review*, offers an expansive analysis of voluntary efforts to review media performance. Comments by *Harper's* editor Lewis Lapham follow Mr. Balk's essay. Henry Geller, communciations attorney and former telecommunications regulator, explores his vision of the fiduciary model, arguing that accountability can be regulated. John Kamp of the Federal Communications Commission offers a critical commentary. Law professor David A. Anderson looks for "the right mix" in the legal model, and newspaper executive John R. Finnegan takes exception. Kenneth Morgan of the British Press Council presents a view from abroad. In an analytical view of accountability, William A. Henry III of *Time* searches for a solution that comports with freedom. A conclusion of one of the editors of this volume sounds an optimistic note and in a philosophical essay, Theodore L. Glasser examines three views of accountability.

Many people contributed to the discussion that made possible this book, including Otto Silha, former publisher of the *Minneapolis Star and Tribune*; Rena Bartos, J. Walter Thompson; Roger D. Coloff, WCBS-TV; Ned Schnurman, *Inside Story*; Osborn Elliot, Columbia University; Margo Huston, *Milwaukee Journal*; Norman Isaacs, author and journalist; John B. Oakes, formerly of *The New York Times*; Hugh Price, WNET-TV; Burton Benjamin, Gannett Center for Media Studies; Robert Schulman, Media critic; David Shaw, *Los Angeles Times*; Robert Siegenthaler, ABC News; Jeff MacNelly, *Chicago Tribune*; Loren Ghiglione, *Southbridge* (Mass.) *News*; Renata Adler, *The New Yorker*; Eleanor S. Applewhaite, CBS; Thomas Winship, Center for Foreign Journalists; Anne Wells Branscomb, communication attorney; John Abel, National Association of Broadcasters; Peggy Charren, Action for Children's Television; Ragan A. Henry, communication attorney; Stephen R. Graubard, *Daedalus*; Bernard Redmont, Boston University; J. Fraser MacDougall, Ontario Press Council; and Lise Bissonette, *Le Devoir* of Montreal.

*Media Freedom
and
Accountability*

The Terrible Burden of Free and Accountable Media

Donald M. Gillmor

Accountability is a concept suspended somewhere between the ideas of law and ethics. *Webster's* defines it as the quality or state of giving an account, of answering, explaining, or of being liable and responsible, terms not unknown to the law. And yet one does not normally associate dire penalties with breaches of ethics or failures to give an accounting. In free societies, absent a law, a person generally has the opportunity to make a moral choice in meeting an ethical obligation or fulfilling a responsibility. This can be a terrible burden.

It can also create a great confusion. What are our ethical obligations and to whom? Who frames them and who has the moral authority to call us to account? Clifford Christians, a leading media ethics revivalist, doubts that people can be called to account for violating their communal obligations in the absence of a system of normative social ethics prepared to assign blame and recognized by both public and profession.

How does this come about in a society as diverse and complex as contemporary America? Does it begin with published codes of professional ethics, newsroom ethicists, media ombudsmen, or citizen news councils?

Is peer pressure sufficient? Or, as David Shaw, *Los Angeles Times* media critic, proposes: would a full explanation of how a publication makes its decisions suffice? Perhaps Christians's solution is collectivist beyond the realities of today's pluralist society. A. H. Raskin, a preeminent labor reporter, would say that the overriding reality is economic—the accelerating capitalist monopolization of the channels of communication.

Milton Goldberg, executive director of Electronic Media Reading Council, does not think ownership makes much difference to the daily diet of news and entertainment because most of it is produced by national syndicates and networks. More and more our standards are national rather than local, he believes, and to lose a rating point is a much tougher penalty than to be sent to Coventry for a moral lapse.

Whatever the current state of our print and broadcast press, and there can be much disagreement about that, there is a vague sense of ethical malaise in the field that makes its appearance in conferences such as this: "Media Freedom and Accountability," held April 4, 1986 at Columbia University's Gannett Center for Media Studies and cosponsored by the Silha Center for the Study of Media Ethics and Law at the University of Minnesota.

Assuming that few among the attentive citizenry are willing to stand pat, the question is how do we combine the attitudinal pieces of our complex mass communication system into an ethical core or center of gravity around which issues of accountability can be addressed? Alfred Balk, consulting editor of *World Press Review* and a longtime observer of the press, recommends an advance on all fronts, not unlike the proposal for concerted action by public, press, and government made by the Commission on Freedom of the Press (the Hutchins Commission) in their 1947 report *A Free and Responsible Press.*

In spite of its unpopularity with major segments of the media, there were few recommendations in the commission report that have been ignored and a good number have been implemented. Whether or not the commission can take credit is a larger question, but it would be difficult to argue that this august body of distinguished private citizens had no influence at all.

First Amendment protections have been extended to newer forms of communication, as the commission recommended. A nonprofit public broadcasting system has been established. News councils have come into being. Revolutionary political views are no longer punishable under law. The search for alternatives to libel law may be reaching its apex. Antitrust laws are still viewed by many as the last best defense of a free press. Efforts are made in the universities to train journalists liberally and some of these programs are centers for advanced study, research, and publication in the field of communication. The value of mutual criticism is appreciated if seldom practiced outside of the opinion journals. Autonomy is recognized as an attribute of the professional journalist. But most important, and the Hutchins Commission can take credit, the word "responsibility" has entered the lexicon of the American press.

Is it possible that we *are* part of a second offensive? As Balk notes, public groups of all kinds are finding the media relevant to their concerns and the press is more inclined to listen and to consider ethical alliances (with bench and bar, for example) than ever before.

But having sounded the trumpet, where do we fall in? The National

News Council ought not to have died and the national press ought not to have helped dig its grave. The press could have supported the council for the most selfish of reasons: the deflection of public criticism. The counterview is that the press should avoid involving itself in any process that allows society or its elected representatives to decide what news decisions are socially responsible. Given the fact that only one state council remains active in the United States, the Minnesota News Council, the latter may be the dominant view.

But are news councils such a bad idea? A number of newspapers representing East, West, and Midwest have inquired about extending the services of the Minnesota News Council. And the British haven't done too badly. While Britain's libel and contempt laws and the Official Secrets Act are substantial burdens for the British press, the press council (a model for the Minnesota council) has had a soothing effect on press-public irritations. It is independent of both press and government, but expert and influential enough so that its judgments carry weight with the press. Its director, Kenneth Morgan, says that it has done the impossible in harmonizing the desire of the nation to have a responsible press with the determination of the nation to maintain a free press. It is funded by organizations of owners, editors, and journalists.

Part of its success is the credibility it gains from its lay and relatively representative constituent membership. In 1984 there were 1,095 nominations for 7 places on the council; in 1985 there were 675 candidates for 6 seats. In 1986 a mortuary caretaker was succeeded by the immediate past clerk of Her Majesty's Privy Council. Ten to 12 percent of some 1,400 complaints a year are given a full formal adjudication. Final determinations are published widely as a matter of moral obligation. A country that has got a tolerably effective, voluntary press council, in partnership with the public, according to Morgan, would do well to keep tight hold of it, for fear of finding something worse.

Certainly no worse are the 40 ombudsmen or readers' representatives scattered throughout the United States. There are, however, more than 1,700 daily newspapers, so it is hoped that a number of other procedures have been developed for handling readers' complaints.

French journalists have a "conscience clause" in their contracts that permits them to quit their jobs with substantial compensation if their honor, reputation, or moral interests are undermined by what their newspapers do. At the same time their readers have a right to reply to personal attacks in the press.

Every Canadian province except Saskatchewan now has a press council. J. Fraser MacDougall, executive secretary of the Ontario Press Council, notes that all 42 English-language newspapers in his province participate and agree to help pay the council's costs, according to circulation, and to publish every decision having to do with themselves. To remain relevant in the public mind the Ontario Press Council carries out studies and holds public forums on ethical questions such as "freebies," pretrial publication, and reporting the names of those charged with lesser offenses.

Balk, and there are many who would agree, calls for a reinstitution of the National News Council with funding that would sustain it. Margo Huston, a Pulitzer Prize-winning reporter for the *Milwaukee Journal* and a member of the National News Council for six years, believes that states ought to serve as their own accountability laboratories by developing arbitration and mediation panels or news councils broadly representative and devoid of cronyism.

John Oakes, former editorial page editor of *The New York Times* and a member of the task force that led to the National News Council, said at the Gannett conference

[I]f we really want to protect our own freedoms [press freedoms], we simply have to face up to the necessity of at least giving some access to the general public to express its views, its sense of grievance in individual cases.... [I]f we don't eventually get around to doing something serious about this ourselves, the public is going to do it for us, and in a way that we don't like.

Finally, Osborn Elliott, former editor of *Newsweek* and dean of the Columbia School of Journalism, noted at the conference that as an editor he was strongly opposed to the idea of a press council, but "[t]he longer I've been removed from active editing, the more I've come to believe that there is indeed a constructive role for a press council to exist."

From a broadcast perspective, Henry Geller sees the recently suspended fairness doctrine and the equal time provision as extraordinary forms of accountability to the public through government. A former lawyer in the antitrust division of the Department of Justice, general counsel of the Federal Communications Commission (FCC), administrator of the National Telecommunications and Information Agency of the Department of Commerce, and now director of the Washington Center for Public Policy at Duke University, Geller is an articulate spokesman for the fiduciary or public trust model of accountability. An attack on the fairness doctrine, which requires that broadcasters provide a reasonable amount of time fairly to controversial issues, is, he believes, an attack on the entire notion of public trust licensing, a notion that has been embedded in the law since 1927.

The argument that the scarcity of frequencies premise underlying the regulatory system is no longer tenable is rejected by Geller:

The scarcity that required this licensing scheme never was a relative one. It was always that more people wanted to broadcast than there were available channels, and that is true today. It's just as true as in 1927. There are no frequencies available in the top 50 markets, radio or television. Stations change hands for half a billion dollars (Chapter 8).

But Geller does not approve of the way the fairness doctrine is administered. While the networks and the larger stations go beyond the minimal expectations of the doctrine in their programming, smaller stations simply avoid the costs of controversy by avoiding controversy altogether. Moreover, by enforcing the doctrine issue by issue, the FCC deeply intrudes into daily broadcast journalism. Preferable would be government intrusion only where there is a pattern of bad faith or a reckless disregard of the doctrine, comparable to the actual malice test for newspapers under the *New York Times v. Sullivan* libel standard.

Geller believes that the equal time provision does chill the larger broadcasters. He would therefore make it applicable only to paid time and only "to significant candidates in the general election (defined as those representing parties that garnered 2 percent of the vote in the state in the last election or, in the case of new candidates, have 1 percent of the vote on petitions)" (Chapter 8).

For the longer term, Geller would scrap the system that requires a broadcaster to serve the public interest. In return for protecting a broadcaster's frequency, Geller proposes a 1 percent spectrum usage fee as part of a multiyear contract. The money would be used for public broadcasting because, as he stated at the conference, "you'll wait until hell freezes over before he [the commercial broadcaster] gives you children's programming, cultural programming, in depth informational programming."

Although he believes new technologies, notably fiber optics, will eventually "save us," Geller is pessimistic in the short run. The scheme of regulation is out of whack with reality, he believes: It's not serving the public interest, and there is a need for revision, but the political clout of broadcasters prevents any revision. According to Geller's statement at the conference, the FCC cannot do anything. The courts will not act (they do not wish to wipe out a half-century of regulation), the Congress won't either, without the consent of the broadcasters, and that consent will not be given.

Recognizing similar distinctions between large and small media, David Anderson, professor at the University of Texas Law School and a former journalist, proposed at the conference a doctrine of proportionality, its premise being that accountability is a response to power, and that different media have different amounts of power, and that we might therefore consider different legal rules for different media.

Anderson believes that today's media enjoy more freedom and less accountability than at any time in the past. Yet a balance between freedom and accountability that works fine for Time, Inc. or CBS may be entirely inappropriate for a small newspaper, a journal of opinion, or a nonmedia speaker. And the Court, said Anderson at the conference, "has been unwilling to give broadcasting the same freedom that print enjoys because it believes broadcasting has the power that requires more accountability than print." Whether print or broadcast, Anderson is very likely correct in observing that public response to the media generally is a response, often negative, to perceived concentrations of power.

Tom Winship, president of the Center for Foreign Journalists and former editor of the *Boston Globe* in its most distinguished period, took strong exception to Anderson's notion of an ever-freer press. The escalating frequency and cost of libel suits, the state-of-mind test for actual malice in determining the level of fault of the journalist in a libel case, and the lack of access to legitimate governmental news are hardly indicators of greater freedom in Winship's view. Nor does he believe the press was held more accountable in the past.

Accountability for Winship and for many journalists is nothing more complicated than accuracy and is "better managed by the press itself." Burton Benjamin, the senior executive producer of CBS who conducted the critical review of CBS practices in the General William Westmoreland case, expressed this convention as "accuracy, accuracy, accuracy," the traditional textbook definition of accountability and a concept a little less elusive and settled in its meaning than "truth."

New York Times v. Sullivan, the landmark 1964 libel decision, was "a disaster of a case," said Renata Adler, a writer who for *The New Yorker* wrote comprehensive analyses of the Ariel Sharon and Westmoreland libel cases and later published them as a book titled *Reckless Disregard*. Neither reputation nor the press, she believes, is protected by the actual malice or negligence tests of the doctrine and nobody understands what the law is. There is much to be said for this position, although the alternatives might give one pause. Adler would welcome a sharper standard of negligence and one that would distinguish the smaller from the larger, and more resourceful media—Anderson's doctrine of proportionality. As to accountability, Adler would explore the differences between speech and press and the freedom of the "nonpress person" who seldom gets a chance to contend, "the problem of non-media speakers and how the press speaker can make room for them."

In response to proposals for revising *The New York Times* doctrine, Anderson said at the conference that he was not ready to accept any principle of judicial certification of truth. "Which of us," he asked, "would be satisfied with any kind of judicial determination that what CBS said [in the *Westmoreland* case] was to was not true? That's a matter to be left to history, to be left to each of us to decide on the basis of our own best information. I just don't think that's the sort of thing we want either judges or juries announcing the truth about."

Reaction to Geller's defense of some form of fairness doctrine was particularly sharp. John Abel, executive vice president of the National Association of Broadcasters, rejected both the doctrine and its scarce-resource rationale. The fairness doctrine, he argued, is not needed and it chills free spech. How is the broadcaster to know what is or is not a controversial issue of public importance? And how many sides does a controversial issue have? What is worse is that ultimately these questions are answered not by the local broadcaster but by a government agency in Washington, D.C. "The whole system," said Abel at the conference, "is an unconstitutional abridgement of First Amendment rights."

Peggy Charren, founder of Action for Children's Television, thought otherwise. As stated at the conference, Charren believes the fairness doctrine sustains the public trustee concept of broadcasting. Self-regulation, she added, does not work for children's programming. "[W]hen the Reagan administration and deregulation came into play, in almost one day, they fired the 20 people in the news department [news for children in a program called '30 Minutes']. They cancelled '30 Minutes.' They got rid of 'Razzmatazz' [a magazine news show for children] and they fired Captain Kangaroo." Neither advertisers nor Congress are interested in diversity in television and "without access, and without the kinds of things that Henry [Geller] suggested, I believe that doing away with the fairness doctrine would ultimately increase the potential for censorship and take power away from people who are pro-choice in speech."

All systems of accountability are supplemental to market or laissez-faire accountability, according to John Merrill, professor of journalism and philosophy at Louisiana State University and a longtime advocate of classic libertarian theories of press freedom. Ultimate accountability is with a public that decides which media die and which survive. But Merrill is not averse to voluntary, self-regulatory systems of ethics functioning in concert with the market. Lewis Lapham is.

Lapham, editor-in-chief of *Harper's Magazine* and a former newspaperman, saw no connection between the market and morality, between the First Amendment and accountability, between freedom and virtue, or between journalism and ethics. "The best press," he said, "is probably the most irresponsible press" (Chapter 7). Mass media, for the most part, he went on to say, deal in entertainment, not education or information. To expect the newspaper to provide, for 30 cents, truth as well as entertainment was for Lapham a fond expectation.

Journalists, in Lapham's view, are storytellers, subject to the conventions of their audience. In order "to keep the crowd's attention [the journalist] has got to tell the crowd more or less what it wants and expects to hear." The market pure and simple—the lost audience and the law-suit—are Lapham's reality. Harsh reality, perhaps, but one that wakes up an audience and carries with it a hint of recognition.

But Lapham's market democracy was too fragile and illusive for Ned Schnurman, senior executive producer for Public Broadcasting Service's "Inside Story," a founding associate director of the National News Council, and a former newspaperman. Freedom, he believes, depends on the climate of tolerance of society. And with respect to television, Schnurman stated at the conference that he would "make the marketplace and accountability fit under one roof and live comfortably together" beginning with a "moratorium on ratings for blocks of prime time to deal with topics that the public should know about."

Roger Colloff, general manager of WCBS-TV in New York, could not fathom why a newspaper readership survey is good and a television audience rating is bad. Why does broadcasting always have to meet the higher standard? Colloff agreed with Merrill that the market model is the foundation of our press freedoms.

"Daily newspapers and most markets are regarded as monopolistically competitive," said John Finnegan, senior vice president and editor of the *St. Paul Pioneer Press & Dispatch*. "That is, while they do not compete directly with other daily newspapers in the same market, they compete with every other kind of media in their marketplace."

While most panelists saw some relationship between freedom and accountability, there were serious misgivings about what accountability really meant and who would, in the final analysis, define and apply it. Lapham would not "try to impose on a rather frail form of storytelling the great burden of truth and righteousness" (Chapter 7).

Although a number of other distinguished media figures participated in the dialogue, these representative threads of the conversation lead back to the problems of defining accountability and of balancing a constitutionally mandated freedom with a growing awareness that the public would be quite comfortable in qualifying that freedom. The essays that follow are an attempt to assess the promises and risks of a range of interventions, some of them ethical, others legal.

Christians delineates and defends a normative social ethic that he believes would seed a renaissance of ethical media performance. Geller searches for fairness within the present structure of broadcast regulation. Balk proposes a new Hutchins Commission and a revived National News Council, both in honor of the spirits of A. J. Liebling and Walter Lippmann. Morgan explains in detail how and why the British Press Council works. Anderson's doctrine of proportionality would expect more accounting, more explaining, and more liability from major media than from their smaller and weaker counterparts. Finally, Merrill locates accountability in the authority of media managers ultimately answerable to people in the marketplace.

This is a dialogue that a free society must pursue if it is to ensure its freedom. But before we become too serious and self-righteous in that pursuit we ought to be reminded again by Pulitzer Prize-winning editorial cartoonist Jeff MacNelly of the *Chicago Tribune* that we, like his *Tribune* editorial page writers in conference, are "some of the funniest people in America."

The Marketplace: A Court of First Resort

John C. Merrill

Critics can, and often do, pick at the edges of the "marketplace model" of media accountability in the United States, but the fact remains that, of all the models suggested, this one is most compatible with American dedication to both press freedom and press responsibility. Market forces may not work perfectly in ensuring accountability, but they do, indeed, bring the public into the ultimate process of accountability through a kind of economic (or "public") determinism that goes a considerable distance in injecting audience values and preferences into the content decisions of our media elite.

Other systems of accountability, of course, can be suggested. The normal array of pressures on the media such as press councils, critical journalism reviews, letters to the editor, codes of ethics, ombudsmen, and litigation do, indeed, have an impact on media activities and serve as important mechanisms of accountability. These systems just mentioned are seen by the "marketplace advocates" as *supplemental*—certainly not contradictory—to market or laissez-faire accountability.

And there are still other forms of accountability, smacking of authoritarianism and state interference. But these are seen as contradictory to the marketplace model because the use of governmental bodies at the national and state levels would have regulatory authority over the media. They would seriously affect media autonomy and editorial self-determinism. We have, with the Federal Communications Commission (FCC), already entered part way into this regulatory area (often called the "fiduciary model"). The marketplace advocate, of course, disagrees with the concept of the FCC beyond, perhaps, the simple process of broadcasting frequency allocation.

The marketplace model provides us with a pluralistically defined press responsibility concept—not perfect, of course, but more consistent with American tradition and ideology than extramedia regulatory or fiduciary models. American society is diversified, having a large number of communications desires; the marketplace model caters to these desires, and in theory—and seemingly even in practice—provides a wealth of this fragmented audience.

The objective of the marketplace model is to permit the maximum of individual and independent editorial determinism in what ideally will be a very pluralistic market system.[1] Media that people accept and support will survive and thrive; media that people dislike or reject will suffer and die. This is *ultimate accountability*. And it is the kind of accountability in harmony with the spirit of individualism, democracy, and freedom.

THE MARKETPLACE APPROACH

Stemming from a kind of synthesis of bits and pieces of the philosophies of John Locke, François-Marie Voltaire, Jean-Jacques Rousseau, John Milton, J. Stuart Mill, Thomas Jefferson, Adam Smith, and Oliver Wendell Holmes, the "marketplace model" (or market model) of communication in society has emerged. Although a broad spectrum of influential persons and movements have had their impact on the market model, it can be said that at least five historical ideas have advanced and perpetuated the model.

They follow, not necessarily in the order of their importance: (1) the philosophy of freedom and individualism coming out of the Age of Reason in Europe, (2) the hard work and competition values of the Protestant ethic (explicated well by Max Weber in *The Protestant Ethic and the Spirit of Capitalism*), (3) the influence of social Darwinism with its concepts of "natural selection" and "survival of the fittest" applied to business competition, (4) Adam Smith's theory of capitalism built on the laissez-faire (free market) approach where the laws of supply and demand determine the flow of goods and services, and (5) Justice Holmes and his "marketplace of ideas" (updating Milton's self-righting process of three centuries earlier), where he spoke of the "power of thought to get itself accepted in the open competition of the market."[2]

The media, in this model, become the market—or serve on the informational and opinion level of society as the main foundation of the market. That the marketplace be as free as possible is considered essential. Because, according to this model, a free market provides the greatest chance to reach the truth, the best way to get a full range of ideas, information, and opinions.

There are 10 principal aspects or characteristics of the market model:

1. The media system should be as free from outside control as possible.
2. The media system should be as diversified (pluralistic) as possible—mainly striving to provide the greatest diversity of information, viewpoints, and opinions as possible.
3. The media system should be competitive, all media striving to gain and keep audience members, and to be economically sound.
4. The media that provide desired services in the competitive market will survive and thrive, and those that fail to do so will languish and possibly die.
5. The economic support of the various media reflects the basic satisfaction, or dissatisfaction, with them on the part of their audiences.
6. The media, therefore, are accountable to the people—to their audiences— for existence and growth.
7. If public support of a certain medium declines, this is a signal to the management that things need to be changed, policy altered, and editorial content is not what it should be. It is a danger signal.
8. If public support increases, this is a signal that the basic policy is all right, that editorial content is at least adequate, and that changes—at least major ones—are unnecessary.
9. The media, in this model, are thereby directed (indirectly, to be sure) by the people. The media managers (similar to elected government officials in this case) must please and represent their constituencies.
10. The media system, then, is an active-reactive mechanism that best reflects the wishes of the people and is, finally, accountable to the people.

After having presented these basic characteristics of the market model, I should mention a few assumptions of the system. The market model assumes that the audience of the media can control these media and keep them accountable for their actions. First of all, the model assumes a knowledgeable and concerned audience and to some degree, a potent and largely monolithic audience as well. Seemingly built into such a model is a kind of Platonic assumption that when people know the good, they will do the good. The market model goes even further and assumes that people, if they know the good, will see to it that others (in this case, the media managers) know and do the good. The acquisition of knowledge and in fact total education, for Plato, are keys here. Through education people will know the good; they will also pursue the good. An obvious question arises at this point: Does such a degree of knowledge and education exist in the marketplace of mass communication?

The market model holds that media are accountable to their publics in the sense that they are rewarded (gain circulation or viewership, and thereby gain profits) or are punished (lose circulation or viewership, and possibly go out of business) as they satisfy or fail to satisfy the desires and expectations of their audiences. It is a simple interaction approach.

This interaction, in the United States, to the degree that it exists, is theoretically the product of the marketplace. As Herbert Altschull says, "If the reader reacts negatively to the content of his newspaper, he will cease to buy it, and the newspaper will be forced to modify its behavior in order to survive in the marketplace."[3] This is how audience members participate in the formulation of news, according to Altschull. And this is the essence of the marketplace theory of mass communication.

The market model can accommodate groups within the audience as well as individual members. Pressures may come from segments of the audiences making up the marketplace. Church groups, militant groups, both left and right, and more conventional groups all may influence the way a publication or station performs. Look at the changes that have come about on "women's pages" in newspapers; they are now quite different from the older home-related "society pages" that dominated the newspaper scene into the 1950s. Also look at the increased coverage of black Americans in the news media. Women and blacks, for instance, as they have organized and become more outspoken—and as they have had access to increasing dollars to use in the marketplace—have had a larger and larger impact on the policies of mass media.

Some writers, such as Hillier Krieghbaum, have pointed out that this kind of action-reaction model can be both good and bad.[4] At best, says Krieghbaum, it represents response to the audience; at worst, it can represent a "buckling under to the threats of boycotts, non-support and inattention."

Now, for a moment, let us look at the concept of "caveat emptor" that is often brought up in connection with the marketplace model. Certainly, the consumer or "buyer" of mass media messages must beware—must, if you will, take his or her chances in the communication marketplace—because in the market there is information that is misleading, untruthful, incomplete, biased, inaccurate, and in some cases, quite deleterious to personal, social, and national well-being and progress. The message is for consumers to take their chances. They decide which messages to expose themselves to, which to retain and take seriously, and which to reject. In this way, the audience member is injected into the market model.

Caveat emptor suggests why the audience member is so very important. It is through this process of relying on the mass media for information, opinion, and analysis that the audience member exercises the maximum personal freedom. Furthermore, the audience member sees the importance of checking one medium against another and of seeking information from a number of sources and perspectives, in short, of becoming a more-intelligent and better-informed individual. The alternative: being taken advantage of by the media in the marketplace.

As consumers of information become more skeptical and better informed about the media and the world about them, the media (at least in marketplace theory) will become more responsive, more pluralistic, and more concerned with fulfilling the ever-rising expectations of their audiences. So in this way, through a kind of mutual education process, the media, in reacting to increasingly sensitive audiences, become ever more accountable to their audiences.

The market model posits that there is a symbiotic relationship between audiences and media: what the people want, the media will provide. If the people demand higher quality, the media will give it to them. As to a possible demand by the public for "lower quality," the model has little to say, for the assumption is that people will become evermore demanding of better information as they themselves develop to higher levels of education and moral consciousness. Of course, the market model could accommodate a lowering of public taste; if such a situation developed, the media in the marketplace, would still be "accountable" for adjusting to the *lower* expectations of their audiences. This is not to say that there would be *moral* benefit in such an adjustment. This would be press responsiveness, not necessarily press responsibility.

In the ideal society (or in theory) this marketplace system should work well. Presumably the people would be the authority—and the agent to which media are finally accountable. And ideally, the people would be knowledgeable and—in the Platonic view—good. They would insist that the media be accountable to them for their actions. They could, then, in a united way, lead or direct the media. The mechanism for this accountability would lie in the economic means of retaliation and reward. The media, through fear and profit motivation, would be forced in this thermostatic relationship to conform to the wishes and expectations of their audiences. And presumably, in society such conformity would ensure media responsibility and morality—determined by the marketplace operating freely and expressing the dictates of a knowledgeable, monolithic, and moral people. Although the people as a whole might not be monolithic, at least there would be groups or segments of the population that would be monolithic enough to serve as potent pressure.

The marketplace model is a truly democratic approach to accountability: the people, speaking clearly through the market, determine to a great degree the content of the media. The main problem is that in the real world the "people" seem to be largely passive or unconcerned about the routine affairs of the media. Feedback of any significant kind—when it comes from the people to the media at all—is episodic and splintered. It offers little or no real guidance for media policies. The media, we can say, are dependent, in a capitalistic society, on the marketplace for financial support but relatively unaffected, at least in the short term, so far as professional and moral guidance is concerned.

MARKET ACCOUNTABILITY: CAVEATS

Market accountability, at least on a moral level, implies that audience groups will want or demand more responsible communication and will insist that the media be more ethical in their practices. In reality, we know that, by and large, audiences know little or nothing about moral quandaries of the media and care little about them. The media are "mixed bags" anyway, with some "irresponsible" segments mixed with "responsible" segments. The public in our society has learned to accept the good with the bad and, in the great expanse of public ignorance, to take on faith the mass of information that lies in the large neutral area between resonponsible and irresponsible journalism.

It is very difficult for a mass audience to respond adequately to perceived irresponsibility in a communication medium. The mass audience is too heterogeneous, scattered, and anonymous to provide a potent (at least, short-term) force of accountability. Some members of the audience may cancel their subscriptions to a newspaper because of perceived media weaknesses or irresponsibilities. But other members will either condone such media activities or, at least, be unconcerned about them. Therefore, the circulation of the newspaper varies very little, if any, because of editorial decisions. Newspapers may pass away, but there is no substantial empirical evidence that they do so because of editorial practices.

If the newspaper were really accountable in the marketplace—or to the marketplace—it could, and would, rather regularly be punished for irresponsible journalism and rewarded for responsible journalism. But too often this is not the case. Take the passing away of the *Washington Star* in the early 1980s, for example. The paper was, in the opinion of media critics, at the zenith of its quality. Was it being punished for its editorial activities? Nobody really believes it was. And take the *National Enquirer* as another example. If it is punished today for its gossipy, sensational manner of playing loosely with the truth, it is through the legal system, not through the marketplace. Readers of this publication get what they want, regardless of the often-fraudulent journalism that the journal may actually contain. There is, in other words, a large enough group in the marketplace to sustain that kind of publication, even if it varies from time to time in its emotional content. There is really little "accountability" working here except, perhaps, in an ethically negative sense. What is working is audience acceptance. Also working is a desire on the part of the editors to provide what they have found to be liked by their audience. If this is considered "accountability" in any kind of ethical context, then it is a very vague and broad concept. In fact, such marketplace sanctioning may actually lead to more unethical and irresponsible journalistic actions in order to expand the audience and to garner larger profits.

The marketplace cannot ensure, in the short-term, either quality or ethical practice. It can, however, ensure considerable freedom for the media managers, and to a lesser extent, it can ensure diversity or pluralism in media content. It may result in some accountability for some media by some members of some audiences. But it is not reliable when it is acting alone, without legal restraints, peer pressure, and the like. In fact, it may be even less reliable than the individual moral consciousness of media managers. And certainly, it is less reliable than the legal system. The sad fact is that in too many cases the marketplace and the profit motive tend to corrupt or set aside the moral sensitivity of media managers.

One other caveat should be given here. Because the market model relies to a considerable degree on media pluralism, the increasing development of huge newspaper groups and multimedia conglomerates poses a threat to the underpinnings of the marketplace system. People might change from one newspaper to another if choices really existed in the marketplace. But in fewer and fewer cities are such choices available. The shrinkage of a pluralistic media system—and some would argue that no such shrinkage is really taking place—does great damage to the marketplace approach. It is true that we need to consider more than simply the number of media in a community, or even the number of separate owners. We need to bring into a discussion of pluralism the very important consideration of *discrete messages*, and the possibility that more messages will reach audience members in a city with one newspaper than will reach the audience of a city with three newspapers.

WEAKNESSES OF THE MARKET MODEL

One of the chief weaknesses of the marketplace approach to accountability is that individual audience members do not have authority or power—even in attempts to pressure the media. The individual audience member is essentially impotent. It is only when individuals can band together to form powerful pressure groups that "the people" have enough authority to insist that the media be accountable to them. An analogy would be workers in a factory and their relationship to management; management would not really be accountable to workers for their decisions and actions unless workers joined together (in a unionized pressure group or power block).

The suggestion that market forces are the best means of media accountability is one that has been supported by many economists and social and political philosophers. Taking such a position, at least to a considerable extent, have been such disparate modern intellectuals as Frederich Hayek, Milton Friedman, Russell Kirk, Jean-Francois Revel, Ludwig von Mises, Eric Voeglin, and Ayn Rand. It would appear that no reputable *moral philosopher* (with the possible exception of Harvard's Robert Nozick) has espoused this market model as one that will lead to responsible or ethical media. It should be quite obvious that the sanctioning of media in a financial way by the public is not the same thing as ensuring moral media actions. Always, from a moral point of view, other accountability approaches must be operating along with the marketplace approach, especially the self-regulating and voluntary resolution approaches.

There has been no real acceptance of the marketplace approach to accountability by American journalists thinking about it in the context of ethics. Most often they don't think of it at all when considering press accountability. This was confirmed by an impressive nationwide study conducted in 1973 that attempted to find out how newspapers hold themselves accountable.[5] The "marketplace model" was not even considered in this study as an accountability system. The study found that editors place accountability in their own newspapers; they are, in short, accountable to themselves and their own efforts to serve the readers. However, in so doing, they did make use of such self-employed systems as ombudsmen, press councils, advisory boards, accuracy forms sent to sources, and corrections. However, 24 percent of the respondents indicated a self-reflexiveness; they referred to "other systems," without naming them.

The market model, despite its inherent ethical problems, is quite consistent with the First Amendment. It relies on the operations of the market solely for media accountability and does not, in any way, condone outside—especially government and legal—measures that would tend to manipulate the media or submit them to prior censorship. There is no reason why the model, if operating in concert with media "self-regulation" and "voluntary resolution," cannot provide considerable accountability for the media system and also be consistent with the provisions and spirit of the First Amendment. But operating alone, it is quite doubtful that the marketplace approach could provide adequate accountability for the media if we are to insist on moral, as well as economic, accountability.

The marketplace model postulates, when related to morality, that the market will control the media and cause them to eliminate irresponsible or unethical activities. It also, among other things, assumes that people can freely exchange ideas and information that will promote the public interest. Robert Picard, in a 1985 book dealing with this subject, questions such a tenet.[6] John Milton and his truth-will-win-out concept to the contrary, there is considerable doubt that in the so-called free marketplace, where falsehood and truth are grappling, truth will actually overcome. There is surely no empirical evidence to support this assumption. Beyond philosophical considerations of such a tenet, there is the question of a restriction-free marketplace. As Picard documents very systematically, restrictions of many kinds tend to disrupt the marketplace.

Many authors such as Picard, Altschull, Dallas Smythe,[7] and Herbert Schiller[8] have contended that choices in the marketplace may be, and have been, removed by a number of factors and that the possibility of truth emerging in the marketplace of ideas and information has been subverted—if, indeed, it were ever possible.

Dennis Brown, of San Jose State University, in a paper for the Freedom of Information Center at the University of Missouri in 1965,[9] questioned the idea that U.S. marketplace philosophy results in fresh winds of discourse blowing through the society. He wrote,

The enormously expensive technology of broadcasting, for example, can be operated at peak economic efficiency only when the very large audiences are being reached. Consequently there is a strong disposition to cater to accepted ideas and to shun the novel or the strange. This aversion to the controversial is by no means restricted to the electronic media. Many scholars in communication have noted a blandness which characterizes the mass communications industry as a whole—perhaps resulting from the commercial nature of its operation and the feeling that it is bad business to stray too far from convention. As a consequence, what is stale and accepted gets public exposure; but what is fresh and controversial often does not.

All negative commentary aside, including Brown's pertinent observations, it still may be that, in the long run, a medium that is grossly insensitive to its audience will suffer, even to the extent of going out of business. And this economic punishment—or potential punishment—in the marketplace is evidently what many mean when they say that the media are accountable to an outside force, in this case: the marketplace.

FREEDOM AND AUTHORITY

This discussion of media freedom and accountability from a market perspective makes no apologies for the lack of scientific foundation. Canadian communications scholar Dallas Smythe believes that much of the present emphasis on "scientism" has led to "an immaturity in research methodology" and to a rather sad state of affairs in communications theory. Smythe, one of the "critical theorists" in communications, believes that "a mature situation in communications research would balance empiricism with a methodological 'open door' policy, welcoming observation and logical rigor outside the controlled-experiment situation."[10]

Such a stance is important and long overdue. Communications scholars—especially in the United States—would do well to "open the door" to larger, more critical, vistas of communications discussion and thought. Our European colleagues are far ahead of us in this respect, as are, surprisingly, some of our fellow students of communication in Asia, Latin America, and Africa.

What is proposed here is that freedom and authority (the accountability agent) are really two sides of the same coin. I am also emphasizing the semantic problems stemming from this complex symbiosis. In short, I am proposing that freedom and authority are inseparable, and that the locus of authority (and accountability) determines the source of the freedom. Let us briefly look at the two main "levels" of media freedom and authority.

Levels of Freedom. Here we consider (1) what can be called "state freedom"—freedom applied to the state authorities (the government-party-press apparatus)—a kind of centralized freedom. Here the state has the freedom to develop and control journalism as it sees fit. There is freedom on the part of the state to see to it that the press is used as an instrument for social stability and national progress and development. From a U.S. perspective, of course, we would call this the "authoritarian" level.[11]

Also there is (2) what is usually called the "free press," or libertarian level. Here we find "freedom" resting with the press. Instead of being government-centered, it is consolidated in an institution and takes on a corporate identity. Freedom really belongs to the press units and basically is a kind of "negative" freedom—freedom of the institution(s) of the press *from* outside interference or control. Freedom in this situation is in the hands of the media owners and managers, with only some freedom filtering down to the lower ranks of journalism. And in this situation, the "people" play their hand at freedom by being instrumental in the marketplace.

Levels of Authority. We come now, as we always do when we are considering freedom, to the subject of "authority." It is important to think of this simultaneously with "freedom." There is a tight relationship between the two concepts. One could just as reasonably refer to each of the levels discussed above relative to freedom as also levels or types of authority. The key question is: Where is the authority centered? The location of the authority determines who has the freedom.

Very briefly, let us look at each of the levels we have just used—the state level and the press level—this time in relation to authority instead of freedom. Because we in the United States consider our press system to be libertarian, slightly more attention will be given to the level that we call press authoritarianism than to the other.

First, there is the authoritarian, or state authority, system. Here the authority, the power, is centered in the government. It is centralized authority, and it is backed up really by the military or the police power; the marketplace is absent, so the people have little to say about the messages they receive or the general demeanor of the media.

Secondly, there is the libertarian, or press authority, system. Here the

authority, the power, is centered in the press itself. This
decentralized authority—with the authority scattered rat
among media managers. This press authority system (which
ertarian) is a kind of institutional, rather than state, author
But it is institutional authority based on the market model, where the
people have an impact on the media managers who have direct (and
constitutional) power.

CONCLUSION

Marketplace accountability is consistent with maximum freedom and is
a basis for people's involvement in media decisions and activities. Rein-
forcing this contention are the related postulates (1) that freedom and
authority each exists at two main levels and are symbiotic, and (2) that
accountability is always related to the locus of the authority, i.e., that the
authorities in the marketplace model are ultimately the people. The
media managers can ignore the people, of course, but at the risk of going
out of business.

The publisher of an American newspaper has much authority; therefore, he or she has much freedom. But according to the market model,
authority and freedom depend on the marketplace: ultimately on the
people.

When we leave the United States and turn to a so-called authoritarian
country such as the Soviet Union, Angola, or Paraguay, it is the state or
the state-party apparatus that is the locus of authority/freedom of the
press. Needless to say, this symbiotic press-party-state system (the authority) is also accountable for editorial decisions only to itself, or perhaps
ultimately to the military forces backing it.

So in a very real sense, we might say that everywhere in the world
there are these two kinds of authority and freedom related to journalism:
state authority/freedom and press authority/freedom. Individual journalists have little real freedom in any system, but probably they are most
free in the market-libertarian countries.[12] Freedom is always related to
authority because authority is necessary for the exercise of freedom.
There are, of course, many people who contend that there is another
authority/freedom level—the *people* level.[13]

Such a belief, to be sure, has spawned both the Marxist concept of
press freedom belonging to the people and also the capitalist-model
concept that states basically the same thing. This, of course, naturally
leads many to the conclusion that "the people" comprise the social entity
to which the media are accountable. In the marketplace approach, the
people have no direct authority over the press; its power is indirect and
largely financial. At any rate, it is important to repeat that the authority
(and the freedom) always lies with the state or with the press itself—or

in a more limited and indirect way, in the market system where the people themselves exercise considerable power as they operate through the market.

In conclusion, the market model contends that the media are accountable to the marketplace and that the concepts of laissez-faire and caveat emptor in journalism both maximize the freedom of the media and, at the same time, make them accountable to the people. This is the model best suited to American tradition and to the U.S. Constitution. It gives media managers much freedom and, at the same time, forces them to consider the people in their audiences.

One final point: the market model may not lead to more responsible journalism. And this is where ethics (and law) must be inserted in the model. Taken together, however, with a respect for law and a moral consciousness, the market model affords the best system for retaining both freedom and authority.

NOTES

1. Merrill explicates the relationship between laissez-faire journalist and pluralism (and presents the classic case for libertarianism) in *The Imperative of Freedom: A Philosophy of Journalistic Autonomy* (New York: Hastings House, 1974).

2. *Abrams v. United States*, 250 U.S. 616, 1919.

3. J. Herbert Altschull, *Agents of Power: The Role of the News Media in Human Affairs* (New York: Longman, 1984), p. 289.

4. Hillier Krieghbaum, *Pressures on the Press* (New York: Thomas Y. Crowell Co., 1972), p. 189.

5. Summary of a study by the American Newspaper Publishers Association conducted by Keith P. Sanders of the University of Missouri: "How Newspapers Hold Themselves Accountable," *Editor and Publisher*, (Dec. 1, 1973): 7–8, 16, 28. See for a full report, Keith P. Sanders, "What are Daily Newspapers Doing to be Responsive to Readers; Criticisms?: A Survey of U.S. Daily Newspaper Accountability Systems," *News Research for Better Newspapers*, 7 (July 1975).

6. Robert Picard, *The Press and the Decline of Democracy* (Westport, Conn.: Greenwood Press, 1985), esp. chaps. 1 and 6.

7. Dallas Smythe, "On the Political Economy of Communications," *Journalism Quarterly*, 37 (Autumn 1969): 563–72.

8. Herbert Schiller, *Mass Communication and the American Empire* (New York: Augustus Kelly, 1969) and *Communication and Cultural Domination* (White Plains, N.Y.: M. E. Sharpe, 1976).

9. Dennis Brown and J. C. Merrill, "Regulatory Pluralism in the Press," *Freedom of Information Center Report 5* (Oct. 1965): 1–4.

10. Dallas Smythe, "Some Observations on Communications Theory," in Denis McQuail, ed., *Sociology of Mass Communications* (New York: Penguin Books, 1979), p. 20.

11. The authoritarian level of freedom is, most likely, not even considered freedom by journalists in the United States. But it, like the other level, implies

freedom for somebody. And it should be noted that it is quite possible for a country to claim press libertarianism (as is true in the United States) without having very much freedom for individual journalists. In other words, "press" freedom or "media" freedom (from government control) is something quite different from "journalistic freedom" in an existentialist sense. Basically then, an American journalist has a very minimal degree of freedom as he or she operates in a system where the media are in "partnership" with government-party authorities who have considerable freedom as regards journalism.

12. One place where this personal or existential impact is discussed at some length is in J. C. Merrill, *Existential Journalism* (New York: Hastings House, 1977).

13. In recent years the idea has found increasing favor that press freedom belongs to the people, not to the press. A few books that have supported this idea (at least to some degree) are Jerome Barron, *Freedom of the Press for Whom?* (Bloomington: Indiana University Press, 1971); William O. Douglas, *The Right of the People* (New York: Arena Books, 1972); William E. Hocking, *Freedom of the Press: A Framework of Principle* (Chicago: University of Chicago Press, 1947); Herbert Marcuse, *One Dimensional Man* (Boston: Beacon Press, 1966); and Bryce Rucker, *The First Freedom* (Carbondale: Southern Illinois University Press, 1968). Many articles and speeches have, of late, extolled this idea of a "people's press." However, many persons find such a concept difficult to comprehend and, in fact, find it contradictory to First Amendment assurances. The First Amendment provides certain freedoms for "the people": expression, assembly, redress of grievances, and religion. But in addition to these explicit people's rights there is the provision that *freedom of the press* (a possessive) will not be abridged.

3

THE MARKETPLACE: A STACKED COURT

A. H. Raskin

We journalists have an infinite capacity for autohypnosis. Most of us are wont to propagate certain articles of faith with all the dogmatism of a fundamentalist preacher, no matter how much contrary evidence must be consigned to hell's fire in the process. Professor Merrill's paean to the market model, I regret to say, suffers from that occupational malady.

He dutifully marshals what impresses me as a devastatingly convincing list of caveats and weaknesses that undercut faith in the marketplace as any kind of sustainer of either quality or responsibility in the press, then blithely disregards them all in proclaiming it the best system for keeping the media both free and accountable. Nothing like adequate cognizance is taken of the miscarriage of the market system that, in my estimation, makes it a particularly grave threat these days to popular acceptance of the belief that running a newspaper or broadcasting organization constitutes a public trust entitled to constitutional protection.

My reference, of course, is to the rapid acceleration in recent years of the trend toward concentration of media ownership that has been gathering momentum ever since the end of World War II—a trend made doubly disturbing by the sudden discovery in Wall Street that the gobbling up of media conglomerates and the manipulation of their stock provide a happy hunting ground for assorted vultures of the financial community whose interest is limited to the prospect of profit, short term or long.

The studied obliteration of competition that has accompanied these developments has gone far toward demolishing the foundation stone of the marketplace theory of mass communication: the notion, to use Professor Merrill's words, that "media are accountable to their publics in the sense that they are rewarded (gain circulation or viewership, and thereby gain profits) or are punished (lose circulation or viewership, and possibly go out of business) as they satisfy or fail to satisfy the desires and expectations of their audiences" (Chapter 2).

Even if one accepts that yardstick as a sufficient definition of accountability, it becomes a mockery in a period when monopoly is increasingly the mode in ownership of the media with the greatest and most regular access to the mass mind. To argue that the needs of our democracy for maximum diversity in the sources of information and opinion have never been better safeguarded than they are today, thanks to the multiplicity of cable channels, counterculture publications, newsletters, specialized journals, and the like, seems to me exceedingly disingenuous.

In terms of credibility, I put that argument by extollers of the market model on a par with the television industry's ritualistic response to its critics that no definitive evidence exists to prove that the omnipresence of mindless violence on the tube stimulates the aggressive impulses of anyone in the viewing audience, least of all children. The reality, as all of us know, is that the people's opportunities for exercising marketplace disciplines through pluralistic choice in the realm of information and ideas has narrowed steadily as control over the fountainheads of mass communication passes into fewer and fewer hands.

Four decades ago, the constrictive effect that centralization of ownership exerted on the flow of public intelligence worried the Hutchins Commission enough to prompt it to cite such concentration as a main prop of its 1947 recommendation for establishment of a new and independent agency to appraise and report annually on the performance of the press. And that recommendation was made before television, spread-eagled by the three giant networks, had emerged as the pivotal instrumentality in determining how much or how little citizens in our democracy know about their world, their nation, and their communities as a guide to intelligent decision making.

By 1978, when the further spread of monopoly in journalism impelled the Bureau of Competition of the Federal Trade Commission to sponsor a symposium on media concentration, Ben H. Bagdikian, now dean of the Graduate School of Journalism at the University of California, Berkeley, reported that 167 chains controlled 61 percent of all the country's newspapers and 75 percent of all daily circulation. Comparable concentration and interlocks in ownership of broadcasting, magazines, books, and movies have created a situation, Bagdikian said, in which fewer than 100 corporate chiefs have ultimate control over a majority of the elements in every mass medium influencing our culture, thought, and politics. He dubbed this select circle of business executives a private "Ministry of Information and Culture" for the United States.

One need not conjure up hobgoblins of thought control to share Bagdikian's apprehension over the vesting of so much authority in so small a group of fallible human beings, whether in industry or government or any other institution. My own concerns along that line stem from no feeling that the principal chains or other media conglomerates now operating have trampled on standards of excellence or community responsibility. On the contrary, I cheerfully concede that there have been instances in which these absentee owners have improved the news organizations they have acquired, although that by no means is universal.

What does concern me is the perception, created by the agglomeration of financial dominance over all branches of the mass media in the tightening circle of rich and powerful corporations, that the dissemination of information and ideas in this "information era" is big business and thus inescapably shaped by the values of the business community. Such a perception ill serves the pluralistic society that seeks to evolve national policy melding of the interests and impulses of widely divergent individuals, most of them operating at the grass-roots level and entrusting the conduct of the governmental functions that touch most intimately to the political machinery of tens of thousands of cities, towns, and counties.

Professor Merrill is candid in acknowledging that the market model adds little to media quality and even less to respect for law in the conduct of journalistic enterprises. "The sad fact is that in too many cases the marketplace and the profit motive tend to corrupt or set aside the moral sensitivity of media managers" (Chapter 2). Worries on that score have been given a forceful new push by the extent to which the last few years have touched off a scramble among investors and speculators devoid of any attachment to considerations of press responsibility or independence for massive stakes in a field they consider open to exploitation as a source of profit and perhaps also of power.

It was possible in the not too distant past for journalists to comfort themselves with the conviction that the bulk of those in command of the great media conglomerates were inheritors of a tradition of impartiality, community service, and enlightenment that gave some color of legitimacy to our pious protestations that the First Amendment was for the public's protection and not a special indulgence to enable the press to ride roughshod over everyone else's rights without accepting any obligation for accountability on our own part.

That concept of editors and reporters as unelected administrators of a public trust never received vast acceptance from many skeptical outsiders, least of all when media executives sought to wrap themselves in the First Amendment as armor against fulfilling duties imposed on corporations, generally under the labor, tax, and antitrust laws. Nevertheless, the plausibility of the case put forward by the concept's defenders was, until recently, considerably enhanced by the presence at the helm of most key news organizations of people who came out of the editorial side or were nurtured from childhood on principles of fidelity to family-founded institutions.

Now, overwhelmingly, those with greatest say in the executive suite are climbers of the business ladder, skilled in scaling down budgets and in maximizing profits by gearing "the product" to the preferences of the type of reader and viewer whom advertisers most want to reach. Given the escalating cost of quality news gathering and the indisputable necessity for keeping the enterprise financially viable, even that shift toward a predominance in top jobs of MBAs, accountants, and lawyers might be defensible provided this new media elite acquires along the way a sense and sensitivity to the distinctiveness of the role the press vaunts itself on fulfilling in society. Something more than the lip service of quick learners is needed to carry conviction in a nation made dubious of the trustworthiness of all institutions by Watergate, Abscam, Vietnam, White House-sponsored "disinformation" schemes, and the myriad scandals that cast shadows over every aspect of our public and private functions.

In any event, what credibility can we expect for our image of ourselves as legatees of an idealistic tradition when the most visible media corporations trade their shares in the open market and have assets valued in billions and when control is increasingly up for grabs by the highest bidder or the shrewdest manipulator?

The homogenization of the print press through the buying out of local ownerships by nationwide chains has proceeded unchecked in the eleven years since the icy resentment of the media mainstream scared the Federal Trade Commission away from conclusions of any kind on what changes in public policy, if any, might be desirable to put a lid on concentration of the dimensions its symposium was initiated to explore. The big shaker of the money tree in the current period has been the Gannett chain. It has gathered into its market basket in quick succession three of the lushest plums in newspaperdom—the *Des Moines Register*, the *Louisville Courier-Journal*, and *The Detroit News*—at a collective cost to Gannett of more than $1.2 billion.

Every premise underlying Professor Merrill's encomium to the market model is brought into question by the differing circumstances that led each of these outstanding dailies to seek shelter in the arms of a journalistic colossus that I still have difficulty remembering is no longer the modest congeries of small papers in up-state New York that it remained until well into my own reportorial career.

But nothing in the sacrifice of independence by all three of Gannett's latest acquisitions more strikingly illustrates the hollowness of the market concept, as it is now being applied in journalism, than the deal Gannett made with Knight-Ridder less than two months after putting up $717 million in cash in February 1985 to win a bidding war for purchase of *The Detroit News*.

Under that deal the two huge chains committed themselves to a century-long joint operating agreement covering *The News* and Knight-Ridder's *Detroit Free Press*, historically the fiercest of rivals, each with a daily circulation of roughly 640,000. If approved by the Supreme Court, the pact would provide for a sharing of profits, issuance of combined Saturday and Sunday editions, and consolidation of advertising, administrative, and publishing operations.

All this evasion of the antitrust laws would be sanctified—Washington willing—by the all-forgiving provisions of the Newspaper Preservation Act of 1970, the so-called failing newspaper act, which the industry lobbied through unabashed by the objections of a few publishers honorable enough to demur at the idea of the press, usually so loud in trumpeting its abhorrence of entangling relations, going to government for preferred treatment.

In the Detroit case, the bundle Gannett turned over for *The News* gave it no pause from joining with Knight-Ridder in publicly declaring that "the market cannot support two high-quality, high-cost, independently published newspapers." When the Justice Department's antitrust division suggested that approval of the joint operating agreement be held up pending a hearing on alternative ways to keep both papers alive, its temerity spurred the two chains to address an urgent appeal to Attorney General Edwin Meese to overrule the notion of open debate on the necessity for waiving antitrust requirements. The right course, they insisted, was an immediate green light for pooled publication.

The battering the market model is taking on the print side is more than matched by the disturbing implications of recent developments affecting command of all three networks, the paramount dispensers of public knowledge and molders of public taste. The ease with which the power center shifted at NBC, CBS, and ABC can only reinforce the widespread perception that the press is a business for sale in the same manner as a meat-packer or a soap company or any other of the big companies on whose advertising the media depend for most of their revenue.

Sometimes the impellent for a Wall Street coup is the attractiveness of the bottom line or the price-earnings ratio, sometimes the chance outsiders see for capitalizing on a downturn in network fortunes through a leveraged buyout, or kindred chicanery, or through shoring up a besieged administration in its efforts to repel hostile takeover. Whether the newcomer wears the plume of white knight or the vulture wings of raider or the standard three-piece suit of the executive suite, the end result in every case has been that someone new—and at NBC and CBS without any expertise or even real association with broadcasting—is exercising the dominant voice in the network's affairs when the dust settles.

To me the most sobering example of the degree to which media properties have become incidental baggage on the corporate trading block was the tie-in sale of NBC to General Electric as a part of that supercorporation's acquisition of RCA. The astonishing thing was how little comment, pro or con, was generated either among the public or inside the media by this transfer of a premier network, with its strategic position in the whole spectrum of communications, to one of the most gargantuan of our multinational industrial enterprises.

The acquisition of ABC by Capital Cities Communications got equally routine press coverage, indistinguishable from that which attended the scores of other mergers of multibillion-dollar corporations that have become a ho-hum part of the day's news. The most noticeable consequence of the ABC sale thus far has been a wave of cost cutting that bit deeply into the staff of ABC news and left many of the survivors still uncertain how long they will be around.

It is true that the palace revolution at CBS, coming as it did on the heels of attempted incursions by Ted Turner and a right-wing coalition inspired by Jesse Helms and Reed Irvine, did get bountiful attention. Jubilation ran high at CBS News, whose stellar performers had chafed under the leadership of Thomas H. Wyman and Van Gordon Sauter— a command team they accused of straying too far from the hard-news tradition of Ed Murrow and Walter Cronkite out of worry over the network's declining profits and audience share.

The probability, however, is that neither Wyman nor Sauter would have been ousted if the morale problems at CBS News had not been accompanied by a run of flops in the entertainment division that turned off advertisers and weakened earnings, a couple of unwise outside investments, a generally soft business environment, and an attempted end run by Wyman, kept secret from the board, to arrange for a merger of CBS into Coca-Cola.

Before exultation over the new order of things at CBS becomes too general, we would all do well to keep in mind that ratings are still the name of the game in broadcasting and that a continued slump in its relative standing and profits would in short order bring insistent new pressure for a change in control. Laurence A. Tisch, the new chief executive officer, made himself the darling of the CBS newscasters by saying all the right things about the importance of their work and of quality programming, but he has an $800 million investment in the network to protect and he did not make himself head of Loews, a diversified corporation with assets even greater than those of CBS, by watching his money melt away. Tisch's own inclinations might be irrelevant in any case. Wall Street teems with scavengers eager to move in whenever they sense vulnerability in a prize as tempting as CBS.

Former Chief Justice Warren Burger did not have to wait for the most recent instances of the cavalier way in which the invisible hand of the marketplace bumps executives, good or bad, out of positions of media control to reach a personal conclusion about the appropriateness of special immunities for the press in the exercise of freedom of speech. His view was set forth in an obiter dictum accompanying the chief justice's separate concurring opinion in the 1978 case of *First National Bank of Boston v. Bellotti*. The majority of that case relied on the First Amendment to affirm the right of corporations to treat as a legitimate cost of doing business expenses incurred in supporting or opposing legislative proposals that might affect the company's financial well-being. Chief Justice Burger was perfectly willing to go along with this extension in the Supreme Court's view of free speech for corporations generally, but he used his dictum to make clear that, in his judgment, the media were just another form of business, entitled to neither more nor less freedom of expression under the First Amendment than any other corporation.

The Burger assertion of parity in First Amendment status evoked predictable expressions of outrage from the journalistic establishment, but in the daily conduct of media corporations it is easy to find confirmation for the chief justice's basic point that they operate by the same marketplace values as any other business.

In the same year as the *Bellotti* case, that identity of values was underscored in a caustic exchange of letters to the *Wall Street Journal* midway through a three-month strike by the press that had shut down all three of New York City's metropolitan dailies. Fred W. Friendly touched off the exchange by blaming the desire of the papers to increase their profits by eliminating pressroom featherbedding for "robbing the world's greatest city of the essential stimuli to its central nervous system—information and probing news analysis."

"What emerges," Friendly said, "is that publishers act just like other businessmen as they mouth platitudes about the people's right to know and their solemn rights under the First Amendment."[1]

In an irate reply, Arthur Ochs Sulzberger of *The New York Times* strongly defended the publishers' position in the strike but took no offense at the other half of the Friendly indictment. "Far from denying Mr. Friendly's accusation that *The Times* is involved in this dispute because it seeks better profits, I affirm it wholeheartedly," Sulzberger said. "A financially sound *Times* is good for our readers, our advertisers, our shareholders and our employees (including, by the way, the very pressmen who are on strike)."[2]

The final sentence of the Sulzberger response put it more succinctly.

Addressed to a question in the initial attack about whether there was not "a moral obligation to maintain the continuity of serious newspapers" came this parting shot from *The Times* publisher, "The only continuity in the poorhouse graveyard is silence."

The multiple tombstones in the poorhouse graveyard—the *New York Herald Tribune, Washington Star, Newark Evening News, Philadelphia Bulletin, Chicago Daily News*, and *Minneapolis Star* to cite only a few of the better-known casualties of the marketplace—have sharpened the resolve of the survivors to fatten their profit margin with the double purpose of staying alive and fending off raiders.

In metropolitan centers, where competition for advertising with television, radio, and other media is especially keen, the pocketbook influence on newspaper content has been unmistakable. The accent has been on attracting readers in the upper-income brackets—business executives and upper middle-class suburban homemakers as the choicest targets—and distributing market surveys to potential advertisers boasting of the rich catch that awaits them if they tap that audience. I won't waste space here rehashing the familiar laments about the emphasis on entertainment, gossip, fashion, and soft features that has marked the quest for affluent readers. Nor is there much point in belaboring the accompanying deemphasis of the problems of the urban and rural poor.

It is not my purpose to carry this jeremiad to the point of suggesting that the press, either print or electronic, has forgotten its watchdog function or that it pulls its punches in going after the malefactors in government, finance, or any other field. But particularly in these days of Dr. Feelgood in the White House, it seizes every opportunity to affirm its basic support for the system—an opportunity it worked itself red, white, and blue in the face exulting over in connection with the extravaganza David Wolper arranged in celebration of the Statue of Liberty centennial. Perhaps the ultimate in the media's orgiastic endorsement of that event was a comment in *U.S.A. Today*, flagship of the Gannett armada, blowing away critics of the vulgarity and commercialism that surrounded the celebration: The paper claimed that bad taste in and of itself was not a vice at the liberty celebration and urged us not to forget that the purchase of liberty goodies was motivated by patriotism. Commercialism, the paper went on, was simply the product of a free market, the hallmark of the United States' charter as the land of opportunity.

I am indebted to Don Gillmor of the Shila Center for reminding me of a forecast by that eminent futurologist Art Buchwald on where this highroad to opportunity is leading communications. Buchwald predicted that in the brave new world of postindustrial capitalism, all mass media would be centered in a great monolith, probably headquartered in Washington and known as the A–Z National Federal Corporation: one voice indivisible, with mush and mash for all.

If we are genuinely devoted to democratic principles, we dare not wait till a market system that has subordinated its creative impulses to the short-term magnification of profits wipes out all competition in mass communications. Legislative restraints on the size of chains of the kind once sought in Congress by Morris Udall and Paul Simon, seem to me at least as valid an expression of concern for the public interest as the Newspaper Preservation Act.

But the real answers must come from within journalism and it is distressing to note a fall-off in the self-criticism bordering on self-flagellation that for several years was the most distinctive feature of the annual conclaves of the American Society of Newspaper Editors and the American Newspaper Publishers Association. The National News Council, on which I was happy to sign aboard after retiring from *The New York Times*, had to abandon its effort to monitor media accuracy and fairness as a result of the wall of hostility built around it by most elements in the media, led by *The Times*. Minnesota is the only state left with any nongovernmental, nonpunitive agency for riding herd on complaints against abuses by the press. Ombudsmen remain a rarity.

Participatory democracy in industrial decision making is becoming commonplace in dozens of industries, with workers and their unions involved at every level from shop floor to boardroom, but the media are very much laggards in enlisting the brainpower of reporters on either the news or business side. A rank-and-file voice in electing top editors is unknown here, although not in distinguished papers abroad.

Professor Merrill may feel it is sufficient to state, as he does, that ethics and law must be inserted into the market model to make it work as a bulwark of freedom and accountability. Because I find the evidence overwhelming that, in its present perverted form, the profit demands of the market model operate to diminish every such consideration of public and professional responsibility, my own conclusion is that it is more enemy than ally of a decent and responsive press.

NOTES

1. The Wall Street Journal, October 5, 1978, p. 24.
2. The Wall Street Journal, October 6, 1978, p. 20.

4

SELF-REGULATION: A CRITICAL ROLE FOR CODES OF ETHICS

Clifford Christians

In the disparaging line of German philosopher Arthur Schopenhauer, news is the tiny secondhand on the clock of history, made of lead. He may be right about the inferior metal and elfin units of time, but no one can doubt the press's contemporary power. The news media appear on every short list alongside such mighty institutions as law, government, medicine, and education.

However, journalistic power has a peculiar twist: it cannot be exercised unless unencumbered. Thomas Jefferson understood that already in 1808, contending for an *independent* information system as "that liberty which guards our other liberties."[1] In his famous dispute over Philip Freneau's role in the *Gazette*, Jefferson argued that no democratic society can function without censors, "and *where the press is free* none ever will."[2] It cannot enlighten and act as watchdog if only repeating establishment dogma. The press must remain untouched in democratic theory or the citizenry cannot be served effectively.

But therein lies a dilemma. Who guards the guardian? Even if the press's noble mission is safeguarding the republic, and even if external restraints violate its very being, why should journalists be uncontrolled? Democracies, by definition, prohibit elite autonomous pockets of power. Loose cannons on the deck of the ship of state are intolerable.

Self-regulation offers one pathway out of the conundrum. In fact, self-regulation has long stood as the only control mechanism forthrightly defended within the news enterprise itself. This essay critically examines the conventional wisdom that a free people can abide no governance except that self-imposed. The general question is what the press can do internally to regulate itself convincingly. Or in more formal terms, what intramedia mechanisms within individual news operations and what intermedia models among associations of professionals can be recommended?

Codes of ethics are normally placed within the aegis of self-regulation, as a visible institutional indicator that the press takes internal constraints seriously. I defend codes of ethics in the paragraphs below, provided they carry enforcement provisions. Ombudsmen—the Rodney Dangerfields of our enterprise at present—and a normative social ethics are also promoted as explicit ways to ensure that the press's immense power will not be abused. Obviously a host of other internal mechanisms have emerged by which reporters, editors, and news directors police their own ranks: office memoranda, staff conferences and training, visits by ethics specialists to the newsroom, journalism reviews, professionals who make media criticism their specialty, and so forth. This essay concentrates on enforced codes—with reference to ombudsmen and ethical theory—as illustrations of the self-regulation motif. I argue that polishing our techniques and inventing new strategies are not as crucial at this stage as a cognitive revolution.

LIMITS OF RESPONSIBILITY

I am deeply concerned with the narrow limits within which media responsibility is often restricted by our Jeffersonian legacy. For all the press's fussing over internal mechanisms of accountability, Aleksandr Solzhenitsyn's impassioned charge remains largely unanswered: "The press has become the greatest power within Western countries, more powerful than the legislature, the executive, and the judiciary. One would then like to ask: By what law has it been elected and to whom is it responsible?"[3] My purpose will be to shift the argument away from codes, ombudsmen, and academic ethics per se to the broader matter of accountability. I contend that the catalyst for advance is a conceptually adequate notion of accountability. Our long-standing debates over codes, ombudsmen, and ethical theory, I believe, reflect a serious misunderstanding of accountability. Clearing away the confusions is the necessary first step before insiders can make any headway toward meaningful self-determination.

SOCIAL HISTORY OF CODES

The first journalistic code of ethics officially adopted by anyone was the Kansas Code, written by William E. Miller and endorsed by the Kansas Editorial Association in 1910. Several state-wide codes soon followed in Missouri in 1921, South Dakota and Oregon in 1922, and Washington in 1923. Local newspapers also prepared their own codes during the

1910s and 1920s—some explicit ("always verify names") and others moralistic ("be vigorous but not vicious").[4] In 1928 the National Association of Broadcasters (NAB) prepared a radio code consisting of eight guidelines designed to encourage broadcasting "in the public interest."

The star among early media codes was the Canons of Journalism adopted by the American Society of Newspaper Editors (ASNE) in 1923, the second year of its existence. Several journalism associations copied or imitated its content during the 1920s. The currently popular Society of Professional Journalists/Sigma Delta Chi (SPJ/SDX) code of ethics, for example owes its origin in 1926 to the ASNE canons.

One year after the canons were formed, the U.S. Senate began checking rumors that government oil reserves in the Teapot Dome were being sold to private oil companies. From that scandal emerged clarification regarding the role of codes among journalism practitioners. That is, one member of this newly formed association—F. G. Bonfils, publisher of the *Denver Post*—allegedly accepted a million dollars in bribes for suppressing information from his reporters about wrongdoing in the Teapot Dome area.

The accusations against Bonfils became a bone in the association's throat. Just one year earlier they had unanimously passed a series of resolutions pledging decency, fair play, sincerity, truthfulness, accuracy, and impartiality. Bonfils had failed on nearly all counts and several of the 124 members demanded that he be punished for clearly violating the code of ethics. The arguments lasted for five years and every conceivable alternative surfaced.

Finally in 1929, frightened by Bonfils's threat to sue them into bankruptcy, the newspaper editors voted for voluntary obedience rather than code enforcement. Some distinguished members contended that adopting a code without provisions of discipline was a mockery. Willis J. Abbot of the *Christian Science Monitor* contended, for example, "It is to my mind utterly indefensible that we should adopt a professional code and make no provision at all for the discipline of the people who refuse to accept the code as part of our fundamental law."[5]

However, the argument that finally prevailed came from Samuel Williams, editor in chief of the *St. Paul Pioneer Press & Dispatch*. "Censorship within the Association violates the free press doctrine. There is in principle," he claimed, "little difference between a judge acting to suppress a newspaper and the power we editors propose to confer upon a small body of our own choosing."[6] Williams's speech was roundly applauded and the ASNE resolved not to construct any provisions to expel.

For reasons too boring and complicated to develop here, for five decades no new codes were written. Then in 1973, SPJ/SDX revised its code, and its adoption became the chief trigger in a new and vigorous wave of code interest among the American press.

But there is no internal enforcement, only the dissemination of the code, that is placing framed copies of it on every newsroom wall. Horatory oratory—we must prevent violations, journalists have a sacred trust, and we must keep good faith with the public. But no punitive power is granted to local or national organizations, no machinery for pushing aside the bandits. Society of Professional Journalists/Sigma Delta Chi chapters have sometimes been alerted to probable violations of the code; but from the 1974 "Guidelines for Implementation" until now none has taken disciplinary action. Members of SPJ/SDX constantly warn each other in speeches, letters, and *Quill* articles about the perils of any enforcement machinery, and the "absolute paranoia" it might cause, and the "potential abuses." The code itself exhorts professional chapters to "prevent violations" and "actively censure," but SPJ/SDX's efforts at implementation since 1973 have been exclusively educational.

This social history of codism generates some disturbing conclusions. Most are obvious and several are understandable, but a serious flaw becomes apparent in the culture of discourse among media practitioners about professional codes. History reveals an unsettling intellectual concern—at least for those of us with a scholarly interest in codes as one aspect of professional ethics. One observes a chasing of tails, reinventing of tiny wheels, and argumentum ad hominem—and in abundance—but little appreciable advance. And the reason, I believe, for this inability to move forward is a failure to understand accountability. Fuzziness over that basic notion has allowed quantity to expand without quality improving. We repeat the same arguments today as they did in the 1920s, not only because of ignorance, but for a want in intellectual precision over accountability. To what extent other professionals have come straight on this notion, I cannot judge. Regarding journalism codes, I think our primary agenda today is an intellectual one. Otherwise we will continue to conflate necessarily distinct issues, misplace our constraints, and mix categories. While housekeeping details such as revision codes are important, I see little virtue in all of us sweeping floors when the foundation has eroded and the building sinks away.

PROTECTING MEDIA INDEPENDENCE

Protecting the media's independence from government intrusion is a distinctive Anglo-American contribution to the world. In general, our visceral commitment to press freedom is not promoted for its own sake, but as vital for providing undistorted news in a complicated age. However, even though it is held on the whole with good intentions, a fierce independence, an absolutist autonomy precludes in the press a genuine appreciation of accountability. The language of responsibility, duty, and obligation we tend to see as alien territory. In the same manner that former President Ronald Reagan fashioned a one-eyed view of foreign policy under Communist expansionism, a stark and uncompromising autonomy may distort our understanding of the press's nature and role.

In principle, press freedom cannot be stressed too strongly. Accepting a dissident press is the mark of a nation's maturity. Yet on the workday level, moral language cannot find a natural home in such a climate. Independence is so much the press's bread and butter that calls for enforced codes, for vigorous ombudsmen, and a strong-minded professional ethics lie forgotten along the road to meeting deadlines and paying the bills.

Democracies need an independent press, desperately so, and we must be vigilant in protecting this independence. Who could quarrel with that? The ongoing struggle to hammer out guarantees against government encroachment is a noble endeavor. Small-minded politicians of all kinds seek to co-opt the media for serving official policy.

But a fixation with what the British philosopher Isaiah Berlin calls negative freedom prevents us from intelligently considering what insiders can do to increase our responsibility. While on a practical level we should continue to debate codes and ombudsmen and ethical theory, I believe our analysis cannot be sophisticated or successful unless we think straight about accountability. In that sense, I do not propose instant remedies. None exists. But I describe the contours of an arduous journey, I ring a bell, establish a discourse, issue a manifesto that motivates us to start traveling. We must begin by contradicting all rhetoric of nonenforcement and by agreeing that in a profound sense, as with all social institutions, the press can legitimately be called to account for its performance.

In what follows, it will become obvious that I am not evangelizing the irresponsible. Journalism has a few deceivers and even some bandits. In staking out a position on codes of ethics by making the concept of accountability intelligible, I do not address the incorrigibles. Those few who abuse freedom or confuse it with autonomy have been placed on the defensive by a long line of philosophers and social analysts who have clarified the intuition that all privilege involves restraint as its dialectical counterpart. My argument is designed for the ovewhelming majority of media practitioners who realize that freedom entails responsibility and who wish to exercise their responsibility through forms of self-regulation. It is beyond my purpose here to specify the kinds of privileges individuals enjoy under the First Amendment; it suffices for the argument below to assume, in a loose and minimal fashion, that while the press has a guaranteed right to disseminate information, it must do so competently and responsibly.

ACCOUNTABILITY OF THREE LEVELS

To say that agents are accountable for their behavior means that they can be called to judgment with respect to their obligations. That is, one can legitimately raise questions or even lay charges if necessary and expect reasonable answers. An account is a reckoning properly requested and given, a statement explaining conduct to legitimately designated parties.[7] And if one attempts to place accountability within the socio-political frameworks in which this notion operates vis-à-vis the media, we must consider it in three different senses: the media are accountable to the government, to themselves as professionals, and to the public.

In its strongest and most explicit form, accountability is to be understood in terms of liability to punishment. In this sense the courts judge persons liable and the state imposes criminal penalties. Those who make such judgments are considered by reasonable persons to administer the punishment legitimately. The persons may be legally and properly blameworthy of civil or criminal offense.

On another plane—in terms of fairly unambiguous communities such as the business, journalism, or legal professions—accountability means disapproval for morally questionable activities. Persons are blameworthy when their offense is considered morally reprehensible by those who share a recognizable community with them. Those who can legitimately pass judgment in this case are peers who punish the offender by public or private censure, by criticism or outrage. We intuitively recognize this form of accountability when distinguishing the moral from the legal, when realizing that although we are not breaking any laws, we have a moral obligation not to violate a commitment or dishonor a relationship.

However, neither meaning of accountability covers a third, more general notion of answerability in that huge social arena constructed largely of custom and convention. Those with power can be legitimately held accountable by the public they serve in the sense that they can be challenged to answer and explain when their behavior appears unacceptable. On this level, the press may be accused of neglect or irresponsibility and punished by scorn or indignation. Answering occurs primarily in the interactionist mode; in this area, claim and counterclaim, clarification and expansion are essential. Those called to account do not stand before a judge's tribunal or a collegial board; they are not being confronted with illegal behavior or violations of formally established moral norms. In the sense of accountability or answerability, an individual or organization merely is being questioned about the failing of omission or commission. As in the other two domains, the calling to account is considered justified; in fact, a public that never debates its institutions comes under blame itself. But this "calling to account" must follow the interactionist pattern to be morally acceptable. If an agent is blamed but not

Table 1
Accountability

AGENCY	TYPE	ENFORCEMENT	MODE
Government	Legal liability	Criminal penalties	Courts
Professional colleagues	Moral sanctions	Censure	Peer review
Public	Answerability boycott	Indignation and such as ombudsmen	Interaction

allowed to explain, an otherwise justifiable beckoning becomes unjustified. News professionals may prove to be blameworthy, but that can only be a posteriori, a possible conclusion when explanations over time prove unsatisfactory.

On the basis of this discrimination of usage, summarized in Table 1, some implications for media codes of ethics become apparent. Before disentangling the details, let me state the conclusion in general terms.

Codes of ethics, in the reconstruction shown in Table 1, reasonably fit into the second category only—that of moral sanction among peers. The National Association of Broadcasters based its rationale for codes almost exclusively on control of broadcasting by broadcasters, believing that if the industry monitors itself, the government will be less likely to interfere. The Television Code, for example, appeared in 1952, the very year that television became a coast-to-coast system after the Federal Communications Commission's (FCC) Sixth Report and Order. In the NAB's own words, the industry "feared the threat of government regulation and the threat of censorship from outside interests."[8] However, to assume that codes will forestall coercive intervention by governments is to commit what philosophers call a category mistake. It is faulty reasoning to take the kind of accountability in domain number two and conclude with the legal sanction of domain number one. Likewise, SPJ/SDX's persistent argument for self-regulation—that First Amendment freedoms preclude enforceable codes—is a category mistake. It also mixes the first area with the second.

Our primary stumbling block is the first definition of accountability: legal liability. The press does have an explicit constitutional prerogative and is entitled to the protection that such legal rights provide. As documented historically by the Anglo-American struggle over freedom of expression, prohibitions against government encroachment in themselves provide little assurance that legal protection will be honored. Already with George Washington there were complaints about the press, and government hostility warrants continuous vigilance. In an age in which media ownership is increasingly concentrated in fewer hands— chains, networks, and conglomerates—the answers cannot be as simplistic as often assumed or hoped. But why delimit the currently vigorous effort in journalism and law to clarify precisely what First Amendment freedom means? I certainly find no reason to be Pollyannaish. Who would deny the value of thorough attention to the press's constitutional guarantees, especially with the Supreme Court often wondering, "What does the press think it is?" Moreover, if one examines any of the recent conflicts between the press and government—the *Pentagon Papers*, the fair trial–free press controversies, and the jailing of reporters over source disclosure, for example—one recognizes immediately the weightiness of this debate, although too much hysteria and paranoia often becloud the warranted concerns.[9]

At this point I only want to reiterate the implausibility of bringing codes of ethics under the aegis of First Amendment rights, as done repeatedly in the libertarian tradition. Three examples for disclaiming any enforcement of SPJ/SDX-type codes are illustrative:

For journalists to seriously contemplate an enforcement procedure designed to punish those who do not conform to someone's preconceived set of moral rules is contrary to the meaning of the First Amendment which these journalists are trying to uphold in a misguided way.[10]

If the press is afforded constitutional guarantees against any restriction on its freedom by Congress, there is no way such restrictive powers (as enforcing codes) could be granted to others.[11]

Enforcement of a code of ethics smacks of intimidation. In fact, it would become an infringement on our First Amendment rights.[12]

Such argumentation scores debators' points because of the media's visceral attachment to their constitutional protection. But to use "Congress shall make no law abridging" as an argument for not enforcing codes is logically fallacious and ignores the distinction between penal action by governments and moral sanction by private organizations. Efforts by a profession to enforce its code of ethics cannot be said to threaten First Amendment freedom directly. Judging one accountable in the second sense of accountability does not in itself, as a newspaper editor once declared, put us "a few steps away from judges and legislators who impose restrictions on the activities of reporters."[13]

Legal counsel at present generally recommends that newspapers and broadcasters not codify their standards. Specific codes, it is argued, may be used as a yardstick in litigation. This is precisely the argument that won the day recently when Casey Bukro's task force recommended a set of grievance procedures to the SPJ/SDX board for violations of the society's code of ethics.[14] The 1983 SPJ/SDX president Phil Record had established a task force to draft a grievance procedure that allows complaints to be aired without harming reputations. He did so on the grounds that when the code was adopted in 1973, it ended with a pledge to try and forestall violations of these standards by censuring them. However, this provision to prevent the code from being just another lofty-sounding document had never been implemented.

A *modus operandi* was submitted to the SPJ/SDX Board of Directors in November 1984 that outlined a four-tier review process that could lead to expulsion of members in extreme cases of ethical misconduct. The board tabled the proposal and requested a survey of chapters to determine their willingness to accept the recommended procedure. With only 19 in favor and an opinion from SPJ/SDX's lawyer that if the code of ethics was upheld the Society would be involved in extensive litigation, the board in May 1985 unanimously rejected the grievance procedure proposal. Instead, it asked the chair of the National Ethics Committee to update code implementation guidelines that emphasize education and heightened awareness.

My analysis suggests that the lawyer's advice and board's decision represent a confusion of categories over accountability. Of course, labeling something intellectually wrongheaded does not in itself confront the legal and political realities. A clear head and upright conscience are not barriers from jail or fines. Obviously in this limited space all the practical dimensions cannot be resolved. But let me at least suggest the general approach my notion of accountability would take regarding explicit enforced codes and the judiciary.

The legal counsel against codes in news organizations is based on what I call power pragmatism. It presumes that written standards provide ammunition to the enemy in the judicial arena and thus weakens the press institutionally. That may be true in the short run, although I know of no specific instances in which written codes have rendered a news operation powerless in court. And as Sam Zagoria of the *Washington Post* has observed, "good newspaper practice is readily demonstrable in the courtroom, with or without a code, and putting standards in writing is evidence of the paper's good intentions."[15]

However, regardless of immediate benefits, the strategy of power pragmatism has little to recommend it over the long term. A policy based on winning legal cases has the potential of undermining the journalism profession at its core, of permitting it to avoid the substantive issues about its logic and purpose. Saving our neck ought not be an occasion for losing our soul. In that sense, there are no guarantees anyhow. Reasonable and legitimate safety is honorable; but without being moralistic, taking risks on occasion in the short term may be unavoidable.

Second, the issue is not written codes or no codes, but the type of codes news organizations adopt. Philosophers have long distinguished the notions blameworthy and praiseworthy. We are blameworthy if we violate an explicit minimum standard, we are praiseworthy if we achieve an ideal. Journalists who risk jail to protect a source may be praiseworthy, but no one is there to blame for refusing to grant confidentiality in particular situations. A journalist who knowingly distorts the facts is blameworthy for falling below the minimum convention of providing facts as we know them. However, journalists cannot be blamed if they conscientiously substantiate their sources and provide an accurate account of what is known to date, without reaching a lofty version of truth. Ideal standards may not be attainable except in unusual circumstances. Those who achieve them are praiseworthy; those who do not reach the ideal are not, therefore, blameworthy. Practitioners who win Pulitzers are noteworthy in that they have reached what is perceived as ideal. Failing to reach that achievement, however, does not imply one is blameworthy.

Journalism professor Deni Elliott has clarified this distinction as applied to journalism codes of ethics. She argues correctly that we should carefully distinguish minimal standards of professional practice from standards as perceived ideals.[16] Our codes to date are mixed through with both—from lofty rhetoric about serving the truth to minimum conventions about checking two sources to verify every story. If we carefully distinguish minimal and ideal codes, we can aid in preventing judges from concluding erroneously that because we have not acted in a praiseworthy manner we are, therefore, blameworthy.

My reconstruction further precludes the use of codes for answerability, that is, as a responsible explanation for the public's legitimate questions about press behavior. In fact, codes are often promoted currently as a signal to a disgruntled public that the press has its house in order. However, to presume that codes improve the media's credibility with society is to conflate two social groupings (professional colleagues and the citizenry). Given the definition of answerability as a blaming and responding process, codes of ethics are profoundly inadequate. The initiator raises a complaint, seeks an explanation, and justifiably requests an accounting; the obligation of the respondent is obviously some response, enough description to satisfy and clarify. Codes, by definition, are static and formally contoured; even in confusing and intractable situations they are beguilingly rigid. They are explicitly sculptured objects in a fluid universe, and therefore asymmetrical and inappropriate.

Certainly this third domain is crucial today. In this age of escalated consumerism, publishers and broadcasters realize instinctively the threat of audience dissatisfaction. And even beyond the economic motivation, the epiologue of the SPJ/SDX code is undoubtedly well meant: "Adherence to the Code of Ethics is intended to preserve the bond of mutual trust and respect between American journalists and the American people."[17] However, given the frame of reference developed earlier, media practitioners should not be surprised that media codes are seen by the general public as a mantle of self-protection and "status quoism." Newspersons point to such words as truth and fairness written all through the codes, and their accusers hear arrogance instead. Especially during embattlement—precisely when codes are heralded as essential by the profession—what we communicate with codes becomes ironically turned on its head. Codes may have enhanced respectability in the 1920s, but whenever the atmosphere becomes highly charged, codes tend to be read as parochial instruments for protecting the tangible interests of the privileged. Ethical codes are structurally flawed as a device for producing that type of accounting I have termed answerability. In reaching this conclusion, I do not dispute that accountability to the public is necessary, only that codes cannot produce it. Letters to the editor, explicit rules for correcting mistakes, ombudsmen, news councils, and other devices are better ways of interacting with the public and taking them seriously.

Thus, in the recent debate between John Quinn of *U.S.A. Today* and Eugene Patterson of the *St. Petersburg Times* over codes of ethics, I obviously side with Quinn's pro-code stand. However, the thrust of his defense is that we must enhance our integrity with the public. "The issue," Quinn says, "is credibility."[18] That rationale I find unconvincing, contending for codes instead on the grounds that professional life needs an epicenter, a center of gravity, and a gyroscope.

Ombudsmen are particularly important agents of this third level of accountability. However, this presumes that ombudsmen are decisively and unswervingly the public's representative. The recent Theodore Glasser–James Ettema study of ombudsmen for the Silha Center indicated sharply divided loyalties among them. Fifteen of the 32 ombudsmen apparently agreed that in the final analysis their loyalty is to the newspaper. An equal number disagreed. Twenty-eight see themselves as neutral mediators between the paper and its readers. One-third claimed it was important to "provide hard-hitting critiques of management's policies and decision."[19]

Obviously we cannot make simplistic, generic judgments about serving two masters. Who among readers or viewers ought to be represented anyhow? And do not the studies suggest that the public sees ombudsmen as advocates of the paper rather than its own representatives?

My analysis of accountability, while not pontificating on all the nuances, does provide a specific direction the ombudsmen issue should take. The public legitimately demands an account, an interaction, or a response to their queries about the best ways to serve the civic good.[20] Ombudsmen are an appropriate agent of answerability whereas codes are not. Given our anxiety over press credibility, ombudsmen carry possibilities that codes do not. With only 35 members among the 1,688 daily newspapers, the Organization of News Ombudsmen is the only journalism association that can fit in one bus with room to spare. An important resource for coping fruitfully with public accountability is unfortunately still struggling for recognition among its peers.

ENFORCED CODES

So far, I have attempted to lay aside journalism's usual objections to enforced codes by contending that such reservations are based on faulty reasoning. This opens the door for considering more precisely the role of codes in the professional domain where accountability implies moral sanction. It is obvious enough that one cannot successfully maintain a community with explicit functions without attaching specific rebukes—such as those formulated in a code of ethics—for failing to meet obligations. Moreover, it seems incontrovertible that the notion of accountability as moral sanction requires peer machinery to apply controls on behalf of the membership. People cannot be called into account for violating their communal obligations unless there are norms by which they can assign obligations and decide innocence or guilt. No accounting occurred without a visible process whereby agreed-on principles function as arbiters of obligation. Clearly no one is accountable to everyone else for everything done. But denying that there are any enforceable codes is tantamount to claiming we are not accountable to others who share our craft. No matter how poorly law and medicine have administered their codes, they have correctly concluded that such instruments are inherent in the very structure of collegial life. Others intend the same idea, although in a more general sense, when they condemn unenforced codes as a charade.

The argument for codes in this second domain—that is, codes among colleagues—hinges on understanding the mass media's organizational structure. The press cannot be reduced to the unfettered decisions of individual managers, editors, and reporters. Newspapers and broadcasting are powerful and technologically sophisticated social institutions. Journalism does not consist of persons and their autonomous actions, but must be seen as an intricate network of interrelated roles, means, and forces that combine into an enterprise, a system. And as students of organizational theory have documented unambiguously, all bureaucratic forms develop a *Geist*, a structural shape, that exists in some fashion independently of the personnel themselves. Max Weber nearly a century ago identified a technical rationality that serves the useful function of providing cohesion and self-sufficiency. However, bureaucratic structures simultaneously tend to create barriers that are impervious to values and socially responsible ends. Contemporary writers such as Jacques Ellul in his *Political Illusion* and Robert Nisbet in *Twilight of Authority* elaborate on the Weberian analysis in such a compelling fashion that no one can glibly assume professionals ought to be left alone to make individual decisions regarding their activities and behavior.[21]

In Irving Janis's version, "group think" characterizes the decision-making process in most contemporary organizations—commerce, military, politics, and education.[22] Janis defines group think as the psychological drive for consensus that suppresses dissent and critical appraisal. Group think is the tendency to conform to norms of the professional group or bureaucratic structure rather than to imperatives of a normative kind. It is the herd instinct in journalism, the concurrence-seeking tendency that makes career advancement more important than integrity and independent thinking.

Whatever else codes of ethics may have to offer, their formulation "represents a modest but important means by which people can discover, before they act, how they would best like to act and imaginatively test in advance some of the difficult choices that lie ahead."[23] Against the centripetal pull of bureaucratic forces, the process of constructing codes of ethics serves to sharpen our corporate responsibility.[24] Complicated professions such as journalism ought to be engaged continually in heightening its moral acumen. In stark cases, such as the Janet Cooke affair, we realize instantly the cheating and deception involved. The heavyweight, once-in-a-lifetime, sensational cases in which we are caught in a malfeasance of duty—such are not worth debating. For Adolf Hitler, Idi Amin, and Al Capone, the case is shut. Ordinarily our consciences refuse to tolerate outright lies, breaking and entering, and stolen money.

But frequently the moral dimension is not obvious or the choices are tragic. Everyday life in a complicated world often leaves us with a forked tongue or a double mind. What about Abscam coverage? The legal questions regarding entrapment may be self-evident, but what is ethical or unethical about using leaked information from the Justice Department outside the context of courts and jury? Or about naming a shoplifter, providing photographic coverage of grieving parents whose four children just died in a fire, writing about the sexual escapades of a senator, exposing a prominent right-to-lifer concealing an abortion, advocating the rights of the oppressed and powerless, or revealing secret information about government policy that contradicts public statements? Identifying the ethical issues here is not always simple.

While the journalism profession as a whole shows moral sensitivity, our ethical awareness needs ongoing improvement. Codes aid in stimulating the moral imagination. Acting on our own without forethought usually results in a minimalist ethics, quandary ethics, or, what is even more counterproductive, in hot-tempered moralism. Codes with a normative bearing, fired by intellectual scope and substance, and contoured by principle are codes that help provide a sense of center and periphery when concrete moral judgments must be made.

My main concern here is to clarify the enforcement matter philosophically. Obviously, as we witness within SPJ/SDX itself, there are complicated problems involved in actually designing a set of enforcement procedures supervised by peers. But once we recognize in good faith that we are inevitably and inescapably accountable as professional colleagues to each other, we will begin cooperating in implementing this commitment intelligently. When our easy arguments are stripped away, common sense and realism on the more precise matters will allow us to finalize the details.

Although with ambiguities, one potentially helpful development at present is the adoption of detailed codes by various broadcasting and newspaper employers. After the National Labor Relations Board ruled in 1976 that the *Madison Capital Times* could impose a binding code of ethics on management and reporters, a host of newspapers formulated their own company policy. Some have been patterned directly after codes from professional associations (the *Milwaukee Journal* Company, for example, adopted the SPJ/SDX Code in December 1973). Others have emphasized particular standards (the *Detroit Free Press*, for example, specifically forbids the acceptance of outside gifts and the *Roanoke* (Virginia) *Times and World News* has exacting guidelines regarding anonymous sources). The 1980 APME (Associated Press Managing Editors Association) Red Book identified four out of five American newspapers with ethics codes of some sort, whereas a 1960 study of APME's Image Committee could locate "little or nothing."

Management at present controls the initiative, and the interests of the Newspaper Guild must be brought more centrally into these company-by-company codes. The guild's secretary-treasurer, Robert M. Crocker, has legitimately complained that typical codes "appear to be directed almost exclusively at the hired hand."[25] The *Jacksonville* (Florida) *Journal* and *Florida Times-Union* did involve the entire staff in preparing its code, but this across-the-board strategy is not typical. Assuming that company codes are not formed and imposed hierarchically, they do have distinct advantages. The codes of national associations cannot be as practical, itemized, and comprehensive. John Merrill legitimately scourges them as vacuous rhetoric.[26] Company-specific guidelines can elaborate the provision in full detail; the *Seattle Times*, for instance, restricts reporters from entering their stories in certain kinds of promotions and contests. Setting local standards helps establish a company mystique and reputation, thereby decreasing the quandary of individuals within it and protecting them from outside wolves who assume everything is negotiable. As a minimum, these codes could halt flagrant breaches of ethics and conflicts of interest, such as occur when columnists receive pay from politicians or financial writers trumpet their own stock. The *Springfield* (Massachusetts) *Republican*, for example, makes inaccurate quotations unpardonable: "When people are quoted, the quoted passage is literally spoken." The *Louisville Courier-Journal* and *Times* refuse all advertisements that "attack, criticize, or cast reflection on any individual, race, religion, or institution." CBS has explicit news standards for "Demonstrations, Riots, and Other Civil Disturbances." Whereas in 1972 only 1.6 percent of 210 newspapers surveyed had a stated freebies policy, the figures had climbed to 35 percent one year after the SPJ/SDX code was adopted. In the *1982 SPJ/SDX Journalism Ethics Report*, Steven Dornfield could claim—although with hyperbole—that freebies are now "as outdated as typewriters and glue pots."

Enforced codes characterized by such specific guidelines can serve journalism professionals on the minimum level of what Henry Aiken labels rule obedience. This essay calls for a continual struggle with the issue of wise and effective enforcement, rather than making the facile assumption that the problem is now safely in the hands of management. If we wish to enhance the professional shape of the press over the long term, writing and enforcing codes must continue vigorously within voluntary associations also.

ETHICAL THEORY

I advocate a radical turn to accountability—meaning radical as radix, the root out of which our entire vocabulary of self-regulation is ramified. Accountability is a radical notion in the manner acetic acid is radical vinegar and granite is radical rock. The notion in radical is not extreme movement toward the edge (as with "left") but straight down to the source.

Enforced codes, ombudspersons, and ethics specialists in the newsroom—all these options have penultimate status—in Dietrich Bonhoeffer's sense. While morally desirable in themselves, they ought not be promoted or introduced as final solutions. If they arise from clearheaded understanding of justifiable accountability, over the long stretch I consider them beneficent. But in an era of revolutionary demands, fixation on codes alone seems petty. Within today's social and economic structures, codes can do no more than clean the house. As household chores are essential for families to function, so codism is desirable for professional life. However, if one weighs the overall significance of these activities, brooms and soap (to continue the analogy) are trivial compared to the need for architecture and footings. The call to foundational work, to conceptual finesse remains the ultimate challenge, the irreducible, nonnegotiable priority.

Hans Jonas's *The Imperative of Responsibility* is widely debated in Germany at present. This book is wall-to-wall argument, with the extraordinary aim of fashioning an ethical theory of compelling force for modern technological societies. Jonas refuses to be cynical or nihilistic. He is especially animated against a narrow and minimalist ethics that refuses to take seriously the magnitude of contemporary crises—our potential annihilation, our global dependency on one another, and our secularized culture. He observes correctly that at the very moment today's vast powers ought to be regulated by norms, our culture has destroyed the idea of norms as such.[27]

The starting point for Jonas, and I believe likewise for us, is establishing ontologically the idea of human responsibility. Irrespective of belief in God, regardless of our politics, he argues, we all are bound to at least one categorical imperative—preservation of life, maintenance of our natural existence. In all respects, *The Imperative of Responsibility* is a *tour de force* and demonstrates the intellectual maturity and substantive theoretical achievement that should also characterize our reexamination of the press as a social institution.

The academy plays a vital role as well. In addition to supporting the SPJ/SDX enforcement effort with this theoretical and historical background, I call on journalism educators to develop a normative social ethics. Constructing a normative ethics with "giving an account" as its focus, can free us from the truncated parameters that confine the issues at present; as a minimum it provides a vocabulary, a framework, the soil from which accountability can grow. Certainly this call to reflection cannot be dismissed as abstract theorizing. My concern is for an intellectual process mediated through practical situations, for moral inquiry that bonds means with ends, that embraces both virtuous action and rational insight.

A generally accepted body of principles would free us from merely reacting to daily pressures when we write the guidelines. It would prevent us from leaning too heavily on constitutional guarantees and from bogging down emotionally in an avalanche of urgent decisions. A finely honed ethics with cognitive substance can prevent overwrought moralism while goading us to recognize the moral issues. What we codify, and how we codify it, can benefit from a reservoir of value theory and informed ethical inquiry.

Serious attention to applied and professional ethics is one catalyst for further advance that can run in fruitful parallel with the adoption of enforced codes by companies and professional organizations. Codes can only have an admonitory function, whereas my option asserts that we need much more pedagogy, more groundwork, more enlightenment on such basic matters as terminology and the worldview underlying our admonitions to moral action. A normative ethics, purged of delusions and personal interests, would raise a stable anchor for daily practice. It represents a fresh start that profits directly from our 60 years of experience with media codes while speaking with a different cadence. It would pester and stimulate us by an authoritative voice. Richard Wasserstrom's convictions about his professional hold for journalism as well: "We might all be better served if lawyers were to see themselves less as subject to role-differentiated behavior and more as subject to the demand of the moral point of view."[28]

Perhaps we can better take our cues here from Walter Lippmann, America's greatest twentieth-century journalist. When faced in the 1920s with collapsing standards and angry assaults similar to today, he responded with a decisive turn in 1929 to his book *A Preface to Morals*. He made no appeal under these strenuous conditions to either the Constitution or codes, but identified the basic problem as his generation's inability to discriminate right from wrong. Realizing that little progress was possible in a moral vacuum, Lippmann searched philosophy, theology, history, and sociology for a system of values strong and relevant to postwar conditions. His reconstructions were not that practical and did not deal with every urgent question. He sought, in fact, a *preface* to morals.

However, under an obsession with events and burdens of profit making, please do not conclude that Lippmann's reconstructions were irrelevant or even bizarre. *A Preface to Morals* became a best-seller (six editions the first year) and a rallying point for a broad exploration into the despair of his time. Lipmann taught us the value of being a scholar in a troubled world who never lets the immediate conundrums tear him loose from the principal domain beneath the turbulent surface. Then, as now, vitality in our minds and conscience can eventually reshape the press's professional contours toward one in which giving an account receives its due and proper focus. In this instance, the longest route around is the best way home.

NOTES

1. Thomas Jefferson, address to Philadelphia Delegates, May 25, 1808. For similar highly quoted passages see his letter to Marquis de Lafayette, November 4, 1823 ("the only security of all is a free press") and his letter to Dr. James Curvis, January 18, 1786 ("Our liberty depends on the freedom of the press and that cannot be limited without being lost").

2. Thomas Jefferson, letter to President Washington, September 9, 1792.

3. Aleksandr Solzhenitsyn, "Harvard Commencement Address, June 1978: A World Split Apart," *National Review*, 30 (July 7, 1978):838.

4. Examples of such newspapers adopting codes: the *Brooklyn Eagle*, the *Christian Science Monitor*, the *Springfield Republican*, Hearst newspapers, *The Detroit News*, the *Sacramento Bee*, the *Seattle Times*, and the *Kansas City Journal-Post*. Iron-

ically, even Warren G. Harding, then editor of the *Marion Star*, adopted a code in the 1920s for his paper.

5. Randy Block, "How Effective Is Our Code of Ethics?" *ASNE Bulletin*, 82 (521) (July 1968): pp. 13, 14; For further reflections on the Bonfils incident and enforcement, see E. Canham, "The American View of Codes." *Problems of Journalism: Proceedings of the 1968 ASNE Convention*, 1968, pp. 73–79 and Vincent S. Jones, "Can We Judge Each Other," *ASNE Bulletin* 82 (520) (June 1968):1, 10.

6. Block, "How Effective Is Our Code," p. 14.

7. For helpful philosophical statements that have benefited my own formulations, see Charles V. Blatz, "Accountability and Answerability," *Journal of the Theory of Social Behavior*, 6(2) (October 1976):253–259. Larry R. Churchill, "The Professionalization of Ethics: Some Implications for Accountability in Medicine," *Soundings*, 60(1) (Spring 1977):40–53 provides a sociological analysis of how medicine has reduced the notion of accountability.

8. National Association of Broadcasters, Television Code, 1952.

9. In the long run, Pulitzer Prize winner Anthony Lewis of *The New York Times*, may be correct in chiding his colleagues: "their struggle with the government pressure is terribly important as a symbol and morale builder." *Editor and Publisher*, 110 (November 19, 1977):34.

10. "Call Your Lawyer," *Editor and Publisher*, 117 (December 8, 1984):6.

11. John M. Harrison, "Media, Men and Morality," *Review of Politics*, 36(2) (April 1974):255.

12. Charles Long, *Quill*, 66 (June 1978):20.

13. SPJ/SDX President McCord, cited in *Quill*, 63 (October 1975):31.

14. For details see Casey Bukro, "The SPJ Code's Double-Edged Sword: Accountability, Credibility," *Journal of Mass Media Ethics*, 1(1) (Fall–Winter 1985–86):10–13.

15. *ASNE Bulletin*, 98 (October 1984):10.

16. Deni Elliott-Boyle, "A Conceptual Analysis of Ethics Codes," *Journal of Mass Media Ethics*, 1(1) (Fall–Winter 1985–86):22–26.

17. Society of Professional Journalists/Sigma Delta Chi, Code of Ethics, 1973.

18. "Why Your Paper Should/Should Not Have a Written Code of Ethics," *ASNE Bulletin*, (October 1984):12–43.

19. "Newspaper Ombudsmen Have Divided Loyalties," *Editor and Publisher*, 118 (June 22, 1985):10–11. See also James S. Ettema and Theodore L. Glasser, "Public Accountability or Public Relations? Newspaper Ombudsmen Define Their Role," *Journalism Quarterly*, 64 (Spring 1987): pp. 3–12.

20. For description of how such interaction between readers and ombudsmen can actually function, see Sam Zagoria, "I, the Jury," *The Quill*, 79 (April 1986):12–16.

21. Clifford G. Christians, "The Implications of Ellul's Bureaucratization for Regulatory Commissions," *International Journal of Contemporary Sociology*, 19(3–4) (July and October 1982):27–44.

22. Irving Janis, *Victims of Group Think*. Boston: Houghton Mifflin, 1972, pp. 2–13, 184–206.

23. Arthur J. Dyck, *On Human Care: An Introduction to Ethics*. Nashville, Tenn.: Abingdon, 1977, p. 29.

24. For illuminating analyses of the notion of corporate responsibility, see

John Ladd, "Philosophical Remarks on Professional Responsibility in Organizations." In A. Flores, ed., *Designing for Safety Engineering Ethics in Organizational Contexts*. Troy, N.Y.: NSF Study, 1982, pp. 191–203; Thomas J. Donaldson, "Moral Agency and Corporations," *Philosophy in Context*, 10 (1980):54–70; and Martin Benjamin, "Can Moral Responsibility Be Collective and Nondistributive," *Social Theory and Practice*, 4(1) (1979):93–106.

25. *Editor and Publisher*, Bill Kirtz, "Conference Held on Media Ethics," 110 (November 19, 1977):27.

26. John Merrill and Jack Odell, *Philosophy and Journalism* (New York: Longman, 1983, pp. 137–145.

27. Hans Jonas, *The Imperative of Responsibility*. Chicago: University of Chicago Press, 1984, p. 22.

28. Richard Wasserstrom, "Lawyers as Professionals: Some Moral Issues," *Human Rights*, 5 (1975):1–24.

5

SELF-REGULATION: REFLECTIONS OF AN INSIDER

Richard P. Cunningham

It is inconceivable, as Professor Clifford Christians says, for a press that is not free to perform the functions that have been assigned to or—perhaps more correctly—taken on by the press in our democracy. It is also true, as he says, that self-regulation is the only model that the American press has so far supported for encouraging accountability.

But self-regulation has not produced the quality of journalism that is demanded by our times. The self-regulated press has not produced an informed, concerned electorate. It has failed to broaden the spectrum of ideas within which political candidates can function with any hope of support. It does not command respect for its morality partly, as Christians notes, because of a pompous tendency to wrap itself in the folds of the First Amendment whenever its morality is questioned, but, more important, because—despite the proliferation of codes of press ethics—the press is not itself clear on what morality is.

Christians calls for us to quit using the First Amendment shield for protection from anything but a true legal threat to the freedom of the press. He asks the press to accept without reservation the responsibility to give an account, to be answerable, a responsibility that goes along with the special privileges granted to the press by custom and by the First Amendment.

He calls for journalists to turn to moral philosophy for the elements of what he terms a normative ethics. And he calls for enforcement, not by law, but by processes to be devised by journalists of the refined codes of journalistic conduct that will flow from that clear body of ethical principles.

Professor Christians is, as he acknowledges, preaching to the converted. His argument that self-regulation is capable of producing the kind of press we need might not convince Aleksandr Solzhenitsyn, whom he quotes. Nor, probably, would it convince a Swede, accustomed to a more regulated press, or even one of the significant percentage of Americans who, irritated by what they perceive as unpatriotic or arrogant behavior on the part of reporters, react by telling opinion surveyors that they do indeed support some limitation on press freedoms.

Even some insiders who have looked with fear on any kind of government interference with the press freedom have begun to worry about whether that freedom can survive nongovernmental threats without government help. Richard Salant, former president of CBS News and former vice chairman of NBC, expressed concern at the purchase of NBC's parent company by General Electric (GE). Salant says internal, but publicly known, rules should be devised to create a wall separating the corporate managers from the news operation when a company as powerful as GE—especially as a defense contractor—buys a news organization. Among those rules should be one requiring that all communications between corporate and news managers be in writing. Certainly the professionalization of journalists implicit in Christians's argument would be no match for power such as that of GE.

But whatever regulation may be necessary to provide for freedom must stop at the point where freedom is provided, and Christians is right that the responsibility for regulation within that freedom must fall on the press itself. Furthermore, the press must show a greater sense of urgency than it has displayed so far.

But Christians has written a disciplined, philosophical paper that leaves us hungry for some how-to thoughts that mix up realistically his categories of responsibility and provide more concrete encouragement than he does for the belief that self-regulation will work. The key words are local and voluntary.

Christians did not write about news councils, because his paper was limited to what insiders might do to make self-regulation a more effective model for press accountability. The National News Council in the United States, which quit in 1984 after failing in 11 years to gain significant press support, was not a product of insiders. It was established with foundation funding, and it took on itself the authority to comment on the fairness and accuracy of journalists' work. (Thirty years earlier editors objected to the recommendations of the Hutchins Commission on the same basis.)

But there are successful news councils in Canada's provinces, successful because they are voluntary. The councils investigate complaints only against those newspapers that are members of the council. The Minnesota News Council, the only state news council in the United States, has functioned successfully since 1971; it was the product of the Minnesota Newspaper Association. Two prominent American editors, Michael Waller at the *Hartford Courant* and Howard H. Hays, Jr., at the *Press-Enterprise* in Riverside, California, support the idea of submitting voluntarily to an appeals panel any complaint that they cannot resolve on their own.

If voluntary councils can find support among American editors, so can voluntary enforcement of ethics codes find support among American journalists. Journalists could band together in local organizations pledged publicly to certain standards of behavior in getting and reporting the news—perhaps those of the Society of Professional Journalists (SPJ)—and could establish mechanisms both for hearing complaints against members and for continuing discussion of the standards.

Members would waive their privileges to sue the local professional organization for publicizing its findings, just as complainants to news councils waive their rights to sue. And the public hearing on a complaint or an issue would be the principal sanction, although the local professional organization might design suspension or an expulsion into its enforcement mechanisms so long as his or her freedom to report was not legally restricted.

Some, perhaps most, newspapers, and broadcast news organizations, will not volunteer for submitting complaints to an appeals panel. Some, perhaps most, journalists will not volunteer to join local professional associations. No matter. The public discussion of principles by those who do commit themselves will gradually have two results: one, increased understanding on the part of both the public and journalists of the subtleties of journalistic problems, and two, the emergence of a body of concepts recognized—at first locally but then, by comparison with the experience of other local bodies, universally—as good journalistic practice.

Christians seems to involve only journalist's peers in enforcing and—although this is not so clear—developing codes of practice. That position flows from his careful differentiation among journalists' responsibilities to the government, to ourselves as professionals, and to the public. But it is a mistake to leave the public out of the development and the enforcement of journalistic codes. Journalism is and ought to be a popular art; indeed, its failures stem largely from its abandonment of that recognition. Journalists are and ought to be responsible to the public to the extent that their codes of conduct reflect a public conscience as well as the conscience of the practitioners of the art. It is foolish to pretend that the public cannot limit the freedoms we now enjoy.

Christians's delineation of three categories of journalistic responsibility is, in this connection, helpful in conceptualizing, but if we stick with it in application, it gets in the way of progress toward making self-regulation a more effective model for assuring media accountability. It is not helpful, for example, to simply label as "category mistake" the fear that voluntary codes of journalistic conduct may be used against journalists. Judges in Nebraska and the state of Washington have used voluntary free press-fair trial agreements as the basis for orders limiting the press's access to pretrial material.

A plaintiff's attorney used both the newspapers' code of ethics and a critical column by the newspapers' ombudsmen against the *Wilmington* (Delaware) *News Journal* in a libel suit. However, while the newspapers lost the suit, there was no indication that the verdict was influenced by the reading of the code or the column. Indeed, it is more persuasive that the adoption of a code and the establishment of an ombudsman or some other method to examine journalistic commitment serves to promote deep regard, not disregard, for truth and responsibility in reporting.

The trick then is to write codes so that they differentiate clearly among what is Caesar's and what is not. Christians notes correctly that one scholar has provided significant help in this regard. Deni Elliott suggests three codes. One would include the established sins such as lying, cheating, and demonstrable conflict of interest for which we all agree a reporter or editor ought to be fired. Another would include ideal characteristics such as energy, initiative, intelligence, and service to the truth and to the community. Journalists might be praised for approaching the ideals on that list, but could not be blamed for falling short. Elliott's two lists would leave at issue those ethical journalistic problems that are dealt with daily in the news huddles of broadcast and print news operations: fairness, accuracy, taste, privacy, a defendant's rights, doing harm, confidentiality, telephone taping, reliability of sources, less obvious conflicts of interest, competition, and a host of others.

And the public ought to be involved in the discussion of those issues. Take conflict of interest, for example. It means one thing to a conservative critic such as Accuracy in Media's Reed Irvine and something quite different to Dan Rather. Yet conflict of interest is definable in the abstract. The public knows that. We ought to accept the responsibility for thrashing out with the public and in public a definition with which we as journalists are prepared to live.

George Bernard Shaw said that every profession is a conspiracy against the public. The goal here is to create a profession that involves the public, a body of people called to the art of journalism and practicing it professionally in the sense that they subscribe to ethical standards. Unlike other professions, however, journalists must not have their freedom to continue as journalists jeopardized by the action of a licensing body. They must preserve their freedom to continue to speak by ensuring that the punishment for failing to meet their own voluntarily accepted standards would be discussion of their alleged failure in a public forum.

That punishment can be severe. Burton Benjamin argues in his internal CBS report that the producer had violated the network's ethical standards in the production of "The Uncounted Enemy," the documentary over which General William C. Westmoreland sued CBS. At the same Media Freedom and Accountability conference, Benjamin said it was a heavy sanction for the producer and the network to have lost a degree of credibility.

That's true, and as a measure of how heavy that sanction is, it is interesting to sample one's own feelings about the credibility of three news organizations after revelations about their reporting. The first is CBS News after the revelations that its producer cheated in the Westmoreland case, another is *Time* magazine after revelation that its reporting was sloppy in the case of Israeli General Ariel Sharon, and the third is the *Washington Post* after revelations that its reporter had snipped at Mobil board chairman William Tavoulareas as he collected information for a story about him. Or in the case of the *Post*, that the Tavoulareas story went into the paper even after a copy editor said, in effect, that the emperor was unclothed, there was no story there.

My own reaction as a newsperson was indignation and a diminution of my reliance on the credibility of each news organization. But part of that was that in each case the revelations had to be pried out of the news organization in a libel suit.

How different the reaction to the *Post*'s revelation that the eight-year-old heroin addict whose story had won the paper a Pulitzer Prize simply did not exist. Also how different the reaction to the *New York Times*'s revelation that a magazine story about guerrilla warfare in Cambodia had been completely fabricated. In both cases, the revelations were frank and complete after the newspapers learned—not under certain threat of a lawsuit—that they had been gulled.

There is a message in the different reactions to these revelations that supports the argument that voluntary self-regulation is effective. It is a message that is borne out by the experience of ombudsmen who have had to hand over to company lawyers complaints about the fairness and accuracy of news stories: When journalistic disputes get into lawyers' hands, tactics become the first concern and the revelation of truth is grudging. Grudging admission is damaging to reputation.

Again, perhaps because he is limiting himself to what insiders can do, Christians does not discuss press criticism as part of the mechanism for making self-regulation more effective. Yet one of the obvious sources of effective press criticism is journalists themselves. There is a reluctance on the part of news organizations to criticize each other. As a result, today too much of the criticism of the press is left to Accuracy in Media

and other organizations with legitimate but limited special interests—
NOW, Right to Life, Pro-Choice, National Association of Manufacturers,
National Rifle Association, and Americans for Democratic Action. More
needs to be done by news organizations themselves along the lines of
the questioning by *The New York Times* of NBC News for its agreement
not to reveal the whereabouts of the terrorist Abdul Abbas, if he would
consent to an interview.

But Christians is right that in order to make self-regulation effective,
criticism and analysis may no longer be based simply on an overlay of
superficial ethics codes disguising a true commitment only to the libertarian tradition of the early American press. There must be something
new to enable the press to fulfill the responsibility laid on it 40 years
ago by the Hutchins Commission to be a socially responsible press. And
that something must come from moral philosophy. It is not enough to
protest that the moral base for most institutions in our society is no
longer simple and clear. In its role as reporter and examiner of ideas,
the press must report and examine what basic moral principles underlie
the journalistic codes whose words we have shuffled and reshuffled for
more than half a century.

To that end, Edmund Lambeth has taken an important step with his
book *Committed Journalism*. He calls for journalistic decisions to be tested
with reference to five principles: freedom, truth telling, justice, doing
no harm, and stewardship of the integrity of the means of communication. Certainly such principles have not been ignored in journalistic
decisions, but they have often been overridden by competitive concerns
and journalistic group think. And too often protests have been answered
with the defensive and incorrect suggestion that the First Amendment
protects the news organization from the requirement to give a moral
answer.

But that may be changing. Ethics courses are multiplying in college
journalism programs just as they are in the academic programs of other
disciplines. The *Philadelphia Inquirer* and the *Louisville Courier-Journal* are
experimenting with an ethics coach in the newsroom. Editors and news
directors are increasingly running into basic moral problems as they
engage in the currently popular pursuit of credibility. It is important to
encourage the search for moral bases, because it is intolerable that the
press—particularly in a postnationalistic time when its patriotism will
increasingly come under question—remain incapable of giving a definition of its function that is based on the most fundamental moral concepts.

6

THE VOLUNTARY MODEL: LIVING WITH "PUBLIC WATCHDOGS"

Alfred Balk

A century and a half ago Alexis de Tocqueville marveled at Americans' predilection for voluntary activities and associations. Other foreigners have observed that at heart we are tinkerers. Certainly any element of our populace regarded as civic-minded seems ill disposed to ignoring institutions that seem not to be fulfilling their responsibilities or whose integrity seems jeopardized.

Over the past two decades these traits—along with prevailing tides of consumerism and the most recent burst of American reformism—confronted U.S. media leaders with an unsettling phenomenon. Citizen groups whom they had inveighed for years to "help defend the First Amendment—it belongs to everyone," began seeking new ways to do so. Public interest groups focused on broadcasting. A national, a state, and several local voluntary media-public press councils were established. And lawyers and journalists joined in state fair trial-free press committees that drafted voluntary courtroom coverage guidelines.

Part of this vision was rooted in the Hutchins Commission, the most famous twentieth-century group to study the U.S. press. The commission, chaired by the charismatic chancellor of the University of Chicago Robert M. Hutchins, grew out of a dinner discussion he had with Henry R. Luce of Time Inc. in 1942. Luce suggested a study on U.S. press freedom and offered $200,000 to support it. The *Encyclopaedia Britannica* also contributed, and by 1947, 12 prominent intellectuals had completed the renowned report, *A Free and Responsible Press*.

The commission, it said, "concludes that the freedom of the press is in danger."[1] "Those who direct the machinery of the press have engaged from time to time in practices which the society condemns and which, if continued, it will inevitably undertake to regulate or control. . . . Freedom of the press for the coming period can only continue as an accountable freedom."[2]

Among other things, it recommended that "the agencies of mass communication assume the responsibility of financing new, experimental activities . . . of high literary, artistic, or intellectual quality . . . from the profits of its other business."[3] The report continued, "non-profit institutions help supply the variety, quantity, and quality of press service required by the American people . . . [and] enlist the cooperation of all who are interested in the cultural development of the country; . . . creation of academic professional centers of advanced study, research, and publication in the field of communications; . . . and the establishment of a new and independent agency to appraise and report annually upon the performance of the press."[4]

Nobody had "elected" the commission, and the press establishment received its report with disdain. "The 1947 transcript [of the American Society of Newspaper Editors convention]," noted the late Herbert Brucker, widely revered editor of the *Hartford* (Connecticut) *Courant,* "reveals twenty-four pages of disputation over how to phrase the anathema to be pronounced upon [it]."[5] By the Kennedy-Johnson years, however, television had become pervasive; the consensus era symbolized by radio's and the great national mass magazines' heydays was fading; the civil rights, ecology, and other movements were active; and reformist euphoria was in the air.

The British press, under Parliamentary prodding, already had helped establish a national press council. In 1967 in the United States, with part of a bequest honoring a former editor of the *Washington Daily News,* four local councils were set up in the West and Midwest; in 1970 Minnesota and Honolulu, spurred by Nixon-Agnew attacks on the press, formed councils; then a Twentieth Century Fund Task Force, which I served as a consultant-rapporteur, midwifed a national council.[6] The genie seemed to be out of the bottle.

But an inevitable political pendulum swing had begun. The assassination wave, Vietnam, Watergate, the oil crisis, the Japanese auto-steel-microchip invasion, global financial readjustments, and the genteel hedonism of the nouveau riche, all became part of it. The swing culminated in the Reagan thermidor. What, then, remains of the latest reformist period's experimentation?

"PUBLIC INTEREST" GROUPS

Consider first "public interest" groups. Originally the term was applied to organizations, generally nationwide, set up as intermediaries between private interests and government agencies. By now the concept's appeal has led to such ready appropriation that definitions of it virtually are in the eye of the beholder.

On general civic and governmental issues there are such broad, self-styled centrist groups as Common Cause and the League of Women Voters (the de facto convenor of the quadrennial televised presidential debates), plus publicized advocacy organizations such as the moral majority and Accuracy in Media. All monitor and lobby the media as well as government.

The U.S. Chamber of Commerce and local chambers monitor business coverage.[7] The chamber, through its Citizens Choice affiliate, convened a National Commission on Free and Responsible Media. The commission's 119-page report, *Responsibility and Freedom of the Press*, released in January 1985, was summarized in an 11-paragraph story in *The New York Times* that concluded with information on where to order the text.[8] Other corporate-funded organizations include the Media Institute, which monitors and issues reports on coverage of business; the Foundation for American Communications (FACS); the Institute for Applied Economics; and the Atomic Industrial Forum.

In the women's field, the NOW Media Project, supported by 250,000 members in 800 chapters of the National Organization for Women, has a $100,000 annual budget to influence coverage of women's issues. Others in the field include Women Against Pornography.[9] In other areas there are almost as many organizations as there are causes, ranging from the Anti-Defamation League of B'nai B'rith, the Arab-American Anti-Discrimination Committee, and the Black Citizens for a Fair Media to the National Gay Task Force and the National Right to Life Committee.

Among the media, broadcasting probably has been influenced most by these groups. In part this is due to the industry's nature. Over-the-air transmission is dependent on channels of an electronic spectrum legislatively defined, because of its finiteness, as public property to be allocated for use in the public interest. Historically, the regulatory Federal Communications Commissions (FCC) tends to become a captive of the interests it is supposed to regulate. The fact that television, with its channel scarcity and pervasive influence, bloomed in the most active postwar reformist era also contributed.

Peter Broderick has summarized the movements' impact in a paper for the Benton Foundation:

In 1966 the Office of Communication of the United Church of Christ won a precedent-setting victory in the U.S. Court of Appeals for the District of Columbia: ... that citizens have a right to participate in Federal Communications Commission proceedings, whether or not they have an economic interest in the matter ... [Subsequently] victories were won at the FCC, in Congress, in the courts, and on the local level. Citizens groups played a significant role in increasing minority employment in broadcasting; developing policies which favored minority ownership; enforcing the Fairness Doctrine; limiting cross-ownership and media concentration; defeating legislation; supporting public access; and fostering positive developments in public affairs and children's programming.[10]

The Reverend Everett C. Parker, then the director of the Office of Communication of the United Church of Christ (UCC), orchestrated the mid-sixties case that established citizens' rights to challenge broadcasting licenses. The decision in the UCC challenge in effect stripped WLBT-TV of Jackson, Mississippi, of its license for documented failure to serve its community's black population. Thus, Parker became widely regarded as what the magazine *American Film* called "the father of the public interest telecommunications movement."[11] Former FCC Commissioner Nicholas Johnson, as head of the National Citizens Committee for Broadcasting (NCCB), was also a movement power of the period.

Both Parker and Johnson now have moved on, Parker to semiretirement as a communications consultant and teacher at Fordham University, Johnson to work as an attorney, professor, and consultant in Iowa City, Iowa. Johnson's NCCB, meanwhile, has metamorphosed into the smaller and less-influential Telecommunications Action and Research Center, whose future has become uncertain with the announced departure of its president, Sam Simon, for consulting work.[12]

Still, the public interest organizational roster remains large, encompassing such groups as the National Council of Churches, the National Catholic Conference, the United Church of Christ, Action for Children's Television, the National Coalition on Television Violence, the Telecommunications Consumer Coalition, the Media Access Project, the National Association for Better Broadcasting, and a number of university-based programs. The university programs include Duke University's Washington Center for Public Policy Research, directed by Henry Geller, former assistant secretary of commerce and FCC general counsel; and UCLA's Communications Law Program, headed by Charles Firestone, formerly of the NCCB.

Of these, Action for Children's Television (ACT) probably is the most conspicuous. Founded in 1968 by Peggy Charren and three other women in Newtonville, Massachusetts, ACT amassed 20,000 dues-paying members and a supporting coalition of 100 national organizations. These included the National Education Association and the NAACP. In 1970 an ACT petition to the FCC spurred an inquiry into children's television. ACT pressure resulted in an end to children's vitamin commercials, product selling by program hosts, and a nearly 50 percent reduction in commercial minutes on Saturday morning television. ACT has published research and handbooks on media for children, its representatives meet regularly with broadcasters and advertisers, and Ms. Charren, who is quoted frequently, writes and speaks to industry and other groups.[13] One of her current campaigns opposes cartoon programs starring brand name toys—"program-length ads," in her description.

In a press conference at a convention of the National Association of Television Program Executives in New Orleans on January 16, 1986, she announced, "ACT [has] filed a petition [with the FCC] for a declaratory ruling requiring television stations to intersperse program-length commercials with a reasonable number of announcements...that the program material is also an effort to promote the sale of the product or products in the story. ACT's petition does not seek to ban or impede the presentation of the programming."[14] ACT, she told me in an interview, "considers itself primarily a defender of the First Amendment, and secondarily of children. We do not advocate suppression. We advocate diversity of choice."[15]

Despite these organizations' accomplishments, Peter Broderick suggests in his Benton Foundation study, all such advocates face a clouded future. In Broderick's words:

The heyday of these groups lasted from the late Sixties until the mid-Seventies. ...They...suffered a major cutback in foundation funding,...Business lobbyists were gaining more financial and organizational support from corporations, ...[and] in the area of telecommunications, business also became better organized in its lobbying.

New policies adopted by an FCC committed to deregulation, and new Justice Department interpretations of antitrust law have cut much of the ground out from under citizens groups...[Telecommunications] technologies and structures are changing rapidly...[and] citizens groups that have concentrated on broadcasting issues are now confronted with a host of new issues involving common carriers and narrowcasting and computers [that] require substantial economic and technical expertise...[Moreover, one respondent in Congress] said the media have done a terrible job covering legal and regulatory aspects.

Whatever the obstacles, there is a critical need for a public role in telecommunications policymaking....These groups have beaten long odds before....[But] they will need all the allies they can find.[16]

FAIR TRIAL-FREE PRESS COMMITTEES

Another phenomenon of the period was what might be called "interprofessional" liaison, through fair trial-free press committees. These began in the sixties after bar and judiciary protests about coverage of the John F. Kennedy assassination and its aftermath, the murder trial of Ohio physician Samuel Sheppard (whose conviction was reversed by the Supreme Court on the grounds that publicity had been prejudicial) and the Reardon Committee report to the American Bar Association recommending restrictions on criminal trial coverage. Over two decades, press-bar committees in nearly 30 states drafted voluntary guidelines for court news coverage, and relations seemed improved. But the movement stalled when a judge in Washington unilaterally made that state's guidelines mandatory, requiring a written pledge of compliance to be "allowed" to cover a 1980 murder trial. The state supreme court upheld him.[17] Nonetheless, says American Society of Newspaper Editors counsel Richard M. Schmidt, Jr., for whatever reason, press-bar relations have improved. "There's a continuing problem," he told me, "but we don't have the big battles we used to."[18]

PRESS COUNCILS

The press—or news—council originated in 1916 in Europe and remains an established institution in Britain, the Nordic countries, Switzerland, and Austria. Worldwide, according to Claude-Jean Bertrand of the University of Paris, Sorbonne, as of 1985, 22 press councils of more than local scope existed in 18 countries,[19] and the movement was dramatically expanding in Canada (Saskatchewan now is its only province without one).[20] In Bertrand's accounting, 14 English-speaking nations in a Caribbean Press Council are counted as a single council.

Essentially a press council is a panel of journalists and public representatives that exists for two purposes: (1) to receive complaints about the accuracy or fairness of specific news reporting—not opinion—and to render public judgment of their validity and (2) to defend press freedom. The rationale is that in a democracy, where the press necessarily must remain free of government control, the citizens and institutions granting that freedom deserve—and, given the nature of modern society and media, require—recourses other than courts or political action. Providing them can benefit both society and the press.

As a general rule, a council requires that the media organization involved first must have been given the chance to resolve a complaint. If it cannot do so satisfactorily, a complainant can obtain a press council hearing by signing a waiver of legal action. The council may, after preliminary investigation, dismiss the grievance, or it can hold hearings and issue its opinion, including its finding of facts and the rationale for its conclusions—often instructive for laypeople and journalists alike. It may also issue reports or statements on matters it believes affect press freedom.

A true press council—as opposed to government-affiliated bodies that, for a government's self-serving reasons, erroneously may be represented as belonging to the genre—has no enforcement authority, only the power of publicity and its credibility. The media, including an organization that is the subject of a complaint, are expected to report the council's findings.[21]

Britain's Press Council usually is regarded as most relevant to us. It was founded in 1951 on recommendation of a Royal Commission, convened by Parliament amid a growing clamor for government action against media ownership concentration, bias, and sensationalism. At first an all-press body appointed by media organizations and given almost no budget, it was transformed, under goading by another Royal Commission in 1962, into a lay-press body with a paid staff and funding by the press. Since then, as British journalist Patrick Brogan notes in a recent study, it has issued annual reports titled "The Press and the People" and it "managed to win grudging acceptance of newspapers and confidence of the general public."[22]

In the United States, local press councils were advocated early in the 1930s by Chilton R. Bush, head of the Department of Communications at Stanford University. But only after World War II did interest perceptibly grow—with the Hutchins Commission report and other proposals. These included suggestions from Stanford and the University of Minnesota for a press-monitoring institute or council, from *Louisville Courier-Journal* and *Times* publisher Barry Bingham, Sr., for local press councils, and from media critic (later *Washington Post* ombudsman) Ben H. Bagdikian for university-based state councils.

With $40,000 from a Newspaper Guild fund bequeathed by former *Washington Daily News* editor Lowell Mellett, four local councils were established in 1967 in small western and midwestern communities. These closed shortly after outside funding ran out, and other small-town councils usually have been short-lived.[23] Honolulu, to break an impasse in relations between the mayor and the press, birthed its council in 1970—the most significant local one to date. That same year, at the height of Nixon-Agnew attacks on the press, a speech by Elie Abel, then journalism dean at Columbia, became the catalyst for the nation's only state council. Abel stressed the need for journalists to "police their own ranks" before outsiders are given the job of doing it. He suggested a Twin Cities press council.

Robert M. Shaw, manager of the Minnesota Newspaper Association, decided that a statewide purview was more feasible. Mainly due to his perseverence, by autumn of 1971 the association's board had launched a statewide council. It had 18 lay and press representatives, including the president of the University of Minnesota, the state's attorney general, and, as one observer put it, a "who's who" of civic and media leaders. Associate Supreme Court Justice C. Donald Peterson was chairman.[24]

In the council's first 17 years it assessed more than 1,000 complaints, of which only 78 by 1989 went to the full council's final decision stage. Sixteen were from public officials or candidates for office, 10 complained about coverage of political organizations, and 17 about news-gathering or reporting procedures. Since 1977 the council, enlarged to 24 members, has handled complaints about radio-television news as well as newspapers.[25] Originally dependent on a volunteer secretary, journalism professor J. Edward Gerald of the University of Minnesota, it now has a paid director, former newspaper and public relations man Thomas Patterson, and quarters furnished by the university.

For 11 years there also was a National News Council (NNC). It was instigated primarily by the Twentieth Century Fund, whose director at the time, the late M. J. Rossant, had served on the staff of *The Economist* magazine and on the editorial board of *The New York Times*. In 1970, he and Lester Markel, former Sunday editor of *The Times* who had been a founding father of the International Press Institute, discussed starting a Northeast Regional Press Council. Then in 1971, amid the antipress clamor of the Nixon administration, the fund's board approved a task force to consider a national council. By the end of 1972, the task force, in whose deliberations I took part, had recommended the establishment of such a national council. It was to focus on complaints against the national suppliers of news—print and electronic—that had been the administration's chief targets. In 1973, with main grants from the fund and the John and Mary R. Markle Foundation, the council began work.[26]

Roger Traynor, former chief justice of the California Supreme Court, was chairman, and Robert McKay, former dean of the New York University Law School, vice chairman. Membership, in which geographical, ethnic, and vocational balance was sought, included William Rusher, publisher of the *National Review;* Joan Ganz Cooney, president of the Children's Television Workshop; Albert Gore, former U.S. Sentor from Tennessee; Dorothy Height, president of the National Council of Negro Women; and R. Peter Straus, director of Voice of America and president of Straus Communications, New York City.

Subsequent chairs included Stanley Fuld, former chief judge of the New York Court of Appeals; Norman E. Isaacs, award-winning former Louisville editor and American Society of Newspaper Editors president; and Lucy Wilson Benson, former under secretary of state and former president of the League of Women Voters. Her term, under a council reorganization, coincided with that of Richard S. Salant, former president of CBS News, as president.[27]

The NNC's decade and one year of existence are discussed in various articles and columns and at length in two books: *Spiked: The Short Life and Death of the National News Council,* by Patrick Brogan and *Untended Gates: The Mismanaged Press,* by Norman E. Isaacs, a longtime champion of media ethics committees and press councils who was the NNC's most vigorous chair.[28] In one article, Professor Robert A. Logan of the University of Missouri provided this summary:

Between 1973–84 the council received 242 complaints and found almost half of them (120) to be unwarranted for hearing and subsequent recommendation. Of the remaining complaints, the council heard 64 cases, while the rest were either dismissed, found to be partially warranted, or withdrawn by the complainant. The NNC also issued 45 statements advocating press freedom, . . . which means the council was a defender of press freedoms as well as an independent evaluator of press performance during its tenure.

The Council heard grievances against AP and UPI, ABC and CBS, several newsmagazines, large metropolitan newspapers, and syndicated columnists. . . . It supported news media complaints against denial of access to government, corporate and institutional records, made a series of recommendations to improve White House news conferences (which were partially adopted), and criticized the Reagan Administration's refusal to let the news media cover the invasion of Grenada.

During its eleven-year history the integrity of the Council's board or decisions was never at issue. A report on journalism ethics by the American Society of Newspaper Editors in 1975 praised the National News Council's selection of jurors and its motivations to improve press performance. The council was described (and acclaimed) by U.S. Supreme Court Chief Justice Warren Burger in *Tornillo v. Miami Herald* as both an independent and voluntary body concerned with press fairness and a means of neutral examination of public claims regarding news media accuracy.[29]

Among other activities, the council also published eight reports on current issues, including (after a Pulitzer Prize-winning *Washington Post* story was exposed as a hoax) "After 'Jimmy's World': Tightening Up in Editing," "Who Said That?—A Report on the Use of Unidentified Sources," and "Protecting Two Vital Freedoms: Fair Trial and Free Press."[30] Starting in 1980 it also published *Excerpts*, a monthly newsletter for the Organization of News Ombudsmen that, among other dispositions, it was found in 1983, was being used in 240 college-level journalism programs.[31]

Yet on March 22, 1984, the council—wracked by tensions between the principals in its revised structure, Richard Salant and Lucy Benson, and unable to finance a fund drive needed to ensure its solvency—voted to dissolve. Its records were bequeathed to the University of Minnesota. The National News Council was history.[32]

Why did the council die? One could cite many contributory factors. Among them are the following.

Lack of a U.S. model. Because there never had been a regional or national news council in the vast and diverse United States, there was no American experience on which to draw. This resulted in perhaps otherwise avoidable suspicion, false starts, lost motion, and sins of omission and commission.

Leadership problems. The council reportedly lost a chance to have former Supreme Court Justice Arthur Goldberg as a co-chairman because, already committed to California Justice Traynor as chairman, it could or would not arrange shared titles and responsibilities.[33] Subsequently its only consistently vigorous leader was its third chairman, Norman Isaacs, who lacked Goldberg's prominence and, on retirement at a critical juncture, was unable to arrange a stable succession.

Underfinancing. Neither the Ford Foundation—the largest grantor for media experiments when the NNC was launched—nor major media (except for modest contributions) supported the council financially, leaving it chronically malnourished. Had it been affiliated with a university and had universities and journalism schools provided research and other services, overhead could have been cut and programs added—but arguably not enough to have saved it.

Media hostility. Although a majority of media were either supportive on the one hand or apathetic on the other, a few prominent ones were actively negative to hostile. Most influential was *The New York Times,* whose de facto blackout of reporting in some periods and emphasis on the negative in others struck, for one, the NCC's second chairman, Judge Stanley Fuld, as behavior that "hardly befits a newspaper of that stature."[34] Ironically, former *Times* editorial page editor John B. Oakes was a dedicated member of the task force that established the council and former *Times* assistant editorial page editor A. H. Raskin was a council executive.[35]

Invisibility. Partly due to the example of *The Times*—perhaps the number one agenda-setter for coverage by other media—the council's proceedings, position statements, and officers' speeches received sparse publicity. (Both AP and UPI wires, however, habitually did report NCC decisions.) Consequently many grievances the council might have heard, including by his own affirmation that of army General William C. Westmoreland against CBS, never got to it.[36] (*The Times,* incidentally, in recent years still has not found press councils and public interest groups newsworthy enough to cover, including a local one called the Listeners' Guild that has gone to court to save the format of *The Times* FM station's only classical music competitor, WNCN.) In hindsight, council representatives now say they might have helped lift the curtain by arranging cable television coverage of their proceedings.

Passive second-tier supporters. Despite a record number of journalism schools and departments, active public interest and civic groups, and foundations that profess an interest in media responsibility—plus council adherents among columnists and broadcasters—most such supporters failed to assist or even speak for the council until after its demise.

A political climate change. With the post-Watergate hiatus in antipress attacks—and indeed a temporary if superficial "canonization" of investigative journalism—the concern among a segment of the press that had helped motivate the NNC experiment died.

The root cause, critics would say, was that the council was a bad idea. That, however, seems oversimplified. In Britain, with Parliament breathing down the press's neck, it took two attempts over a generation to implant a stable lay-press council. Councils do survive elsewhere, and in the United States new ones continue to be proposed.

Wisconsin and Kentucky, for example, both have considered press councils in the past few years, and although they were initially rejected, supporters in both states remain active.[37] Groups in Massachusetts, California, and Nebraska have requested information from the Minnesota News Council, and it now may offer to cooperate in hearing complaints or demonstrating its *modus operandi* wherever asked. The editor of the *Kansas City Star* and *Times,* for one, has expressed interest in using the council's services.[38]

More plausible explanations of the NNC's fate, it seems, lie in these two realms: the nature of the American media, and the priorities of the U.S. academic and philanthropic communities. Despite popular image, the typical media organization no longer is a family-owned newspaper or radio station on Main Street. Chains and conglomerates dominate. Among newspapers, according to analyst John Morton, 1,175 of the nation's 1,699 daily newspapers are owned by 155 chains, and the 10 largest chains represent almost half of the total American daily circulation of 62.6 million.[39] Newspapers and broadcasting are enormously profitable—"the hottest plays on Wall Street," according to a *Business Week* report.[40] "Indeed," analyst Merrill Brown reported in *Channels* magazine, "according to a study by *Forbes* magazine, over the last five years the media led all other fields in earnings growth, while ranking third in both profitability and sales growth."[41]

Martin Pompadur, managing general partner in Television Station Partners, has been quoted as estimating that "established independents [in television] usually have margins of 30 to 40 percent, while margins for network affiliates in the same market showed between 35 and 55 percent."[42] *Fortune* magazine in its April 14, 1986 issue estimated the three television network companies' total return to investors for comparable 12-month periods: at Capital Cities/ABC, 37 percent; CBS, 64 percent; and RCA (NBC) 65 percent.[43]

Such megaprofits are achieved in three ways: by astute management, economies of scale, and—alas for the First Amendment imperatives—shirking of social responsibility. Except for the Newhouse Organization, which still is family owned (but rigorously profit oriented), the chains' and broadcast groups' primary obligation is widely seen as serving outside shareholders, many of them institutional fund managers, whose business is business—i.e., short-term profits, stock-price escalation, takeovers or takeover defenses, and management preservation. In a capitalist economy, hardly economic sins, but priorities that leave the media unmotivated to look beyond the present, in which credibility surveys show them increasingly vulnerable to charges of trading constitutional obligations for megaprofits—and future trouble for us all.

History and common sense suggest that a time will come when constitutionally protected institutions so profitable as these must begin to answer to society for such habits as inadequate staffing (under chain ownership, average newspaper staff sizes have decreased), pay (a median starting salary for journalism graduates about equal to that for promising stenographers),[44] staff diversity (development of nonwhite staff members, among others, is persistently underfunded), news holes (small- and medium-size cities' dailies—almost all without competition—have shrunk to flimsy department-store flyer size), broadcast public affairs coverage (television network prime-time documentaries now are virtually only memories), and local newscasts (most are tabloid-quality, disaster-oriented picture presentations).

As for the academic and philanthropic communities, despite ritual pronouncements by both about the centrality of an enlightened press to healthy democracy, media development, analysis, and criticism remain stepchildren on campuses and at foundations. When the philosophers of the press are discussed, only Walter Lippmann and A. J. Liebling spring to most minds—because they are almost the complete list.

There never has been an infrastructure for scholars, writers, and analysts in the field. Its periodicals, such as the *Columbia Journalism Review*, which this writer was privileged to edit for four years, are underfinanced and only intermittently socially relevant—which helps perpetuate the convenient myth on newspapers that, of all institutions, the press does not merit regular coverage because it lacks "interest" or importance to readers or could not be done objectively without being "destructive."

Social science research on the structure and economics of the press, its staff resources, and journalism's interface with society is on the whole sparse, superficial, and of only marginal relevance. Universities tolerate inferior, underfunded, poorly led journalism departments and schools; interdisciplinary endeavors, if they encompass the press at all, usually do so as an afterthought; and administrations fail to plan and fund institutes or centers that could affect the vicious circle.

New Everest-profile foundations such as MacArthur in Chicago appear on the horizon, but no foundation of any size, except for the medium-scale John and Mary R. Markle Foundation, either specializes in this field or—since the calamitous abdication of Ford in the seventies—allocates enough of its resources to have real impact. Nor do affluent media's philanthropic arms attempt to fill the gap. Hence potential breakthroughs are either underfunded or stillborn.

However, incentives for both the press and these institutions to change seem imminent. First of all, the First Amendment is only what the courts say it is. The lower federal courts already have been changed ideologically by five years of Reagan appointments, the Supreme Court is only one or two appointments away from a sea change.

Moreover, libel suits have become so prolific and costly that the media soon may find them harder to ignore—especially in light of such research as a foundation-funded study at the University of Iowa. It shows that only about a quarter of libel plaintiffs sue for money damages rather than for hearing of an unresolved grievance; that libel litigation lasts on the average for more than four years; and that, although the media win 90 percent of the cases, in the end they spend more than the plaintiffs.[45]

General Westmoreland's 1985 speech at the National Press Club also seems significant. In it he urged an alternative to the courts for settling disputes between the press and public figures—specifically, "something like a National News Council." He added, "The media itself (*sic*) must do something to help sustain public confidence in its ability to exercise the awesome responsibility of protecting the public's right to know."[46]

In the long run, the press and public can mutually profit from enlightened citizen action and lay-press intermediaries. The marketplace of ideas works: the cranks and "know-nothings" get sorted out, and both the media and society are better for the attendant dialogues.

Faltering, sometimes false starts have been made in responding to the Hutchins Commission's challenge. But none of these fragmented attempts is worthy of a great nation or of the press that a great nation deserves—and now requires. Indeed, I contend that press councils, public interest groups, and fair trial-free press committees have had to struggle in part because such experiments have been too little and too late. The United States never has created vehicles for integrating them into a philosophical whole.

Therefore I submit this modest proposal: that the Gannett Center join with Columbia University's president and journalism dean to select a nationwide steering committee of university, media, and foundation leaders to convene a successor to the Hutchins Commission. Its specific charge should be finally to bring to reality—with Ford, MacArthur, and Carnegie-scale funding—the commission's vision of "a new and independent agency to appraise and report annually upon the performance of the press"; to coordinate "the creation of academic-professional centers of advanced study, research, and publication in the field of communications"; and to emphasize "the widest possible publicity and public discussion on all the foregoing."[47] This should include an adequately funded monthly journalism review, public television or C-Span and videocassette distribution of appropriate forums, and MacArthur Foundation-magnitude multiyear grants to experienced analysts who would return the spirit of Lippmann and Liebling to our newspapers, magazines, books, and classrooms.

This nation's foundations and individuals of means have the resources. What is lacking are the vision and the will. Let us make this the generation that provides them.

NOTES

1. Commission on Freedom of the Press, *A Free and Responsible Press*. Chicago: University of Chicago Press, 1947, p. 1.

2. Ibid., p. 19.

3. Ibid., p. 93.

4. Ibid., pp. 97–98, 99, 100.

5. Herbert Brucker cited in Norman E. Isaacs, *Untended Gates: The Mismanaged Press*. New York: Columbia University Press, 1986, p. 103.

6. Alfred Balk, *A Free and Responsive Press: The Twentieth Century Fund Task Force Report for a National News Council*, background paper. New York: Twentieth Century Fund, 1973, pp. 33–51.

7. Lois Breedlove, Jeff Burbank, Anthony Heely, Denise Palesch, Tim Race, and Shelby Sadler. "Media Monitors: Most Are Simply Vigilant, But Some Are Vigilantes," *Quill*, (June 1984): 17–22.

8. B. Drummond Ayers, Jr., "Responsibility in the Press Assessed," *The New York Times*, Jan. 19, 1985, Sec. I, p. 7.

9. Breedlove, et al., "Media Monitors."

10. Peter Broderick, "Last Stand or New Offensive: The Struggle for Public Representation in Telecommunications Policymaking," a discussion paper. Prepared for the Benton Foundation, Washington, D.C., 1983, pp. 3–5.

11. Henry Geller, "Diversity Nipped in the Bud," Interview with the Reverend Everett C. Parker, *American Film*, (December 1984): 77.

12. Caroline E. Meyer, "Simon Says: Enough," *Channels*, 5 (March 1986): 16.

13. John and Mary R. Markle Foundation, New York. *Annual Report*, 1985, pp. 41–43.

14. "Remarks of Peggy Charren," Press Conference, National Association of Television Program Executives, New Orleans, Jan. 17, 1986. (Action for Children's Television, Newtonville, Mass.).

15. Telephone interview with Peggy Charren, Mar. 1986.

16. Broderick, et al., "Media Monitors," p. 15.

17. "Justices Allow Censorship Agreements." *The News Media and the Law*, (June–July 1982): 5.

18. Telephone interview with Richard M. Schmidt, Jr., Mar. 1986.

19. Claude-Jean Bertrand, "The Ideal Press Council," *The Quill*, (June 1985): 38–41.

20. Marcia Ruth, "Does Anyone Miss the News Council?" *Presstime*, 7 (March 1985): 32.

21. Balk, *A Free and Responsive Press*, pp. 27–28.

22. Patrick Brogan, *Spiked: The Short Life and Death of the National News Council*,

a Twentieth Century Fund paper. New York: Twentieth Century Fund, 1985, p. 105.

23. Balk, *A Free and Responsive Press*, p. 32.

24. Alice Olson, "Why the Minnesota News Council Is Alive," *The Observer* (quarterly publication of the Minnesota Newspaper Foundation, Minneapolis, Minn.) (Spring 1985): 7–8.

25. Ibid.

26. Brogan, *Spiked,* pp. 19–33.

27. Ibid., pp. 111–116.

28. Ibid.

29. Robert A. Logan, "Jefferson's and Madison's Legacy: The Death of the National News Council," *The Journal of Mass Media Ethics,* (Brigham Young University, Provo, Utah), (Fall/Winter 1985): 68–77.

30. Brogan, *Spiked,* p. 127.

31. Isaacs, *Untended Gates,* p. 139.

32. Brogan, *Spiked,* p. 86.

33. Ibid., pp. 23–24.

34. Isaacs, *Untended Gates,* p. 120.

35. Brogan, *Spiked,* pp. 111–116.

36. Westmoreland to Richard Cunningham, former National News Council assistant director, at American Bar Association Convention, 1985.

37. "News Council Idea Still Alive in Kentucky," *Editor and Publisher,* 118 (Feb. 9, 1985): 16.

38. Telephone interview with Thomas Patterson, Mar. 1986.

39. Alex S. Jones, "Newspaper Sale: A Trend Continues," *The New York Times,* Feb. 1, 1985, sec II, p. 7.

40. John Wilke, Mark N. Vamos, Mark Maremart, "Has the FCC Gone Too Far?" *Business Week* (Aug. 5, 1985): 48.

41. Merrill Brown, "The Reign of the Money Men," *Channels,* 5 (Mar. 1986): 21.

42. Martin Pompadur cited in Thomas C. Hayes, "Hot Independent TV Stations," *The New York Times,* June 25, 1985, p. D1.

43. "Investor's Snapshots," (table) in Stuart Gannes, "The Phone Fight's Frenzied Finale," *Fortune,* 113 (Apr. 14, 1986): 27.

44. Isaacs, *Untended Gates,* pp. 170–171.

45. Randall P. Bezanson, Gilbert Cranberg, and John Soloski, "Libel and the Press: Setting the Record Straight," Silha Lecture, University of Minnesota, May 15, 1985, pp. 11, 25–32; also see same title, *Iowa Law Review,* 71 (Oct. 1985): 215–233.

46. James E. Roper, "Westmoreland Reflects," *Editor and Publisher,* 118 (Mar. 23, 1985): 7.

47. Commission on Freedom of the Press, *A Free and Responsible Press,* p. 102.

7

Against Accountability:
First and Last Resorts

Lewis Lapham

On the question of the media in relation to their markets, I am a strict constructionist. I think the market not only the court of first resort but also the court of last resort.

To the best of my knowledge markets haven't got anything to do with morality. Nor do I make any necessary connection between the First Amendment and accountability. As I remember the First Amendment, it simply mentions free speech, not accountability. Nor can I think of any apparent connection between journalism and ethics. The two words would look strange to me in the same paragraph, much less the same sentence. Nor again, to continue the separation of powers, can I think of any necessary connection between freedom and virtue.

I don't know what accountability means. I'd be very interested to know. Does it mean that you got the press release properly down on paper? Does it mean that you haven't offended the people likely to sue the newspaper? Does it mean that your version of events is accurate?

The version of events is not apt to be accurate because at newspapers you are working against a very short deadline, and in television you are working against the very compressed space of time. That doesn't mean that the media can't be very good and very interesting. But why should the news necessarily be definitive or true? Or responsible? I don't see why it is necessary to make so blind a leap of faith. I don't think the media are responsible for running the country or telling people what to think. I think that the American public, which is many publics and many audiences, is intelligent enough to discriminate between what is true and what is false.

When we talk about the media we usually end up talking only about three television networks, two magazines, and maybe eight newspapers. But in the United States, the media are much larger than that, comprising the immense range of trade journals, magazines, newsletters, reports, and libraries of all kinds of descriptions. If somebody wants to be truly informed on a subject, he or she can resort to an almost infinite number of reliable sources. I don't see why most of the information in newspapers or on television should be any more or less correct than most of the other information with which one is presented every day in other quarters of society. Most of the information that one receives in the course of the day is probably wrong, whether it's a presidential speech, a press release, a doctor's diagnosis, or a tip on the stock market. I don't mean to offend anybody, but it seems to me wrong to try to impose on a rather frail form of storytelling the great burden of truth and righteousness. I don't think the media can carry such a burden.

When I hear people speak of the media as a collective moral force accountable to some notion of truth, I tend to become suspicious. I don't think of the mass media as instruments of either education or information. The media deal in entertainment. I don't think journalism is a profession. I think it's a craft, a trade, and sometimes an art. I think journalists are storytellers subject to the superstitions of their audiences. Like any other storyteller, the journalist is obliged to drum up a crowd. To keep the crowd's attention, he's got to tell the crowd more or less what the crowd wants and expects to hear.

Were I the editor of *National Review* I couldn't publish pieces about the American romance with crime. Were I the editor of *The Nation* I couldn't publish pieces extolling the United States as a happy country club. The audiences of the two journals belong to different constituencies and hold different conventions.

I have never met a historian who would write history on the basis of what he had read in newspaper accounts. After various periods of time, sometimes only a few days or a few weeks, newspaper accounts can be seen to be patently wrong. I think it was President Harry Truman who said that he truly pitied anybody who depended upon the newspapers for a reliable account of the events passing in his or her time.

I love the newspapers. I even like looking at television, but in neither circumstance do I expect to be adequately informed. If I seriously want to learn something about a subject I will have to read the literature—documents, the professional journals, and the major historians.

A few years ago Carol Burnett sued the *National Enquirer* for libel because the paper published a gossip item that associated her with drinking in a Washington restaurant in the presence of Henry Kissinger. If my memory serves me, the court awarded her at least $1 million—a wonderfully preposterous judgment because the *National Enquirer* is a newspaper that routinely publishes citings of UFOs and interviews with the late Elvis Presley. To expect such a newspaper, or any other newspaper to provide, for 30 cents, the truth as well as entertainment seems to me a very fond expectation.

So I have no problems at all with the market. I think the best press is probably the most irresponsible press. As soon as the press begins to try to be responsible, it suffocates itself under the blankets of its worst pretentions. Journalists are not statesmen. The questions of accountability can be answered in two ways—by a libel suit or by the loss of an audience. To me that is the nature of a democratic system, which I am prepared to defend in an uncompromising, absolutist, and strict constructionist sort of way.

8

THE FIDUCIARY MODEL: REGULATING ACCOUNTABILITY

Henry Geller

The outstanding example of the fiduciary model is of course the present scheme for regulation of broadcasting. This scheme has spilled over somewhat into the cable television regulatory picture, but with no great practical effect. The ensuing discussion will therefore focus largely on the commercial broadcasting.

THE BASIS OF THE MODEL

It is important to recognize the basis of the fiduciary model in broadcasting. In the 1920s, when there was ineffectual governmental regulation, engineering chaos resulted: People were jumping frequencies or powers, with the result that no one could effectively broadcast. The government therefore stepped in with a licensing scheme. As the Supreme Court pointed out in the seminal *NBC* case (*NBC v. FCC*, 319 U.S. 190, 226 [1943]), radio is "unique" in that it "inherently is not available to all"; more people want to broadcast than there are available frequencies.

The government had several options in implementing this licensing requirement. It could have simply auctioned off the frequencies, with the highest bidder thereafter having full ownership rights; or it could have auctioned long-term leases; or adopted a common-carrier requirement.[1] Instead, in the Radio Act of 1927 and again in the Communications Act of 1934 (47 U.S.C. 151 *et. seq.* (Title III)), Congress decided on a short-term public trustee scheme. Licenses (originally for three years and now for five in television and seven in radio) would be awarded applicants who volunteered to serve the public interest and demonstrated to a government agency, the Federal Communications Commission (FCC), that they had done so in order to obtain a renewal of license.

This public trustee scheme inevitably affects broadcast journalism because it necessarily leads to the fairness doctrine. The doctrine imposes a twofold obligation on broadcasters: First, to devote a reasonable amount of time to issues of public concern and, second, to do so fairly by affording a reasonable opportunity for contrasting viewpoints.[2] While it was developed by the commission under the public interest standard, it is now codified in the act in the proviso to §315(a) (citing the obligation of the broadcasters under the act "to operate in the public interest and afford a reasonable opportunity for the discussion of contrasting viewpoints on controversial issues of public importance").

The first duty stems from the public interest consideration that broadcasters must contribute to an informed electorate, so crucial to the proper functioning of a democracy. Indeed, the commission has stated that it has allocated an inordinate amount of spectrum to broadcasting as against other claimants precisely because of this need for informational programming.[3] It follows that broadcasters must devote a reasonable amount of time to issues of public concern, or the allocation process is undermined.

Suppose the broadcaster does that but decides to present only those viewpoints with which he agrees. To give a specific example, in the 1960s, one of the two television stations in Jackson, Mississippi, WLBT-TV, was run by a racist. Even though 45 percent of the population of Jackson was black, the station would broadcast programming that gave only the segregationist point of view on the then raging issue of integration.[4] How could such a station be called a public trustee "given the privilege of using scarce radio frequencies as proxies for the entire community" (*Red Lion Broadcasting Co. v. FCC*, 395 U.S. at 394)? The second part of the doctrine thus stems also from the congressional decision to treat broadcast licensees as public fiduciaries.

Chief Justice Warren Burger stressed in the WLBT-TV case that compliance with the fairness doctrine is the sine qua non of every broadcast license, if it is to obtain renewal.[5] And in *Red Lion*, the Court stated: "Congress need not stand idly by and permit those with licenses to ignore the problems which beset the people or to exclude from the airways anything but their own views of fundamental questions" (395 U.S. at 394).

PRESENT IMPLEMENTATION OF FAIRNESS DOCTRINE

The commission has stressed the great discretion afforded licensees in fulfilling their obligations under the fairness doctrine. The licensee determines what issues to cover, the format, the particular viewpoints, the appropriate spokespeople, etc. The commission will intervene only if a complainant has met a high burden as to an initial showing that the licensee has not afforded reasonable opportunity for the presentation of contrasting viewpoints on a controversial issue of public importance. Then, and only then, will the complaint be referred to the station for its comments. And while the commission will review the matter, it will weigh the licensee's judgment on each facet (e.g., whether a controversial issue was presented and reasonable opportunity) and will upset that judgment only if it is found to be arbitrary. As a result, out of thousands of complaints each year, less than a hundred are referred to the station, and in only a handful of cases is the licensee found to have violated the doctrine.[6]

There are three corollaries to the doctrine that are of special importance. First, under *Cullman* (*Cullman Broadcasting Co.*, 40 FCC 576 [1963]) the commission held that where a broadcaster has presented only one side of a controversial issue of public importance—say, a series of paid commercial spots—and has no plans itself to present the other side, it cannot reject an otherwise suitable spokesman for the contrasting view on the ground that it wants payment. The "paramount right" under the Communications Act is that the public be informed—not that the licensee, which volunteered to serve the public interest, always gets its "buck" (*See Red Lion*, 395 U.S. at 390 "It is the right of the viewers and listeners, not the right of the broadcasters, which is paramount"; *Green v. FCC*, 447 F.2d 323, 329 (D.C. Cir. 1971) "the essential basis for any fairness doctrine . . . is that the *American public must not be left uninformed*"). It is critically important to recognize that the licensee is not a common carrier: it *chooses* to permit the presentations of one side because of its judgment that the public should receive information on this issue. The licensee having done so, *Cullman* follows from the public fiduciary scheme.

The commission has also developed a personal attack rule, which provides that when a licensee, in the course of discussing a controversial issue of public importance, makes a personal attack on the integrity, character or some like quality of a person or group, the latter should be notified of the attack within a week and afforded a comparable opportunity to respond. The licensee, as a public trustee, has an affirmative obligation to encourage and implement the presentation of the opposing view. Here there is an obvious way to make that affirmative effort— notify the person or entity attacked. Significantly, there are exemptions from this rule for the area of fast-breaking news, such as newscasts, on-the-spot coverage of news events, or news interviews. These areas come under the general fairness approach, which means, in practical effect, that the licensee itself can supply the other side and need not notify the person attacked.

The political editorializing rule applies to a station editorial that supports or attacks a candidate. Again the station must notify the candidate attacked or those not supported and afford a comparable and timely opportunity for response.

EVALUATION OF THE FAIRNESS DOCTRINE: PROPONENTS

Proponents of the doctrine point out that after the *WLBT-TV* decision, no licensee operates in such a racist fashion; that this case and the decision in WXUR (where Reverend Carl McIntire thought he had a license from God rather than the FCC and engaged in a pattern of repeated and flagrant violation of the doctrine)[7] have had the prophylactic effect of ensuring overall operation in the public interest in this most important area.

Proponents also stress that without the doctrine and its *Cullman* corollary, the affluent would set the agenda and swamp the public debate. More and more, participatory democracy with its use of legislative referenda is coming to the fore. If the oil companies can inundate the public with commercials on Proposition X, the entire process will be skewed. With fairness there is some reasonable balance of viewpoints presented—perhaps a five to one ratio—so that the public debate stays within reasonable bounds.

As to the matter of government intervention, proponents such as the Media Access Project (MAP) assert that in the vast majority of cases, there is no resort to the FCC. Rather, the matter is worked out in a reasonable, good faith effort by both sides, and the public gains enormously. Significantly, experienced broadcasters such as Westinghouse and ABC have not sought repeal of the doctrine. Indeed, Westinghouse has said that a responsible broadcaster must and does operate in compliance with fairness.[8]

Proponents strongly aver that there are no chilling effects. Even if a broadcaster is found to have violated the doctrine, that only means that it must afford some more speech; its license is not in jeopardy except for flagrant operations such as WLBT-TV or WXUR.

They point out that the FCC has set out its experience with the doctrine in 1974 with its overview,[9] in 1976 on reconsideration,[10] and again in 1979.[11] Each time the commission has concluded that the doctrine has worked well, and that conclusion—not the one reached in the 1985 review[12]—is sound. Just as the commission has done, proponents stress the great leeway afforded the licensee to make reasonable judgments on all aspects of the doctrine's obligations, and that its process for handling complaints is deliberately geared to reducing the burden on the licensee, by requiring the complainant to "present prima facie evidence of a violation" (*See* 1974 *Fairness Report*, 39 F.R. at 26374–75; *ASCEF v. FCC*, 607 F.2d 438,445–47 (D.C. Cir. 1979), affirming the importance of this high standard for complainants and noting that in a typical fiscal year "the Commission received approximately 2,400 complaints and determined that only 94, or four percent, required the filing of a response. See *Fairness Report,* 48 FCC2d at 8").

EVALUATION OF THE FAIRNESS DOCTRINE: OPPONENTS

First, opponents assert that the doctrine does chill robust, wide-open debate. Indeed, they point out that it resulted in stifling the strong voice of WXUR (McIntire's station in the Philadelphia area), despite the 35 or more competing radio voices in the area (*see* dissenting opinion of Chief Judge Bazelon in the WXUR case, *supra* note 7).

Above all, opponents rely on the recent fairness report of the FCC (*see supra* note 12), *the* expert agency in the field. After voluminous comments, the FCC concluded that for three reasons, the fairness doctrine, as a matter of policy, no longer serves the public interest.

First, the agency found that in recent years there has been a significant increase in the number and types of information services. For example, cable television is now approaching 50 percent penetration of U.S. television homes and provides a great diversity of programming. The broadcast industry itself has grown substantially, and may be augmented by new services such as Direct Broadcast Satellite, Low Power TV, Multichannel Multipoint Distribution Services (MMDS), Satellite Master Antenna service (SMATV), etc. The commission concluded that the development of this information-services marketplace makes unnecessary any governmentally imposed obligation to provide balanced coverage of controversial issues.

Second, the FCC found that the evidence in the proceeding (adduced mainly by the National Association of Broadcasters (NAB) and strongly disputed by MAP) shows that the doctrine actually thwarts the laudatory purpose it is designed to promote, because broadcasters opt not to present controversy in an effort to avoid the burdens associated with the requirement to provide reasonable opportunity for opposing views. For example, this is particularly the case as to presentation of a series of spot announcements dealing with a controversial issue.

And third, the FCC concluded that the restrictions on broadcasters' journalistic freedoms resulting from the doctrine's enforcement contravene fundamental constitutional principles, afford a dangerous opportunity for government abuse, and impose unnecessary economic costs on both broadcasters and the agency. The FCC clearly believes that the doctrine is unconstitutional.

The commission took no action to eliminate or revise the doctrine, including consideration of alternative implementation approaches, for the agency is a creature of Congress and the latter wants the doctrine to continue. The commission, therefore, after noting that "Congress has shown an intense interest" (a lovely euphemism for saying that "Congress will blow off our heads if we touch the doctrine"), stated that it is affording Congress the opportunity to review the doctrine in light of the record adduced in the proceeding. In short, the commission is looking to the courts for relief, and has indeed inspired two suits—*RTNDA v. FCC*, Case No. 85–1691, D.C. Cir. and *Meredith Corp. v. FCC*, Case No. 85–1723, D.C. Cir.

EVALUATION OF THE DOCTRINE: MY VIEWS

The Critical Public Fiduciary Notion

I believe that opponents fail to take into account how fairness ties in with the public trustee concept. The two are integrally linked together. When they argue that the fairness doctrine can be eliminated, they are in effect saying that WLBT-TV can operate in a wholly racist fashion and still be renewed as a public trustee. That makes no sense at all.

Furthermore, because of the existence of this pervasive public interest regulatory scheme (e.g., renewal, comparative hearings, and regulations such as prime time access or multiple ownership), elimination of the fairness doctrine would not accomplish the goal sought by its critics—placing broadcast journalism in the same position as to the government as print journalism. There have been legitimate concerns and cited examples of how government might use improper means to chill critical journalistic efforts.[13] But the fairness doctrine is an unlikely tool for government control or abuse. Skewed fairness rulings would shine like a dead mackerel in the moonlight, and would not survive judicial scrutiny. An administration with an improper purpose would thus be far more likely to use approaches that directly affect the economic health of the network or licensee in important respects—for example, by delaying renewal, changing the station ownership rules applicable to networks or large VHF stations, changing the network or large VHF stations, or changing the network programming process through prime-time access and syndication rules. I therefore believe that so long as the public interest licensing-regulatory scheme is maintained along the current line, elimination of the fairness doctrine will not insulate broadcast journalism from the possibility of improper government activity, and the egregious case of public trustee failure such as WLBT-TV will be left without a remedy.

I leave discussion of the scarcity argument to the section on constitutionality of the doctrine (below). I will treat here the issue of chilling effects.

In *Red Lion*, the issue of the chilling effects of the doctrine was "strenuously argued." The Court, however, rejected the argument that because of the doctrine's operation, licensees would avoid controversial issues on several grounds—that "the possibility is at best speculative"; that the industry and, in particular, the networks have in the past presented controversial issues and have insisted that they will continue to do so; that "if experience with the administration of these doctrines indicates that they have the net effect of reducing rather than enhancing the volume and quality of coverage, there will be time enough to reconsider the constitutional implications"; and finally, that this seems unlikely, because "if present licensees should suddenly prove timorous, the Commission is not powerless to insist that they give adequate and fair attention to public issues" (395 U.S. at 392–3).

It is now 15 years later. In *FCC v. League of Women Voters of California,* 104 S. Ct. 3106, 3117, n.12 (1985), the Court again indicated that it would review the matter in light of any new showing of chilling effects. So it is appropriate to do so at this time.

First, I place little reliance on the findings of this commission in its 1985 report, FCC 85–459. The Fowler Commission has from the outset (1981) stated its strong belief that the entire scheme is unconstitutional and that broadcasting is entitled to the same First Amendment protection as print (*see,* for example, Remarks of Chairman Fowler before the Oregon Association of Broadcasters, June 12, 1981 and before the National Radio Broadcasters Association, September 15, 1981). In light of this ideological tilt, it is to be expected that the commission would find chilling effects on the record evidence.

Second, I believe that the Supreme Court's observation in *Red Lion* is still apt: it is most unlikely that the large commercial broadcaster—for example, the multiple station owner or the networks—is in any way chilled by the doctrine. Some, like Westinghouse or ABC, may accept the doctrine, while other like CBS or NBC may strongly resent governmental intrusion into broadcast journalism. But I know of no evidence that the news departments of these large owners avoid or skew their treatment of some issue because of the fairness doctrine.

Third, the commission cannot properly ascribe the overall blandness of so much of commercial broadcasting to the fairness doctrine. Rather, in my view, it stems from the dependence of the commercial broadcaster on advertising for support and consequently on reaching the largest possible audience (and thus of avoiding offense to any significant segment of the public).

I am not saying that there are no First Amendment costs in the fairness area. There clearly are. First, as Judge Wright aptly pointed out in *Straus Communications, Inc. v. FCC,* 530 F.2d 1001, 1008 (D.C. Cir. 1976), "the . . . doctrine . . . [does], after all, involve the Government to a significant degree in policing the content of communication." Was a personal attack or a controversial issue of public importance presented? What views were presented on that issue? Was there reasonable balance as to overall time, frequency of presentation, nature of audiences reached (e.g., prime time or early morning)? Governmental review of these facets can constitute a deep intrusion into daily broadcast journalism.[14] Thus, it can have a burdensome effect on the smaller station and can reinforce the above noted tendency to avoid real controversy.

I have previously documented that effect by citing one example gleaned in a six-month study of all FCC fairness rulings.[15] The significance of this example is that it is a *routine* ruling by the commission in favor of the licensee, so the agency could argue that there is no chilling effect. Yet, as my analysis (set out in an appendix attached hereto) shows, there can well be an inhibiting effect on the smaller station.

The Renewal-Only Approach under a *New York Times v. Sullivan* Standard

The present manner of implementing the doctrine thus raises a serious problem. As to what should be done, it is agreed by all what the proper test is here: "The abiding First Amendment difficulties, . . . along with an appreciation of Congress' intent in enacting the Communications Act, have engendered an important corollary: the licensee is to have the maximum editorial freedom consistent with its position as public trustee of a portion of the airwaves" (fn. citing *CBS v. DNC* 412 U.S. at 109–11, 126, 132; *Pensions,* 516 F.2d at 1113; *Straus Communications, Inc. v. FCC, supra* 530 F.2d at 1008). The commission should therefore ask itself: Has it afforded the licensee maximum editorial freedom? What is needed to ensure that the licensee meets its public trustee obligation?

I believe that the answer to these questions is clear: the licensee today is not being afforded maximum editorial freedom because the commission will review the reasonableness of the broadcaster's judgment on issue after issue—a deep intrusion into daily broadcast journalism. And what the commission is now trying to ensure is fairness on every broadcast issue—not that the licensee has acted consistently with its public trustee obligation.

The commission has lost sight of the goal—the licensee must operate as a public fiduciary and show at renewal that it has done so. That is the essential holding of the *Red Lion* case. A licensee cannot act as WLBT-TV did—with malice in the fairness area (i.e., bad faith or reckless disregard of the doctrine's obligation)—and then claim renewal as a public trustee. But when the commission goes beyond this critical issue and seeks to ensure fairness on each issue broadcast so that the public is better informed, however well intentioned the effort, it is then necessarily intruding deeply into daily broadcast journalism, contrary to the act's intent as the Supreme Court has forcefully stated (*CBS v. DNC*, 412 U.S. 95 (1973)). I therefore strongly urge that with one exception (*infra* at 19), the commission review fairness only at renewal under a *New York Times v. Sullivan* (376 U.S. 254) standard—whether the licensee has acted with malice in this area (i.e., deliberately violating the doctrine—bad faith as shown by independent extrinsic evidence such as the evidence of a station news staffer—or a pattern of acting in reckless disregard of the doctrine).

This would not gut the doctrine. The responsible broadcaster would still recognize its fairness obligations and act accordingly, without regard to FCC oversight, as is the case today with the very great majority of fairness issues. Most importantly, if an operation involves deliberate disregard of the doctrine or a pattern of sloughing aside responsibilities in this important area, it will still be the subject of action, either at renewal or, if appropriate, revocation. *For the licensee would not be acting consistently with the notion of public trustee.* And such commission action denying a license to WLBT-TV is not only proper but has ramifications far beyond the case. No one now operates a broadcast station as if it were a racist newspaper.

Consider, however, what it would mean for cases such as *Pensions* or *ASCEF*. There was no real question in these cases of malice—bad faith or reckless disregard of the doctrine. Rather, the issue was whether the American people had been fully or adequately informed by the licensee concerning a contrasting viewpoint on the particular issues involved. This type of case—even if there were a score of them—would simply be found not determinative of renewal (i.e., not involving the critical public trustee issue) and hence not necessary to be resolved.

It may be argued that this leaves the people uninformed on these issues. First, I point out that having some different audience eight months later hear some further presentations on these issues is not really the be-all or end-all of the democratic process.[16] But in any event, the short answer is that yes, there may be a good faith fairness violation so that there should have been this further presentation, but the effort to establish this—to ensure perfect fairness issue by issue—has a cost that is not required by the act and indeed disserves the act's essential thrust "to maintain—no matter how difficult the task is—essentially private interest broadcast journalism held only broadly accountable to public interest standards" (*CBS v. DNC*, *supra* 412 U.S. at 120).

Stated differently, the focus would be on whether the licensee has fulfilled its essential public trustee role, not on whether it has made an "honest mistake or error in judgment" in affording reasonable opportunity for contrasting views on some particular issue (*Report on Editorializing by Broadcast Licensees*, 13 FCC at 1255). The FCC eschewed the search for "perfect fairness" (*Gary Lane*, 39 FCC 2d 938 (1973)) in 1949, when it held that each program need not be balanced to ensure that the same audience hears both sides (*Id.* at 1250–51). Such a rigid search for strict fairness would run counter to the goal of promoting unrestricted debate. Similarly, there are unlikely to be benefits in any particular "balance" case from some different audience hearing an additional presentation of the contrasting viewpoint that would outweigh the fundamental detriments noted above.

The oddest opposition to my proposal comes from a group of broadcasters who assert that it is better to resolve complaints as they come in, rather than pile up at renewal where they might jeopardize the station's continued operation. First, *all* complaints meeting the FCC's high standard will be referred to the broadcaster so that they can act one way or another. Second, any complaint really putting the renewal in jeopardy (i.e., involving malice) will be processed as it comes in. Finally, it is incredible that responsible broadcasters would fear renewal under the test proposed here—a *New York Times v. Sullivan* test most heavily weighted in the broadcaster's favor. (Cf. *Editorializing Report, supra,* 13 FCC at 1252: "[T]here can be no doubt that any licensee honestly desiring to live up to its obligation to serve the public interest and making reasonable effort to do so, will be able to achieve a fair and satisfactory resolution of these problems. . . . ").

Indeed, under the present system complaints, even though resolved on an ad hoc basis, do not go away. As shown by the WLBT case[1] they are considered at renewal, if resolved against the licensee, and renewal is not under a *New York Times v. Sullivan* test. In every respect, the broadcaster is worse off under the present system. I believe that the opposition is really based on the fact that these broadcasters want elimination of the doctrine, and anything short of that—even if it substantially ameliorates the situation—is rejected. Stated differently, it is a matter for them of being treated like print journalism or to hell with any halfway or three-quarters relief.

The one exception from the above policy would be in the ballot area. As to candidates, the legislative history of the 1959 Amendment to Section 315(a) indicates fairness should be available as a back-up protection in the area of the Section 315 exemption (See S. Rept. No. 562, 86th Cong., 1st Sess., at 5). And indeed the Commission has assured Congress that fairness rulings in this area will be timely made within the election period, and has kept that promise. There would appear to be little reason to separate out one part of the ballot (candidate) from another part (ballot propositions), where again timely rulings have been made. Therefore, in this one area (ballot), for pragmatic political reasons, fairness complaints meeting the FCC's present standards would continue to be processed and timely resolved.

I believe that the foregoing approach, along with a return to general fairness principles in the area of political editorializing and personal attack, would go a long way to meeting the congressional purpose here and serving the goal of promoting robust, wide-open debate. And such an approach would be valid under existing law. Indeed, from the time of the 1949 *Editorializing Report* until 1962, the commission did follow a renewal-only approach. It follows that when Congress ratified the fairness concept in the 1959 Amendments, it did so at a time when the overall renewal-only approach was being used. Furthermore, *CBS v. DNC (supra)* lends strong judicial support if indeed it does not compel adoption of this approach.

Use of Voluntary Access Approach

Another way of alleviating the strains involved in implementation of the fairness doctrine is through broadcasters' widespread use of a voluntary access approach. Thus, the broadcaster might set aside an hour a week for short presentations (spots or a few minutes) and one half-hour program. The broadcaster would remain the editor, just as a newspaper is the editor of its op-ed page (e.g., Saturday's *Washington Post*).

Such an access approach could make a large contribution to achievement of all fairness goals. Thus, as noted, the first duty under the fairness doctrine is to cover issues of public importance. Of course the licensee as editor wants to select issues to be covered and will continue to do so. But access allows others to bring to the fore issues that the licensee might overlook or fail to appreciate their growing importance. Furthermore, the issues are then presented in a *partisan* fashion by those who believe strongly in them—again a commendable plus (*see CBS v. DNC.*, 412 U.S. at 112, 131; *Red Lion, supra* 395 U.S. at 392, n. 18; *DNC*, 25 FCC 2d 216, 222–223 (1970), requiring that partisan spokesmen be allowed some reasonable access; *Fairness Doctrine Inquiry, supra*, 74 FCC 2d at 177).

Finally, access helps immensely on the second duty of the fairness doctrine—to cover the issues fairly. That second duty does not require that reasonable balance be achieved—only that reasonable opportunity be afforded and that the licensee affirmatively encourage such reasonable opportunity (*see Fairness Doctrine Inquiry, supra*, 74 FCC 2d at 1278). Access can thus fully satisfy the second duty in the great majority of situations *without the need for governmental intervention and content examination*. Troublesome cases such as *Pensions (supra)* or *Wilderness Society* (31 FCC 2d 729 (1971)) cease to be raging controversies. Those wishing to add some further views simply do so on the access programming.

I recognize that access will not solve every fairness problem—for example, those that might arise from a very extensive editorial advertising campaign (*see Public Media Center v. FCC*, 587 F.2d 1322 (D.C. Cir. 1978)). But as the commission itself acknowledged, its contribution can be large "Such a [voluntary] system if properly structured and administered by a broadcast licensee, may serve to maximize the expression of controversial issues of public importance and truly partisan viewpoints on such issues, while minimizing governmental intrusion into the licensee's journalistic judgment" (*Fairness Doctrine Inquiry, supra,* 74 FCC 2d at 177). In the same proceeding, the commission noted that NTIA suggests that many of the problems associated with access

largely disappear if access is viewed as strictly voluntary, completely structured and controlled by the licensee, and merely supplementary to the licensee's own efforts [at meeting its obligations under the Fairness Doctrine]. . . . The licensee would remain the public trustee, and could, of course, reject material on such grounds as poor taste or total lack of significance. . . . We, therefore, do not urge access as a substitute but as an important voluntary complement to the licensee's own programming efforts (Ibid.).

The most responsible newspapers employ ombudsmen and, most importantly, extensive use of "op-ed" space, as well as letters to the editors. Surely the responsible broadcaster should emulate this pattern.

THE EQUAL OPPORTUNITY PROVISIONS OF SECTION 315

Because the broadcaster is a public trustee, Congress decreed in the Communications Act that if the broadcaster allows one candidate for office to use its facilities, it must afford equal opportunities to all other qualified candidates for that office. The difficulty arises because of the fringe party candidates—the Socialist, Socialist Labor Vegetarian, Prohibition, etc. (e.g., in the 1960 presidential election, there were 14 candidates on the ballot in several States). If then the broadcaster presented a clip of one of the major party candidates in the evening news, it would have to afford precisely equal time to these other candidates. Because a 1959 FCC ruling so required, Congress amended Section 315 to exempt appearances of candidates on four news-type programs: (1) bona fide newscasts; (2) bona fide news interview shows; (3) bona fide news documentaries (if the appearance of the candidate is incidental to presentation of the subjects covered); and, (4) on-the-spot coverage of bona fide news events (e.g., the political conventions).

The exemptions have certainly helped; indeed recent FCC constructions of the fourth exemption have made possible coverage of the presidential debates and press conferences. A recent court ruling, *King Broadcasting v. FCC* (Case no. 88–1367, D.C. Cir.) decided on November 1, 1988, has opened the possibility of one or all three networks presenting the two major party candidates for president in a series of back-to-back speeches on major issues (e.g., one session on the economy; another on social issues; another on foreign policy; still another on defense). But if the broadcast activity does not fit within an exemption, it can be blocked by the Section 315 requirement that hours of prime time to be afforded the fringe party candidates—and many worthwhile programs do not fit. For example, the following types of broadcast journalism are blocked: in-depth interviews with the major candidates, documentaries delving into their positions and backgrounds with extensive use of interviews or clips (so it might not fall within the present exemption with its emphasis on *incidental* appearance), or the appearance of a candidate on an "Advocates"-type program. The list could be extended greatly because it is not possible to forecast all the formats to which broadcast journalism might turn.

It is important to bear in mind that in these circumstances the Section 315 requirement accomplishes nothing: The program is not presented so the fringe party candidates receive no time, and the public is simply deprived of many informational programs about candidates in whom it is really interested.

There are ready ways to deal with this problem: simply make equal opportunities applicable only to paid time, and thus free all bona fide broadcast journalistic programs. Or make it applicable only to significant candidates in the general election (defined as those representing parties that garnered 2 percent of the vote in the state in the last election or, in the case of new candidates, have 1 percent of the vote on petitions). Or, add a fifth exemption for any joint or back-to-back appearance or bona fide journalistic program under the full control of the licensee (*see* FCC *First Report*, 48 FCC 2d 1, 46 (1974)).

Congress balks at these obvious reforms because it is made up of incumbents who do not really want to free the broadcaster to better illuminate the campaign choices. The less time, the better off the incumbent is. Because Congress is unwilling to act, one wonders why the broadcasters do not sue to invalidate this provision of §315 as overly broad and restrictive for its purpose.[18] It is ironic that the networks and large broadcasters have attacked the validity of the fairness doctrine (which, in my view, does not really inhibit them—*see* note 12, *supra*) but not the equal opportunities requirement, which does significantly restrict broadcast journalism at all levels.

THE CONSTITUTIONALITY OF FAIRNESS

I have dealt above with the "chilling effects" argument for invalidating the fairness doctrine. Here I discuss the FCC's conclusion in its 1985 fairness report that there has been a significant increase in recent years in the number and types of information service, and thus there is no longer a scarcity basis for the doctrine. This claim, along with the other

FCC findings, is now the basis of the two pending cases in the Court of Appeals for the District of Columbia Circuit seeking to have fairness declared unconstitutional: *RTNDA v. FCC*, Case No. 85–1691 and *Meredity Corp. v. FCC*, Case No. 85–1723.

The FCC completely misunderstands the basic concern of the Supreme Court in the *Red Lion* decision and indeed of the commission in implementing the fairness doctrine over the years (*see Red Lion v. FCC, supra* 395 U.S. at 388–90; *Fairness Report,* 48 FCC 2d 1, 4 (1974)).

As noted the basis for the fairness doctrine—and the public trustee scheme—is clear: The airwaves are not inherently open to all and therefore the government must license; it can constitutionally do so by conditioning the licenses on fulfillment of fiduciary obligations by broadcasters (*Red Lion,* at 389). This is just as true today as it was in 1934 or 1969: not everyone who wishes to can broadcast. And although the number of media outlets is clearly increasing and more efficient use of the electromagnetic spectrum is being made, there is still an indisputable scarcity of valuable broadcast stations.

Most significantly, there are no AM, FM, or television frequencies open in the top 50 markets where almost 80 percent of the U.S. population resides. If a radio or television frequency opened tomorrow in a top market, there would be a dozen applicants for it. Furthermore, the television industry has not grown dramatically. Since 1965, only about 250 commercial television stations have been added. The VHF station, particularly, remains a most powerful medium in short supply (441 VHF stations in 1960, 508 in 1970, and 518 in 1980).

Corroboration of this is given by the one source in which the commission seems to place the most trust: the marketplace. Thus, in *Broadcasting Magazine*'s wrap-up of the 1983 station sales, there is the following: "$342-million record-setting purchase of KHOU (TV) Houston, and $245-million purchase of KTLA (TV) Los Angeles, [excluding these two sales] the average price of the 37 VHF sales in 1983 was $24,024,714, bettering by 37 percent the previous high set in 1980 . . . $136-million purchase of UHF WFLD-TV Chicago" (January 9, 1984, at 74–82). The figures are even more dramatic for 1985: $510 million for a Los Angeles VHR independent, $450 million for a Boston VHF network affiliate. These figures shout scarcity, scarcity, scarcity.

The comparison made by the FCC and others between the number of daily newspapers or magazines and the number of broadcast stations is inappropriate and irrelevant. In its seminal *Fairness Report,* the commission itself noted:

This scarcity principle is not predicted upon a comparison between the number of broadcast stations and the number of daily newspapers in a given market. The true measure of scarcity is in terms of the number of persons who wish to broadcast and, in Justice White's language, there are still "substantially more individuals who want to broadcast than there are frequencies to allocate" (*Red Lion*, 395 U.S. at 388; *Fairness Report*, 48 FCC 2d 1, 4 (1974)).

The fact remains that, economic factors aside, broadcasters depend on spectrum space that cannot accommodate everyone. It is on this basis that the government licenses broadcasters. The crucial discussion in *Red Lion* is still just as apt today (*supra* 395 U.S. at 388–90).

I believe that the foregoing is wholly dispositive of this issue. But in any event, reliance by the commission on the new alleged technological abundance is unwarranted. First, several of the new technologies cited are little more than future prospects at present. For instance, as the FCC noted, of over 10,000 Low Power TV applications, only 206 stations are presently in operation. Similarly, videotext and teletext are little more than promising experiments. Much of the promise of Direct Broadcast Satellite service (DBS) is clouded. Furthermore, event cable television— the most likely source of a "video of abundance"—now reaches only 45 percent of U.S. homes with a substantial number of the cable systems capable of delivering only 12 channels or less.

Second, most of the new video distribution technologies are limited to entertainment fare and thus contribute little to the "information distribution marketplace." Rather than presenting controversial issues of public importance—speech that is central to our democratic society (*Buckley v. Valeo*, 424 U.S. 1, 14 (1976))—services such as MMDS and STV (Subscription Television) primarily feature movies, variety shows, and sports events. While the FCC recognizes the entertainment orientation of videocassettes and disks, it fails to note the general paucity of nonentertainment offerings available from all the new technologies. What was true in the past still remains essentially true today: Broadcast television remains by far the principal electronic medium for dispensing information, and the fairness doctrine with its obligations concerning the presentation of controversial issues remains crucial to the public trustee concept.

Surveys show that "67 percent of all Americans get most of their news from television" (*Telecommunications in Transition: The Status of Competition in the Telecommunications Industry, A Report by the Majority Staff of the Subcomm. on Telecommunications, Consumer Protection, and Finance, 235–390,* 97th Cong., 1st Sess. (Comm. Print 1981) [hereinafter cited as *House Staff Study*] at 347). There is no comparable survey showing primarily, or any, reliance on MDS, DBS, Low Power TV, cassettes, disks, etc., in this crucial regard.

Indeed, only cable television is significant here. Services such as Cable News Network (CNN) do contribute, and their contribution will undoubtedly grow in the future. But CNN today reaches only about 30 percent of U.S. television homes and has a share of roughly 2 percent in those homes (or only 0.6 percent for all television homes). Compare that with the roughly 30 percent share reached by the combined three major network evening news programs, or 13 percent for the morning network news shows (the Washington Post, Jan. 12, 1984, at 12, Sec. D), or roughly 30 percent for the three local early evening news shows (6–7:00 P.M.) in Washington.

I do not say that the trends here are irrelevant. In radio there are over 9,000 stations, with many more in the offing. As the Court noted in *League of Women Voters (supra* note 11), Congress might well want to revisit the public trustee-fairness standards in this new context. But note that this is a matter of revisiting the public trustee notion—not just fairness and that this is a matter for Congress. For there are large policy issues involved: even with abundance there are gaps in the commercial radio marketplace (e.g., children's educational programming and in-depth informational fare). Congress, therefore, might well deregulate radio only on the payment of a modest spectrum usage fee, to be used to fill these gaps (*see House Staff Study, supra* at 342).

As for television, Congress might well await the experience with radio deregulation before proceeding. Thus, the *House Staff Study* concluded that "the future of competition in video is promising"; that the "revolution is clearly underway, but it is just beginning to make inroads in the most densely populated urban areas"; and that if "deregulation of broadcast television [sweeping away the most fundamental regulatory concepts such as diversification] is warranted today, then it must be justified by a completely different rationale" (*House Staff Study, supra* at 25–26).

It is important to keep in mind that the broadcasters, including CBS, NBC, and others now clamoring to be relieved of fairness responsibilities, all volunteered to be public trustees, and thus obtained their channels without any payment therefor. These licensees would be first to seek government protection if someone caused them interference. Yet they strenuously resist any notion of a spectrum usage fee, in lieu of the public trustee obligation, and simply ask that all regulations except those protecting their channels be gutted. The word for their position is *chutz-pah.*

CABLE TELEVISION

I will briefly treat the regulatory scheme in the most important new medium, cable television. Regulatory policy here is set by the Cable Communications Policy Act of 1984.

While soundly ruling out programming regulation, that act seeks to foster the public interest through a structural (content neutral) approach aimed at diversifying the sources of information over cable. It thus proscribes local cross-ownership of cable by broadcast or telephone entities, requires that systems with 36 or more channels set aside 10 to 15 percent of capacity for leased access for video programming, and permits the franchising authority to specify channels for public, educational, and governmental use (PEG), with facilities support and a franchise fee not to exceed 5 percent of overall cable revenues. The cable operator is to exercise no editorial control over the leased or PEG channels.

In my view, this structural approach to cable with its greater channel capacity is sound—far superior to the broadcast, content-focused scheme. The flaw lies in its incomplete or inadequate implementation in the act. Thus, while the franchising authority may not establish requirements for specific video programming or other information services, it can enforce requirements in the franchise "for broad categories of video programming or other services" (§624(b)(2)(B)). This is not only content regulation but even can become quite specific, because there can be only one news, music, etc., channel.

Even more important, the new act fails to deal with some existing provisions that make cable subject to broadcast content requirements. In 1972, Congress amended §315 to provide that for the purposes of the section, "the term 'broadcasting station' includes a community antenna system" (47 U.S.C. 315(c)). This apparently makes fairness and equal opportunities applicable to cable, although there is no discussion of this result in the legislative history (and there has been no implementation because of a dearth of complaints to the FCC). There is also a dispute as to whether §312(a)(7), calling for reasonable access for candidates for federal office, applies to cable (*see* 34 FCC 2d 510, n.2; but *see* FCC Report to Sen. Goldwater, *Cable Television and Political Broadcast Laws.* Jan. 1981, at 24–26). These content provisions should not be made applicable to cable with its abundance of channels; the least intrusive method should be employed to accomplish the diversification goal, and that is access, not fairness or equal time.

The act also has flaws in implementing the structural (access) approach. Thus, a video programmer complaining that the terms for leased access are onerous is forced to go to court and win against a "presumption" that the terms are reasonable "unless shown by clear and convincing evidence to the contrary" (§6122(f)). But the programmer needs immediate access; it cannot afford lengthy court proceedings, with the dice so loaded against it. As a practical matter, the leased access provision is thus not apt to be much used. An alternative was suggested—to use compulsory arbitration in the event of a dispute, with the programmer obtaining immediate access, but the cable industry strongly resisted this approach.

The PEG provisions also contain a serious flaw. The problem here was never provision of channel capacity on these large modern systems, but rather financial support. The FCC rule in existence at the time of the act permitted a 3 percent franchise fee (to defray regulatory costs) and an additional 2 percent if used for cable-related purposes, almost always for PEG. The act, however, allows the cities to have a 5 percent fee with no requirement that it be used for cable purposes (§622(h)(3)). The cities insisted that there be no strings, and Congress was indifferent to a proposal that there be a 1 percent for national access programming and 1 percent for local fare. But without adequate funding, access is an empty shell. The act is thus a step backward from the prior regulatory scheme. Cable subscribers are being taxed with no assured benefits. Indeed, this raises a most serious constitutional issue (*see Minneapolis Star & Tribune Co. v. Minnesota Commissioner of Revenue*, 460 U.S. 575 (1983)).

CONCLUSION

In my view, the fairness doctrine is integrally tied to the public trustee concept. It follows that elimination of the doctrine really depends on ending the public trustee scheme for broadcasting—an unlikely event in light of broadcaster opposition to the notion of a compensating reasonable spectrum usage fee (e.g., 1 percent of gross revenues fixed in a long-term lease contract). Eventually we will get to video publishing, with the print model of regulation applicable to all video, but we may have to await further technological inroads (e.g., the rewiring of the nation by telephone companies with a fiber optic broadband highway—the so-called broadband integrated digital service network [IDSN]). In the meantime, steps should be taken to reduce the chilling effects of the present methods of implementing §315(a) of the Communications Act. I believe that the proposals set forth here, while no panacea, would be most helpful in promoting robust debate.

APPENDIX: Analysis of the FCC's KREM-TV Fairness Ruling (*Complaint of Sherwyn H. Heckt*, 40 F.C.C. 2d 1150 [1973])

Station KREM-TV, Spokane, Washington, one of whose top officials was associated with an Expo '74 proposed for Spokane, editorialized strongly in favor of the project and its supporting bond issue. There was considerable disparity in the amount of time actually afforded the antibond viewpoints, and the station rejected one of the spokesmen for that viewpoint. The station had a reasonable explanation for its rejection (i.e., the spokesman did not appear to represent groups for which he claimed to speak), and showed that it solicited opposing viewpoints.[19] The station also actively sought to obtain the views of leading spokesmen for the opposition and did present them. On the basis of these facts, the FCC staff found that the licensee had afforded reasonable opportunity.

However, the FCC process for resolution of the significant issues was a long, arduous one—the complaint was filed with the FCC on September 8, 1971; the licensee responded to the complaint on October 12, 1971; the complainant filed a reply on October 31, 1971; the FCC conduced a field investigation on June 5 through 9, 1972; the FCC sent a letter of inquiry to the licensee on October 6, 1972; the licensee's response was filed on February 6, 1973; and finally the FCC staff's decision was issued on May 17, 1973—21 months after the August 28 and 29, 1971 broadcasts (40 F.C.C. 2d at 1150–1151). The licensee's letter of February 6, 1973 concludes:

Finally, apart from the merits of the controversy engendered by the Hecht complaint, we desire to comment briefly upon the procedures followed here. With due respect for the Commissions' important responsibility in administering the fairness doctrine, we think there is a grave question whether it serves the public interest to require a station to account in such minute detail for everything it has said and done on a particular issue. We cannot believe that such a requirement contributes to an atmosphere of licensee independence of robust presentation of issues; we know that it is tremendously burdensome. We hope the Commission can find a way to give reasonable consideration to individual fairness complaints without the kind of exhaustive investigation that has apparently been thought necessary here (KREM-TV letter of February 6, 1972, at 31–32 (FCC files)).

In order to quantify the extent of burden, a Rand study inquired of the licensee as to the amounts of time and money expended in the handling of this fairness complaint. The licensee reported legal expenses of about $20,000, with other expenses (e.g., travel) adding considerably to the total. This is not an insubstantial amount, in light of the fact that the total profits reported by all three television stations in Spokane for 1972 were about $494,000.[20] However, from this licensee's standpoint, the important factors were the amount of time spent by top level station personnel and the emotional strain on them.

Thus, during the period from September 14, 1972 to May 18, 1973, the president and vice president of the station devoted a total of about 80 hours; the station manager, 207 hours; and six members of his staff, an additional 194 hours. The station pointed out, "In round numbers, then, 480 man hours of executive and supervisory time was spent on this matter. This, of course, does not include supporting secretarial or clerical time attendant to the work carried out. This represents a very serious dislocation of regular operational functions and is far more important in that sense than in the simple salary dollar value."[21]

Finally, there is the factor of deferral of license renewal. The KREM-TV renewal would normally have been granted on February 1, 1972; because of the fairness complaint, however, its application for renewal (and that of its company's AM station) was placed on deferred status until May 21, 1973. The FCC has recognized that placing the renewal in jeopardy because of licensee activity in the news field can have a serious inhibiting effect and should be done only when a most substantial and fundamental issue is presented.[22]

NOTES

1. *See Red Lion Broadcasting Co. v. FCC*, 395 U.S. 367, 390–91 (1969).
2. *Id.* at 377.
3. *See,* for example, *Storer Broadcasting Co.*, 11 FCC 2d678 (1968); *Report on Editorializing by Broadcast Licensees*, 13 FCC 1246 (1949).

4. *See Lamar Life Broadcasting Co.*, 38 FCC 1143, reversed and remanded, *UCC v. FCC*, 395 F2d994 (D.C. Cir 1966) [hereinafter cited 25 *UCC*].

5. *UCC, supra* at 1003 (Ch. J. Burger):

A broadcaster has much in common with a newspaper publisher, but he is not in the same category in terms of public obligations imposed by law. A broadcaster seeks and is granted the free and exclusive use of a limited and valuable part of the public domain; when he accepts that franchise, it is burdened by enforceable public obligations. A newspaper can be operated at the whim or caprice of its owners; a broadcast station cannot. After nearly five decades of operation the broadcast industry does not seem to have grasped the simple fact that a broadcasting license is a public trust subject to termination for breach of duty.

6. *See infra* 7–8; *Fairness Report*, 48 FCC 2d 1, 8, 17–21 (1974).

7. *Brandywine-Main Line Radio, Inc. v. FCC*, 172 F.2d 16 (1972), *cert. denied*, 412 U.S. 922 (1973).

8. Thus, Westinghouse Broadcasting Company stated to the FCC that operation under the fairness doctrine is simply responsible broadcasting. *See Fairness Report*, FCC 85–459, at ¶ 59, note 142.

9. 1974 *Fairness Report*, 39 Fed. Reg. at 26347 ("In the years since *Red Lion* was decided, we have seen no credible evidence that our policies have in fact had 'the net effect of reducing rather than enhancing the volume and quality of coverage' ").

10. *Memorandum Opinion and Order on Reconsideration of Fairness Doctrine*, 58 FCC 2d 691 (1976).

11. *Fairness Doctrine Inquiry*, 74 FCC 2d at 168–177.

12. 1985 *Fairness Report*, FCC 85–459, at 16–46 (Aug. 23, 1985).

13. Bazelon, *FCC Regulation of the Telecommunications Press*, (DUKE L.J. 213, 214–15 (1975).

14. *See* Geller, *The Fairness Doctrine*, The Rand Corp., R–1412-FF, 1973; Simmons, *The Fairness Doctrine and the Media* (1978); Rowan, *Broadcast Fairness* (1984).

15. *See* Geller, *The Fairness Doctrine, supra* at 36–43.

16. The Rand study, *supra* at 37, showed that on the average it took eight months to resolve a fairness complaint.

17. *See Lamar Life Broadcasting Co.* (WLBT), *supra* 38 FCC at 1145–48; *cf.* Sen. Rept. No. 562, 86th Cong., 1st Sess., at 12 (1959).

18. *U.S. v. O'Brien*, 391 U.S. 367 (1968); *Hynes v. Mayor of Oradell*, 425 U.S. 610 (1976).

19. The station contacted 22 area organizations, and mailed the station's editorial, with an offer of time to respond, to 194 community leaders and 400 members of the public (40 F.C.C. 2d at 1152).

20. See H. Geller, *The Rand Study, supra* at 41; TV Broadcast Financial data, 1972, FCC 05693, Table 17.

21. Letter to J. Roger Wollenberg from Jay Wright, Office of the Vice President Engineering, King Broadcasting Company, reprinted in Randy study, *supra*, Appendix E. at 134.

22. See *CBS ("Hunger in America"), supra* F.C.C. 2d at 150.

9

The Fairness Doctrine Is Bad Public Policy

John Kamp

This statement is intended to respond both directly and indirectly to Henry Geller's positions about the fairness doctrine in the foregoing article. The central thesis of the Geller piece is that the fairness doctrine is an appropriate and constitutional way to give life to the fiduciary model for the regulation of broadcasting.

Responding directly, the fairness doctrine is bad public policy and likely unconstitutional. It is bad public policy because it does not meet the ends it was designed to serve, i.e., increased discussion of public questions. Its questionable constitutionality stems from the fact that it makes the government the arbiter of "fairness" in broadcasting, thus intruding into the editorial rights of broadcasters, to the detriment of the public and, perhaps, the political process. Even accepting the fiduciary standard as Geller does, the fairness doctrine was appropriately struck by the FCC. Its absence does not leave the public interest standard of the Communications Act without substantive force.

Responding less directly but more fundamentally, the better view of the public interest standard is that the Communications Act of 1934 does not require a fiduciary model for broadcast regulation, just as such a model is not required of others licensed under Title III of the Communications Act. Instead, we urgently need to create and scrutinize new models and theories of regulation, lest we lapse into implementation of communications policy where no model or theory of regulation marks the promise or progress of this new era of telecommunication technology and today's information-rich social order.

BACKGROUND

In his article, Mr. Geller claims that the public interest standard of the Communications Act and the public trustee system set by the Federal Communications Commission (FCC) to enforce that standard necessarily led to the fairness doctrine. This statute and the public trustee scheme are assumed to inevitably imply the essence of a twofold obligation imposed on broadcasters: to devote reasonable time to issues of public concern and to do so fairly by affording reasonable opportunities for contrasting viewpoints.[1] Mr. Geller claims that the doctrine is embodied in §315(a), where broadcasters are obligated to "afford a reasonable opportunity for the discussion of contrasting viewpoints on controversial issues of public importance." However, current federal court decisions are to the contrary.[2]

Without clear legislative mandate, the question becomes not whether the existing fairness doctrine is incorporated in the Communications Act, but whether it is good public policy and consistent with the First Amendment. Recent rule-making decisions by the FCC have found against the doctrine as good public policy (*see*, for example, *1985 Fairness Report*, 102 F.C.C.2d 143 (1985)). Furthermore, in its most prominent recent judicatory decision on the matter, the commission found the public policy and constitutional issues joined and, thus, refused to enforce the doctrine against a broadcaster found in violation (*Syracuse Peace Council*, 2 FCC Rcd 797 (1987)). That case is now before the D.C. Circuit Court of Appeals and could well reach the Supreme Court given the gravity of the First Amendment issues involved. The FCC concluded that the fairness doctrine is unconstitutional, in that it conflicts with the First Amendment rights not only of broadcasters but of those possibly denied access to information because of broadcasters' reluctance to deal with issues attracting FCC scrutiny. As a result, the agency eliminated the doctrine. It now no longer relies on it in any way to enforce the public interest standard of the act.

DIRECT RESPONSE

There are three direct responses to Geller's legal and policy case favoring the fairness doctrine: that it is (1) counterproductive; (2) improperly intrusive into the editorial process; and (3) unnecessary to enforce the public interest standard of the Communications Act.

Counterproductive

In his article, Mr. Geller often cites *Red Lion Broadcasting Co. v. FCC*, 395 U.S. 367 (1969), in which the Supreme Court upheld the FCC's judgment that the fairness doctrine enhanced First Amendment goals by increasing the amount of public issue programming and ensuring some editorial balance in that coverage. However, in that same opinion the Court also warned that the doctrine's constitutional implications would be reexamined should the results of enforcing it effectively reduce broadcast speech (*Id.* at 393). Experience has borne out the Court's worries. The fairness doctrine not only did not increase speech, it decreased it. In substantive due process terms, the means of the law did not create the desired ends; thus, the doctrine failed to meet one of the most elementary standards of law. It did not work.

While it is highly difficult to prove that controversial issues have been avoided because of government regulation, the commission was, in fact, presented with many such instances during its investigation into the doctrine that resulted in the *1985 Fairness Report.* These examples came from broadcast station personnel who had declined to air programs on controversial topics, from surveys of local broadcasters and from organizations denied access to paid time in which to air their viewpoints because of fairness regulation concerns (brief for Respondents at 30–31, *Syracuse Peace Council v. FCC* [867 F2d 654 (D.C. Circ. 1989)]). This "self-squashing" had gone so far that less than half of all broadcasters in a nationwide survey had aired an editorial in the previous two years. With everyday news coverage and advertiser demands, apparently it had simply become unwieldy to invite government scrutiny by opening public on-air debate of local topics, even with something as innocuous as a station editorial hedged about by disclaimers.

Improperly Intrusive

Fairness doctrine enforcement inevitably leads to case-by-case investigation, regardless of whether the FCC uses its current approach or the actual malice variant suggested by Geller. While the language Geller quotes as codification merely urges a "reasonable opportunity for the discussion of contrasting viewpoints," the long-term, broad concept of fairness has been reduced to probes into individual complaints and a stopwatch, number-crunching practice of determining ratios among various sides of an issue. An example is the *Syracuse Peace Council* case itself, where the decision rested on the staff's count of minutes spent on each side of the nuclear power issue (*see* Letter of April 15, 1987 from Chairman Mark Fowler to John Dingell; Chairman, House Energy and Commerce Committee).

This sort of practice not only destroys any idea of broad, overall fairness, it more dangerously interjects the commission into a judgmental role in controversial issues, many of which are inherently local and which it can know little about. To interpret fairness, the commissioners must decide what issues are controversial, what the significant viewpoints are, how those have been treated and what constitutes "reasonable opportunity" for all sides. Obviously, such determinations entail judgments on program and advertising content, which should immediately raise First Amendment fears. One prominent liberal jurist recognized the danger of giving a government agency responsibility for such decisions:

Truth and fairness have a too uncertain quality to permit the government to define them.... [I]n order to determine what the "other side" is, one has to have an objective concept of truth against which to compare the challenged speech. And who in this country is in possession of this objective concept (Bazelon, *FCC Regulation of the Telecommunications Press*, 75DUKE L.J. 213, 236–37 (1975)).

Furthermore, where the government is deciding the truth, it can often become governmental truth. In fact, the D.C. Circuit Court has criticized the commission in the past for attempting to use a fairness doctrine complaint to force greater coverage for the political party in power (*Columbia Broadcasting System, Inc. v. FCC*, 454 F.2d 1018, 1036 (D.C. Cir. 1971)(Tamm, J., concurring)).

The fact that penalties for noncompliance with the fairness doctrine were seldom invoked does not lessen the First Amendment danger created by its existence. An individual's ability to remain in the broadcast business depends on continued possession of the broadcast license. The agency with the power to enforce the doctrine is also the agency with the power to withdraw that license. Therefore, the potential invocation of the doctrine hangs over the editorial chair of broadcasters like Damocles's sword. One commentator who has aptly articulated the problem notes that "the value of the sword of Damocles is that it hangs, not falls" (Lucas Powe, *American Broadcasting and the First Amendment* 120 (1987)). Abuses of the licensing process have occurred during both Republican and Democratic administrations, and some of these are ably reviewed by Powe.

The most direct and dangerous abuses may be within the election process. It has been said that free speech is the operational principle of self-government because it ensures that voters have unrestricted access to information in elections. There is more than a casual relationship between the fairness doctrine and the continued efficacy of §315 (*see* Letter of September 14, 1987 from Congressman John Dingell to congressional colleagues (on the need to codify the fairness doctrine)).

Geller correctly notes the equal opportunities requirement for candidates in political campaigns "significantly restrict[s] broadcast journalism at all levels," and that "Congress balks at...obvious reforms because it is made up of incumbents who do not really want to free the broadcaster to better illuminate the campaign choices" (Chapter 8). That incumbents wish to protect their incumbencies seems axiomatic. That the First Amendment was designed to stop Congress from using its power to protect incumbents by restricting speech should be a modern axiom of free speech and free elections.

Geller questions why broadcasters do not sue to invalidate §315. No neophyte to the halls of Congress, Geller must have smiled while writing those words. The history of the fairness debate among Congress, the FCC, and the broadcast industry has been marked by almost unprecedented contention. Furthermore, FCC legislation proposals to modify or eliminate §315 have been, at best, ignored by Congress. For broadcasters to pursue such reforms, even through the courts, in the face of congressional opposition would amount to folly or even political suicide.

Meanwhile, the practical concerns of running broadcast newsrooms remain. By lifting the weight of fairness doctrine enforcement standards, the FCC moved broadcast operations closer to the more free and unencumbered debate of print journalism.

For better or worse, editing is what editors are for; and editing is selection and choice of material.... Calculated risks of abuse are taken in order to preserve higher values. The presence of these risks is nothing new; the authors of the Bill of Rights accepted the reality that these risks were evils for which there was no acceptable remedy other than ... a sense of responsibility—and civility—on the part of those who exercise the guaranteed freedoms of expression (*Columbia Broadcasting System, Inc. v. Democratic Nat'l Comm.*, 412 U.S. 94, 124–25 (1973)).

Thus, the commission chose to apply a more traditional First Amendment approach; broadcasters themselves decide which local issues are controversial and how to present them fairly. Dropping the doctrine should facilitate those judgments and protect the First Amendment rights of broadcasters, viewers, and listeners.

Unnecessary

Elimination of the fairness doctrine should not cause fears among those sharing Mr. Geller's love of the public trustee model for broadcasting; it yet lives. "Geller's contention ... that the Commission's action has 'wiped out' and made 'a joke' of the Communications Act's scheme of regulation is, while perhaps colorful, completely inaccurate" (brief for Respondents, *SPC* at 45). Broadcasters must still provide "issue responsive" programming for their communities, as well as programs designed to meet the needs of children (for examples, *see Commercial TV stations*, 98 F.C.C. 2d 1076, 1091 (1984) and *Children's Television Programming*, 96 F.C.C. 2d 634 (1984)). The equal time provisions of the act governing political access also remain in force. In striking down the fairness doctrine, the commission made it clear that broadcasters' efforts, or lack of them, in areas of public interest in their communities will still be scrutinized heavily at license renewal time (*SPC Recon.*, 3 FCC Rcd at 2037, 2039; *Syracuse Peace Council*, 2 FCC Rcd 5043, 5064 n.91, 5065 n.101 (1987)).

The decision to drop the fairness doctrine was a narrow one, based on findings that it was unconstitutional and contrary to the public interest served by broadcasters. There is no reason to believe that other fiduciary obligations are also eliminated by the commission's action or, necessarily, that the decline of the doctrine spells the end of the fiduciary model.

THE GELLER ALTERNATIVE

Mr. Geller urges the continued enforcement of the fairness doctrine although he admits it can inflict real First Amendment damage. He too, dislikes the case-by-case investigation practice and would instead use an "actual malice" *The New York Times v. Sullivan* standard, laid on only during the license renewal process. He advocates two questions be answered by the commission: Has it afforded the licensee maximum editorial freedom? What is needed to ensure that the licensee meet its public trustee obligation? His primary concern is for cases such as *Red Lion*, in which a station blatantly favors one viewpoint consistently.

However, there is no difference from a First Amendment standpoint. Whether decided on individual complaints or every five or seven years, it is not the proper role of a government agency to judge program content, define issue perspectives, or mandate their treatment. Mr. Geller says his approach would not gut the fairness doctrine; he is right. Its enforcement would still violate the First Amendment.

The commission's response in the *Syracuse* record fully addresses the problem with Geller's approach. It interpreted the fiduciary model to mean that broadcasters must operate in the interests of the public at large, providing a platform for all speech, not just that seen as "safe" under fairness doctrine constraints. "Fundamentally, the practical effect of [his] alternative is not to support the exercise of those speech rights that are the essence of open debate, but to withdraw in some measure the debate from the court of public opinion and to rechannel it to the court of administrative review" (*Syracuse Peace Council Reconsidered*, 3 FCC Rcd 2035, 2041 n.54 (1988)).

INDIRECT RESPONSE

The more fundamental response to Geller begins with his assumption that the fiduciary model for regulation of broadcasting is the best way to implement the public interest standard. Geller notes correctly that

Congress initially had other alternatives for a frequency distribution scheme, such as license auctioning or common carriage. Incorrectly, however, he assumes that the public interest standard of the act requires that the licensing scheme chosen be accompanied by a public trustee model that "inevitably affects broadcast journalism because it necessarily leads to the fairness doctrine" (Chapter 8).

Although the Communications Act requires the FCC to license broadcasters in the public interest, it does not set forth a comprehensive list of programming obligations fundamental to that concept. The standard has often been characterized as "a supple instrument for the exercise of discretion by the expert body which Congress has charged to carry out its legislative policy" (*FCC v. Pottsville Broadcasting Co.*, 309 U.S. 134, 138 (1940)). Congress has granted the FCC broad authority to determine how best to pursue the public interest goal of the act, including the goal of securing "the maximum benefits of radio to all the people of the United States" (*National Broadcasting Co., Inc. v. U.S.*, 319 U.S. 190, 217 (1943)).

The fiduciary standard is not a necessary incident of licensing. Consider, for example, that the FCC under the act has licensed over one million persons and corporations in private (personal, business, and public safety) radio services alone, without regard to the content of their communications. Meanwhile, as Geller notes, the 1984 Cable Act imposes a separate scheme of licensing on cable operators, and this country's common carriers operate under a scheme of regulation that is more akin to the Cable Act than to broadcast regulation.

Similarly, the standard is not the inevitable result of broadcast spectrum scarcity. Although electronic engineers note that there is theoretically an unlimited spectrum resource, the practical reality is that broadcast frequencies have value; "scarce" is therefore accurate in that they must be allocated and apportioned among competing users and uses. So does every resource where demand exceeds supply. To say that this scarcity of broadcast spectrum requiring licensing sets in tone the public trustee scheme is to ignore the ability of Congress to change the act. Instead, what licensing does is provide public-policy makers an opportunity to allocate in such a way that meets public policy goals of whatever type the social and political realities of the times may compel.

The time may well have come to make some changes in either the act or its interpretation. The time has definitely come to give new meaning to the public interest standard, at least by eschewing theories of broadcast regulation that lead to content control by the FCC. Five reasons spring to mind, the first three arising from the above discussion of the fairness doctrine. In the context of fairness, at least, content control (1) doesn't work, (2) impinges on the First Amendment rights of broadcasters, viewers and listeners, and (3) can compromise the free flow of information.

Ancillary to this third reason is the broader problem of making the control of broadcast content a part of the larger political process. This issue deserves further elaboration because it is not yet widely understood, much less fully articulated and described. One example illustrates the scope of the problem. During the one-hundreth Congress, a veto by President Ronald Reagan frustrated attempts to codify the doctrine. After that action many legislative leaders refused to even consider other legislative initiatives being urged by broadcasters. In effect, Congress told broadcasters that no matter how legitimate other requests may be— license renewal, "must carry," and copyright concerns—nothing would move in Congress until broadcasters accepted a statutory fairness doctrine.

The First Amendment is not properly the subject of such a trade. At worst, because broadcasters are for the most part pragmatic business-people, some might acquiesce for the sake of more tangible and financially rewarding legislation. From this angle, public rights are in the hands of private parties. At best, it makes these issues the subject of negotiated compromise rather than constitutional principle. Meanwhile, it is not inconsequential that the power to regulate content can allow some legislators to garner more PAC (Political Action Committee) money to finance their own campaigns.

Two additional reasons argue against continued regulation of broadcast content. First, it may no longer be necessary as a means of ensuring that the public be informed. Second, it may put broadcasters at an unfair business disadvantage. Both these stem from the fact that broadcasting has not only grown considerably since the trustee concept was first developed, it has also become only one among many forms of mass media. However, it is still virtually the only one so regulated.

All this means that consumers continue to have increasing control over program content; the greater the number of choices, the more responsive each provider must be to the desires of the viewer. Without viewers, revenue from subscriptions and advertisers drops. The business may eventually fail, to be replaced by one that is more responsive to its audience.

Distinctions among mass media are also blurring at a rapid rate. Newspapers increasingly use electronic transmission techniques while broadcasters and cablecasters perform many of the traditional functions of newspapers. Telephone companies have already become "information service" businesses aside from their traditional functions; they provide all sorts of data transmission, much of it increasingly sophisticated and thus "edited" rather than merely transmitted. Policymakers, meanwhile, are looking at the possibility of melding cable television and these telephone businesses into a single-wire service into homes.

Why then regulate broadcast content and not that of others? Can regulated media compete? If not, is that not a sign that the unregulated media better serve the needs and interests of their audiences? FCC Chairman Dennis Patrick also warned members of the International Radio and Television Society against trading content control for other government protection.

Broadcasters can tolerate new restrictions—even seek them out—in exchange for a special, protected relationship. But if broadcasters accept these kinds of restrictions, when their competitors are free to give audiences what they want, the effect on their market share and revenues will be almost immediate.... Broadcasters will find themselves with a very special, very protected and very small market share (Address by FCC Chairman Dennis R. Patrick, International Radio and Television Society luncheon, September 22, 1988).

CONCLUSION

Debate about the public trustee concept and the fairness doctrine will not be quelled by the counterstatement to Henry Geller, nor should it be. It is about principle: about the First Amendment freedom of all people, of all the press, to be able to speak openly about the issues of the day without interference from the federal government; about the First Amendment right of all of us as voting citizens to hear about timely issues and about political candidates from a free, robust, and uncensored press. Without these freedoms, free elections and democratic self-government are hollow.

Meanwhile, the most practical point about the fairness debate is that it may be largely moot in the political arena, regardless of all the past, present, and future political folderol. Regardless of actions by the FCC, legislation in the next Congress, or political posturing by the industries involved, the issue will almost certainly be settled in the courts, perhaps the Supreme Court. Although definitive resolution may be profoundly sought by all sides, it may be the least likely of the outcomes. More likely is a decision settling some issues but returning others to the Congress, the commission, and the industry. Perhaps those remaining issues will be more sharply focused and less likely to distract interested parties into partisan fights rather than engaging in reasoned and enlightened public-policy making.

Meanwhile, continuing debate over the doctrine, especially in Congress, mistakenly creates the illusion of a significant public policy question, and while doing so, gives powerful members of Congress reason or ruse to avoid the more significant and politically difficult issues of telecommunication policy. It is dangerous to continue to put these aside, because without significant changes in the Communications Act, public policy in this area will continue to be made on an *ad hoc* basis. The important question is not whether the fairness doctrine is good public policy; rather, it is how best to regulate broadcasting and the other media, old and new, that are under the jurisdiction of the federal government.

NOTES

1. If the words sound familiar, it may be because they come from the commission's own *Fairness Report* of 1974, one of several reports supervised by Geller in which the doctrine was upheld. For the sake of full disclosure, it should be noted that the author of this statement took a similar part in the report of 1985 that came to several contrary conclusions.

2. See *Meredith Corp. v. FCC*, 809 F.2d at 873 n.11; *Telecommunications Research and Action Center v. FCC*, 801 F.2d 501, 516–518.

10

THE LEGAL MODEL: FINDING THE RIGHT MIX

David A. Anderson

The activities of the mass media generate a wide array of demands to hold them legally responsible for the harms they cause. Let me list a few examples.

- A businessperson, falsely accused of having ties to organized crime, seeks damages for harm to his/her reputation.
- A private individual, catapulted into the public spotlight by events beyond his control, has his homosexuality revealed to the world by the press; he seeks damages for invasion of privacy.
- An adolescent girl is raped by a gang of teenagers who the night before watched a similar attack on network television; her parents believe the network should be held accountable for inciting the violence against their daughter.

Most of us, at some point in our lives, probably will wish for some mechanism to hold the media legally accountable, if not for one of these wrongs then for some other transgression. And no one doubts that the media can be held accountable for at least some harms. Not even Justice Hugo Black would have exempted the press from all legal control; while he considered freedom of speech and press to be an absolute, his limited definition of the concept made many forms of expression subject to governmental control.[1] It is equally clear that the press cannot be held legally accountable for all its errors or all the injuries it causes. Even if we agreed that it is desirable to do so, the litigation volume would be too great even for as litigious a society as ours.

The issue, then, is one of degree: how much legal accountability is appropriate? This question has answers grounded in both principle and pragmatism. We limit accountability on grounds of principle, because we understand that it is the converse of press freedom; to the extent that media are held legally accountable, by so much is their freedom diminished. We do not hold media accountable for criticizing government because we believe that would abridge an essential freedom.

We also limit accountability for the same reasons that we limit the law's role in other areas of life, because the cost of intervening is thought to be too great. We might well decide that providing a remedy for misquotation violates no essential principle of freedom of expression. But we choose not to do so, probably because we believe that trying to determine whether a person has been misquoted, and what the law should do about it, would be more trouble than it is worth.

We have wondered for 200 years how the framers of the First Amendment intended to answer the question of how much accountability there ought to be.[2] The Supreme Court has faced the question in dozens of variations and has never been able to formulate a comprehensive answer. Scholars such as Zachariah Chafee,[3] Alexander Meiklejohn,[4] and Thomas I. Emerson[5] have proposed answers, but none has carried the day.

We will suggest some ways we might go about evaluating the appropriateness of the balance we have struck between accountability and freedom. One method is historical: we can examine the kinds and amounts of accountability we have imposed on the media in the past and then ask whether the product is too free or too restricted. Second, we can compare our current balance of freedom and accountability with that of other societies and ask whether we like their results better. Third, we can compare the accountability of the media with that of other speakers in our own society and ask whether the experience of these others makes a case for more or less media accountability.

HISTORICAL EVALUATION

At first blush, it seems obvious that the American press was held more closely accountable in the past than today. Through most of our history the Supreme Court did little to discourage attempts to control the press. Not until 1925 did the Court recognize the First Amendment as a limitation on the states' power to hold the press accountable.[6] No act of Congress was ever held to violate the First Amendment until 1965.[7] In 1919, Justice Oliver Wendell Holmes's belief that citizens could not be punished for criticizing the government was a dissenting opinion.[8]

Until 1964, libelous statements were excluded from any constitutional protection,[9] and until 1931 local authorities could shut down a newspaper they considered malicious, scandalous, and defamatory.[10] Obscenity was unprotected until 1957,[11] and commercial speech was not protected until 1975.[12] Until the 1940s, judges were free to use their contempt power to punish editors who criticized their judicial conduct.[13]

One must be cautious, however, in assuming that the law as declared by the Supreme Court is an accurate measure of the extent to which the media are legally accountable in fact. For one thing, the Supreme Court may lag behind the lower courts. In our own time, for example, the Supreme Court has refused to extend First Amendment protection to reporters' claims of a privilege to protect confidentiality of sources.[14] In a sense, the Court has thus preserved the power of courts to hold the press accountable: judges can at least compel reporters to testify to the same extent as other citizens. But in fact, the Supreme Court has been subverted by lower courts. Seizing on dicta in a concurring opinion, many state and federal lower courts have developed a conditional privilege that often relieves reporters of the need to breach the confidence.[15] The result is that the press in fact is less accountable in this respect than the Supreme Court decisions would lead one to expect.

Second, reported decisions (whether of the Supreme Court or lower courts) do not always reflect what the law is doing in practice. Again, the confidential source issue is illustrative. Until the late 1960s, one would have been hard pressed to find any reported decisions protecting confidentiality. The reason, however, was not necessarily that courts were hostile to the claim. Rather, it was that until the Nixon administration began a systematic program of issuing subpoenas to reporters in 1969, such subpoenas had been rare.[16] Thus, what appears to be an absence of legal protection was in fact an absence of a problem.

Third, it is often hard to know how effective a new doctrine designed to limit accountability really is. We tend to assume, for example, that *New York Times v. Sullivan* worked a revolution in libel law. Harry Kalven, Jr., quoted Meiklejohn calling it "an occasion for dancing in the streets."[17] William Prosser thought it was "unquestionably the greatest victory won by the defendants in the history of the modern law of torts."[18] Yet, after 20 years, there are some who believe the press today enjoys less protection from defamation suits than it did before *Sullivan*.[19] This writer disagrees, but no one can doubt that reports of the death of libel were highly exaggerated. Moreover, it is beyond dispute that the *Sullivan* doctrine is less effective in protecting the press today than it was during its first decade of life, even though not one syllable of the doctrine has been changed. What has changed is the membership of the court and its enthusiasm for the *Sullivan* rule. In the 10 years following *New York Times v. Sullivan*, the Court decided 12 libel cases all but one of them for the defendants.[20] In the next 12 years, the Court decided 10 more cases, only 2 of which went for the defendants.[21] The degree of media accountability obviously depends not only on doctrine, but on the attitudes of those who apply the doctrine.

For all of these reasons, comparing the present with the past is not merely a matter of asking how much the Supreme Court has curtailed media accountability. And so far we have considered legal accountability only in the context of the print media. The flowering of broadcasting, largely within our own lifetimes, makes a comparison of the past and present even more difficult. The most pervasive media of our time simply did not exist through most of our history. One therefore must attempt to compare apples with apples *and* oranges. Although broadcasting developed during a period when the Supreme Court was reducing the accountability of other media, radio and television did not benefit as fully from this movement. Except for its very early years and very recent years, radio was a closely regulated industry. When television came along after World War II, it was subjected to the same regulatory regime, and it continues to be subject to the equal time provision and other control mechanisms from which the Supreme Court has refused to extend the full protection of the First Amendment.[22]

Yet it seems clear that even though most of the regulatory apparatus is still in place, broadcasting today is in fact far less accountable legally than it was even 20 years ago. Again, the reason is less doctrinal than attitudinal. In the late 1960s the fairness doctrine, comparative license renewal, and community service requirements reflected not only the law, but values that the regulators, the Congress, and perhaps much of the public believed in. The Federal Communications Commission (FCC) occasionally was willing to take away a license,[23] and the United States Court of Appeals for the District of Columbia was trying to force the commission to exercise its regulatory role even more aggressively.[24]

Today, most of the regulations are still on the books, but no one has much interest in enforcing them. The FCC seems to have won its war with the court of appeals, and is now less interested in regulating the industry than in campaigning for abolition of the regulations. Sometime in the 1970s, perhaps during Watergate, the television networks sensed that the will to employ the regulatory mechanisms had waned. Then in the late 1970s and 1980s, the growth of cable and the onrush of new communications technologies mooted many old controversies and monopolized the attention of people who otherwise might have insisted on keeping tighter control of broadcasting. Thus, although the Federal Communications Act remains unchanged and the First Amendment still permits more regulation of broadcasting than of other media, the law's power to hold broadcasting accountable has been greatly weakened.

Despite the difficulty of comparing the mixed media of today with the print media of the past, and notwithstanding the discrepancies between real and apparent accountability, I think that overall the media today are less accountable legally than they have been at any time in our history.

It is true that libel verdicts are enormously larger than they were even a generation ago,[25] but the media that are the most frequent targets are enormously richer, too. It is true that the medium from which most Americans get their news is subject to governmental regulation, but television has the power and resources to stand up to the regulators in a way that the press of our forefathers could never have done. On a few issues the press may be less free today than it was a generation ago, in the heyday of the Warren Court. But in the long view and considering the full range of free press issues, I think it is undeniable that the media of the late twentieth century are less accountable legally than their predecessors were. In the last half-century the First Amendment has become a formidable barrier to efforts of courts and legislatures to hold the media accountable.

Through the nineteenth and early twentieth centuries, the formative period in our politics, institutions, and culture, the media were subject to far more legal accountability than today. One might therefore conclude that the freedom from accountability that the media enjoy today is not essential to a free society as we know it. The America we remember is largely a product of a value system in which freedom of expression was not exalted over other values to the extent that it is today.

Indeed, one might go further and argue that the present extent of media freedom is inimical to the preservation of American political culture and institutions. If the America we know is a product of a more restrictive system of law, one might infer that today's less-restrictive system is likely to produce something different. John Kennedy, Dwight Eisenhower, Harry Truman, Franklin Roosevelt, and their predecessors were products of a legal system that protected them from defamatory attacks as fully as it protected the private citizen.[26] If *New York Times v. Sullivan* has had the effect that the Supreme Court intended, the subsequent generation of politicians has been subject to far more "vehement, caustic, and sometimes unpleasantly sharp attacks."[27] This surely must have affected American politics. If one believes the political system that produced John F. Kennedy had found the proper balance between robust discussion and the protection of official reputation, then the present level of press accountability may threaten an important value.

While the present extent of media freedom probably is not essential to the preservation of a free society, on balance it has produced a better society than we had through the first 150 years of our national existence. The appropriate comparison is with the America of a half-century ago, after the explosion of new technology and libertarian First Amendment jurisprudence had begun but before they had greatly changed the society. It was the world of FDR, baseball, and big bands. Newspapers were highly competitive and mostly mediocre.[28] The most important national publications were *The Saturday Evening Post* and *Life*.[29] On radio were Edward R. Murrow, live drama, simulated Martian invasions, and goat-gland hucksters.

The media were not particularly aggressive, but neither were they obviously oppressed. They enjoyed a more or less peaceful coexistence with government. The press tacitly agreed not to photograph Franklin Roosevelt in situations that showed his disability, and White House reporters played poker with Harry Truman. Through World War II, the press would voluntarily acquiesce in government censorship of military matters.

It was also a time of isolationism, in which Americans and their media did their best to ignore Adolf Hitler's rise in Europe and Joseph Stalin's oppression in the Soviet Union. It was a time when racism was practiced and supported by the media in half the country and acquiesced in by most of the media in the rest of the country. Labor activists and political dissenters could not expect a fair shake from the press. From "Amos 'n Andy" to "Blondie and Dagwood," the media perpetuated and reinforced the stereotypes of the culture. William Randolph Hearst and Henry Luce and their counterparts in local communities used their presses shamelessly to punish their enemies and advance their favorite causes.

America today is not a better place in every respect. The level of civility, generally and in the media, is probably lower. The racial, ethnic, and gender stereotypes are not quite so blatant, but the debasement of the culture by pornography, violence, and willful ignorance has increased. The integrity and competence of public officials is not conspicuously better. Enormous advances in the variety, sophistication, and impartiality of the media do not seem to have produced comparable improvements in the intelligence, interest, or judgment of the electorate.

These losses are all attributable in some degree to increased media freedom. Civility is an inevitable casualty of the contentiousness that we expect a truly free press to stimulate. When we no longer allow the authorities to be arbiters of taste, we are choosing to let the tastes of the marketplace govern. Politicians who are subjected to closer scrutiny may turn out to have more warts than we thought, and the result may disenchant the electorate.

Increased media freedom has produced some immense benefits, however. When the courts ruled a half-century ago that the post office could not ban *Ulysses*,[30] they started a revolution that eventually unshackled the arts, stimulating an outpouring of creativity and variety in everything from movies to ballet. The same revolution allowed human sexuality to escape from the brothel and the imported postcard—a development that may have been a prerequisite to the present revolution in sex roles.

The press now has achieved some freedom to scrutinize private centers of power. The extension of some constitutional protection to commercial speech,[31] defamatory statements about private persons,[32] and actions for invasion of privacy[33] has helped to open up the activities of nongovernmental elites, such as business, the professions, local social oligarchies, foundations, and private universities.

Most importantly, the press has finally become powerful enough to exercise a real check on the other three estates. Many share Vincent Blasi's belief that the framers of the First Amendment viewed the press clause as a means of checking the tendency of government officials to abuse their power.[34] But the press as the framers knew it, with only the freedoms that they envisioned, would have been no match for government as we know it today. In part for reasons of economics and technology, but more so because the expansion of First Amendment protections in the last half-century has finally given the press the power it needs to be an effective fourth estate. The "puny anonymities" whose pamphlets Oliver Wendell Holmes wanted to protect in *Abrams*[35] have not become the "formidable check on official power" that Justice Potter Stewart described as an organized, expert, institutional press that can bring to bear on government "a conspiracy of the intellect, with the courage of numbers."[36]

This latter development moots whatever controversy might otherwise exist as to the desirability of the expansion of press freedom. If the press had any less power, the government could simply overwhelm it. We know of one instance—Watergate—in which an administration came perilously close to escaping the checking function of the press, and there undoubtedly have been other administrations that succeeded. Watergate shows how crucial a single rule can be. Without the protection of *New York Times v. Sullivan*, the *Washington Post* could not have maintained the scrutiny—sustained, lonely, and sometimes flawed—that eventually brought down the Nixon administration. For me, the possibility that the administration could have won that battle is sufficient proof of the need for a press no less powerful than today's.

OTHER SOCIETIES

A second method of measuring the optimum degree of media accountability is to observe the levels that other free nations have arrived at. Since I am not a comparative law scholar and have no personal knowledge of the system of press freedom in any other country, I can only make some general observations based on the work of others. I rely primarily on a recent book, *Press Law in Modern Democracies*, edited by Pnina Lahav.[37] It is a collection of essays describing and evaluating the state of press freedom in seven countries: Great Britain, the United States, France, West Germany, Sweden, Israel, and Japan.

These essays offer striking evidence that a society can be reasonably free despite press restrictions that we would consider hopelessly repressive. West Germany has no aversion to prior restraints. There is no general presumption against them, and in some context they are the preferred remedy, on the theory that it is better to prevent harm than compensate for it after the fact.[38] Sweden and Israel require all potential publishers to first obtain a license from the government and Israel engages in outright censorship.[39] The French have reached a conclusion exactly the opposite of ours on the issue of protecting public officials' reputations. Officials receive special protection, not available to private citizens, on the theory that the burdens of public service are onerous enough without the additional irritation of defamatory attacks.[40]

France and Germany apparently do not reject the concept of seditious libel. The German criminal code prohibits attacks on the president, the republic and its symbols, and members of federal and state legislatures.[41] French law imposes penalties for defaming or insulting governmental bodies.[42] In Japan, Israel, and Sweden, criminal prosecutions for libel are more common than civil suits.[43]

The British have their Official Secrets Act and its "D-notice" and other devices that enable the government to suppress information to an extent that our government can only envy.[44] They find it unnecessary to give the press any special freedom to criticize public officials.

The power of these governments to hold the press accountable pales beside that of Israel, however. The Israeli government can compel newspapers to publish its pronouncements and its denials of material previously published. It can suspend newspapers that pose a likely danger to public peace, and its powers of censorship are so broad that the press is forbidden even to publish white space indicating that something has been censored. When the Israeli government designates particular subjects as secret, the press must submit articles on those subjects for prior review. Seditious libel is a crime punishable by termination of the newspaper, and truth is no defense.[45]

The Israeli system sounds so repressive it is hard to believe the society that tolertes it could be called free. Yet friends who have lived in Israel assure me that the press seems quite free in some respects, most notably in its willingness to criticize vigorously those in power. In any event, the other countries mentioned are certainly "free," and some would be considered among the enlightened nations of the world.

A society, obviously, can be free without choosing precisely the same accommodation between media accountability and freedom that we have chosen. Even principles that we consider central—such as no prior restraints or no seditious libel—may not be as indispensable as we thought. If freedom can coexist with prior restraint, seditious libel, licensing, or official secrets acts in other societies, perhaps that indicates we have gone further than necessary in protecting the press.

Again, however, caution is in order. In every country, press freedom is a product not merely of laws, but of traditions, habits, and attitudes. Legal rules reflect the needs, experiences, and values of the country, and the same rules may produce very different results in different cultures. Americans have viewed government as a threat and an adversary since our earliest days. It is not surprising that our system reflects a general distrust of public officials. The British, on the other hand, have far more faith in their officials, particularly the civil service. Without speculating as to whether British officialdom is in fact more trustworthy than ours, one can nevertheless understand why the British rules inhibiting scrutiny of officials might not work in a society that lacks the British civil service tradition. Licensing of the press undoubtedly seems quite innocent in Sweden, where the culture accepts a far larger government role in many of the affairs of life. In the United States, where one needs no governmental permission to engage in most activities, a scheme for licensing the press would have much different connotations.

One cannot assume, therefore, that a particular free press principle is unnecessry because another society is able to get along without it. But the fact that *so many* free societies are able to do without *so many* rules that we consider essential suggests that we may be wrong to think freedom would vanish if we permitted prior restraints, or seditious libel, or an official secrets act. Perhaps freedom of the press is the product not so much of particular legal rules, but of a matrix that includes all the rules, plus our traditions, values, and myths.[46] It may well be that in a mature society such as ours, the very idea of press freedom has a power of its own that does more to protect the press than the rules themselves. If this is true, then perhaps we need not cling quite so tenaciously to the particular doctrines that we have come to consider central to our system.

OTHER SPEAKERS

A third suggestion for gauging press accountability is less comparative than analytical. Because we generally have not held the press any more or less accountable than other speakers,[47] there is no different body of jurisprudence or experience to compare with. This need not be so, however. The media are by no means the only important speakers in our system. The individual, speaking to his neighbors, his governors or constituents, his business and professional associates, his coreligionists, or his fellow citizens, is at the core of our attachment to the principle of freedom of speech. There are other important voices: corporations, foundations, associations, universities, churches, and political parties. The government itself is an immensely important voice, indoctrinating children in the schools, advising farmers and homemakers, instructing taxpayers, directing those it regulates, and speaking to the general public through innumerable bulletins, studies, reports, press releases, press conferences, and speeches.[48]

Treating the press differently from these other speakers is an idea we resist for several reasons. First, it offends our egalitarian instincts. Equality is a powerful value in our society, and one that is served by the idea that the lonely pamphleteer and the mightiest publishing empire are equals before the law.[49] A second reason is that treating the press differently embroils us in a definitional stew: who qualifies as press?[50] Third, some people fear that singling out of the press, even for favorable treatment, would inevitably lead to invidious treatment.[51]

We must not minimize any of these objections. However, there are some countervailing concerns. One reason we want to hold media accountable is the same as the reason we want to hold government or business accountable: power. The more powerful the institution, the more likely we are to insist that it be subject to some check. The press, as has been noted, must have more freedom today because government is so much more powerful today.

Some kinds of speakers obviously have more power than others. A giant utility company is a more powerful speaker than the individual consumer, a fact that may tempt the state to try to exert greater control over the company than the individual.[52] Likewise, some media are more powerful than others. The pamphleteer whose printing press consists of access to a photocopy machine does not generate the same demands for accountability as a national television network.

It is suggested that appropriate degrees of legal accountability may differ for different types of speaker, including different types of media. A balance between freedom and accountability that works fine for Time Inc. or CBS may be entirely inappropriate for a small newspaper or journal of opinion. A comparison of two libel cases—*Sharon v. Time Inc.*[53] and *Green v. The Alton Telegraph*[54]—illustrates the point. *The Alton Telegraph*, a small daily in Illinois, was forced into bankruptcy by a $9 million libel verdict. The paper once seemed on the verge of folding, but eventually it settled the case for $1.4 million and the paper is still publishing today.[55] General Ariel Sharon sued *Time* Magazine for $50 million but lost when the jury found that although *Time*'s story was false and defamatory, it was not published with reckless disregard for the truth.

The general reaction of the press and some segments of the public to *The Alton Telegraph* case ranged from consternation to outrage. The case was widely—and correctly—viewed as an example of libel law run amok.

The *Sharon* case, on the other hand, produced a very different reaction. Many observers, including some from the media, viewed it as a healthy exercise, giving General Sharon some measure of vindication and exposing to public view some of the practices of newsmagazine journalism.[56] Yet the *Sharon* case cost *Time* at least $5 million in defense costs—far more than *The Telegraph*'s settlement.[57]

The reasons for the difference in reaction all reflect a belief in *proportionality;* we feel that the result in *Alton* was out of all proportion, while the result in the *Time* case was not. It is not merely that $5 million means far less to Time Inc. than $1.4 million means to *The Alton Telegraph* or that *Time*'s loss was insured, while *The Telegraph*'s was not. Rather, the reaction reflects something deeper: a sense that what is good for *Time* is not necessarily good for *The Telegraph*.

For one thing the defamation in the *Alton* case was contained only in an unpublished memo, while *Time*'s allegation reached millions of readers. The *Alton* case was really a nonmedia case, a private defamatory communication from individuals who happened to be reporters to law enforcement officials. It is hard to believe that a communication so limited requires the same legal response as *Time*'s publication.

Second, there seemed to be a sense that *Time* needed a chastening, or at least a public undressing, because for so many years it has represented itself to so many millions of readers as knowing so much that the rest of the media did not. The rest of the media showed little sympathy for *Time*'s travail.[58] This may have reflected not just pent-up resentment of *Time*'s legendary arrogance, but also a belief within the journalistic community that because of *Time*'s power as a molder of public opinion, its brand of journalism deserved the dose of legal accountability it received. Perhaps no one (except, no doubt, the plaintiff and his attorney) believes *The Alton Telegraph* deserved its dose.

The media by and large have denied that they should be treated any differently than nonmedia speakers, and the bigger media, at least, have resisted the idea that different media might be treated differently. This commitment to symmetry gives the large media a powerful mode of argument: "the proposed restriction might not harm us, but it must be rejected because of the effect it would have on the smaller media."[59] The proposition has endless variation, one of the most familiar of which appears in the "chilling effect" argument. Rarely does an editor or his lawyer admit that the threat of a libel suit might cause *him* such a failure of courage that *he* would decline to publish a story. Rather, the danger is always that some weaker soul will be chilled.

The chilling effect is real, and it is not just the weak who are chilled;[60] the argument here serves the harmless purpose of allowing editors to point out a danger without admitting their own weakness. But as a general proposition, the large media's insistence on equal legal treatment of all media is suspect because it serves their interests better than it serves those of the weak and powerless.

There are two important areas in which the Supreme Court has engaged in differential treatment. One is commercial speech. After insisting for many years that commercial speech required no constitutional protection, the Court now holds that it requires some, although not as much as "true" speech.[61] Differences between commercial speech and other varieties, the Court said,

suggest that a different degree of protection is necessary to insure that the flow of truthful and legitimate commercial information is unimpaired. The truth of commercial speech, for example, may be more easily verifiable by its disseminator than, let us say, news reporting or political commentary, in that ordinarily the advertiser seeks to disseminate information about a specific product or service that he himself provides and presumably knows more about than anyone else. Also, commercial speech may be more durable than other kinds. Since advertising is the *sine qua non* of commercial profits there is little likelihood of its being chilled by proper regulation and foregone entirely.[62]

Although the distinction expressed is between different types of speech, the rationale is one that distinguishes between different types of speaker. The reason the advertiser is better able to ascertain the truth of his speech has less to do with the content of the speech than with the relationship of the speaker to the subject matter: it is because he is in a position to know the truth. The news reporter describing the activities of third persons may not be in this position, but many other noncommercial speakers are: the politician describing his own record, the institution describing its own policy, and the publisher describing his own affairs.

And the reason commercial speech may be more durable depends not on the nature of the speech but on the strength of the speaker's motivation. Other speakers may have motives that make their speech as unchillable as that of the advertiser; the political candidate, for example, has powerful reasons to speak about his opponent. Similarly, some media activities are more durable than others. Despite the legal campaigns waged by Carol Burnett, Shirley Jones, and other celebrities,[63] the *National Enquirer* has not abandoned its style of journalism. *Penthouse* and *Hustler* seem to be able to fend off libel, privacy, and obscenity actions all over the country and still have energy and money left over to sue each other.[64] "60 Minutes" remains on the air even though it has generated many lawsuits, some of them costly.[65] In each case, the speech is durable because the speaker has strong economic incentives to speak, just as the advertiser does.

The Supreme Court recognized this, at least tacitly, in 1985 in *Dun & Bradstreet v. Greenmoss Builders, Inc.*[66] The question was whether defamatory credit reports require constitutional protection. The Court refused to treat such reports as commercial speech or to distinguish between media and nonmedia speakers. And it refused to protect the reports on the ground that they do not involve matters of public concern. Yet the rationale again rests on a distinction between different types of speaker.

Nothing in the nature of the report—a statement that the plaintiff corporation had filed for bankruptcy—precluded its being a matter of public concern. Were the same report to appear in the local newspaper, it might well be characterized as a matter of public concern. The Court conceded as much by assuring us that even another credit report might be a matter of public concern, depending on its content, form, and context.[67]

The speech in question was denied protection not because of anything inherent in its content, but because of the medium in which it appeared. The Court gave four explanations for its decision that the report was not a matter of public concern. Two were the commercial speech arguments from *Virginia Pharmacy*: credit reports, like advertising, are more durable and ("arguably," the Court said) more objectively verifiable. Another was that the speaker's motivation was solely economic self-interest—its own and that of its subscribers. The fourth was that the report was circulated to only five subscribers, each of whom was contractually forbidden from repeating it; the communication therefore did little to promote the free flow of commercial information or debate on public issues.[68] These are all reasons that have more to do with the nature of the medium than with the content of the speech. Implicitly, the Court is treating different media differently.

In broadcasting, the Court has drawn a distinction based explicitly on the nature of the medium. Broadcasting may be regulated in ways that print media may not, just because it is a different medium.[69] The original justification was that because of spectrum limitations, the airwaves were an inherently scarce resource, which the government had to allocate and regulate.[70] If that justification was ever valid, it has long since evaporated. New technology has made available to most communities more than enough broadcast outlets to meet the demand, and the real scarcity is in the number of daily newspapers.[71]

But differential treatment of broadcasting has persisted, and the explanation lies not in scarcity but in power. The Court has been unwilling to give broadcasting the same freedom that print enjoys because broadcasting has a power that requires more accountability than print. Despite misgivings about the rationale, many Americans have shared the Court's reluctance to deny government the ability to control such unprecedented concentrations of communications power as the networks once enjoyed.

The power may be dispersing now. Cable has broken the monopoly of over-the-air broadcasts, and ABC, CBS, and NBC now have to share their power with superstations, cable networks, and pay channels. The time probably has come to stop discriminating against broadcasting. But the Court may not have been wrong, from the 1940s through the 1960s, to insist that broadcasting might require more accountability than other media. Although the FCC rarely tried to call the networks to account, and almost never succeeded, the fact that it had the power to do so may have helped preserve a precarious balance during a transitional period in which the networks otherwise might have achieved an unbreakable stranglehold.

This is not to argue that our experience with broadcasting proves the desirability of different levels of accountability for different media. But it does give us one clear-cut precedent, and whether the experiment has been wise or not, it shows that differential treatment does not bring down the Republic. Regulation does not seem to have made the network news notably more progovernment than the daily newspapers; network White House correspondents do not seem less independent or aggressive than their print colleagues. Local television news is frequently awful, but so are local newspapers, and in both cases the causes seem to have more to do with greed and lethargy than regulation. Like our own historical experience and the experience of other free societies, the limited experience we have had with differential treatment of media suggests that a different mix of freedom and accountability is not unthinkable.

CONCLUSION

None of these three methods of gauging the legal accountability of the media proves that we have either too much or too little. The media in America today probably enjoy more freedom than at any time in the past and are probably freer than the media in any other country, but that does not prove they are too free. From the historical experience, one could as well conclude that it is important for media freedom to continue expanding as it has over the past 50 years; the future no doubt will produce as many new threats to freedom as the past. And there is nothing wrong with having the freest press on earth; despite the differences noted above, in general other societies have looked to America as their exemplar in matters of freedom of expression. If we are to continue that role, our system of freedom of expression must continue to evolve.

Likewise, comparison of media freedom with that of other speakers may well persuade one that the media need more, not less. The insistence that media be treated no differently than the general public may interfere with the development of desirable rights. The area of access to information provides an example. There is much to be said for the proposition that the government should not be allowed to conduct military operations against another government without any on-the-spot press coverage. Yet one cannot plausibly insist that any member of the public who wishes to accompany the troops to Grenada must be allowed to do so. In practice, of course, the press enjoys preferential treatment in hundreds of ways every day.[72] If we were to accept the notion that different speakers may require different legal treatment, it would be impossible to ground press access on something more than custom and mutual need.

The mix of media freedom and accountability we have today is the product not of any grand plan, but of hundreds of rules fashioned at various times to resolve controversies of many different kinds. For the most part, the choices were made without much concern for the effect they would have on the total mix; ours is not a planned legal system. Nevertheless, perceptions as to the appropriateness of the total mix have an effect on specific decisions. Libel lawyers say they see this at work in jury verdicts: Jurors may react less to the merits of a particular case than to their belief that the press in general is too powerful.[73]

Judges also respond to their overall perceptions. Justice Byron White's skepticism about the need for more press protection in defamation cases is grounded in his observation that the press seems vigorous, successful, and powerful enough under the existing rules.[74] Chief Justice Warren Burger was influenced not only by the "vast wealth and power" of some media enterprises, but also by the possibility that "such media conglomerates as I describe pose a much more realistic threat to valid interests than do [nonmedia corporations] and similar entities not regularly concerned with shaping popular opinion on public issues."[75]

One need not share these views to understand that such perceptions do influence specific decisions. For that reason, it is useful to develop methods for evaluating the overall balance between media freedom and accountability, even though we know the balance will continue to be determined by individual decisions in specific controversies and not by any master plan.

NOTES

David A. Anderson is Rosenberg Centennial Professor, University of Texas Law School. The author wishes to thank Sarah Pierce for research assistance in the preparation of this paper.

1. *See Cohen v. California*, 403 U.S. 15 (1971); *Associated Press v. United States*, 326 U.S. 1 (1945).

2. *Compare* L. Levy, THE EMERGENCE OF A FREE PRESS (New York: Oxford University Press, 1985) with Anderson, *The Origins of the Press Clause*, 30 U.C.L.A. L. REV. 455 (1983).

3. *See* Z. Chafee, GOVERNMENT AND MASS COMMUNICATIONS. Chicago: University of Chicago Press, 1947.

4. *See* A. Meiklejohn, FREE SPEECH AND ITS RELATION TO SELF-GOVERNMENT. New York: Harper & Bros., 1948.

5. *See* T. Emerson, THE SYSTEM OF FREEDOM OF EXPRESSION. New York: Vintage Books, 1970.

6. *See Gitlow v. New York*, 268 U.S. 652 (1925).

7. *Lamont v. Postmaster General*, 381 U.S. 301 (1965).

8. *Abrams v. U.S.*, 250 U.S. 616, 624 (1919).

9. *See New York Times v. Sullivan*, 376 U.S. 254 (1964).

10. *See Near v. Minnesota*, 283 U.S. 697 (1931).

11. *Roth v. United States*, 354 U.S. 476 (1957).

12. *Bigelow v. Virginia*, 421 U.S. 809 (1975).

13. *See Craig v. Harney*, 331 U.S. 367 (1947).

14. *See Branzburg v. Hayes*, 408 U.S. 665 (1972).

15. *See*, for example, *Zerilli v. Smith*, 656 F.2d 705 (D.C. Cir. 1981); *Spiva v. Fernandez*, 303 So.2d 363 (Fla Dist. Ct. App. 1974). Many more cases are discussed in Goodale & Moodhe, *Reporter's Privilege Cases*, 2 COMMUNICATIONS LAW 5 (Practising Law Institute 1985).

16. Blasi, *The Newsman's Privilege: An Empirical Study*, 70 MICH. L. REV. 229, 229–30 (1971).

17. Kalven, *The New York Times Case: A Note on the Central Meaning of the First Amendment*, 1964 S. CT. REVIEW 191, 221 n. 125.

18. W. Prosser, HANDBOOK OF THE LAW OF TORTS. St. Paul: West Pub. Co., 4th ed. 1971, p. 819.

19. Don Reuben, a Chicago media lawyer, advanced this view at the annual Media Law Conference of the Practising Law Institute in New York on November 7, 1985. Another exponent of the view is Arthur B. Hanson, former general counsel of the American Newspaper Publishers Association.

20. See *Garrison v. State of Louisiana*, 379 U.S. 64 (1964); *Henry V. Collins*, 380 U.S. 298 (1965); *Rosenblatt v. Baer*, 383 U.S. 75 (1966); *Linn v. United Plant Guard Workers of America*, 383 U.S. 563 (1966; *Curtis Publishing Co. v. Butts*, 388 U.S. 130 (1967); *St. Amant v. Thompson*, 390 U.S. 727 (1968); *Greenbelt Cooperative Publishing Association v. Bresler*, 398 U.S. 16 (1970); *Monitor Patriot Co. v. Roy*, 401 U.S. 265 (1971); *Ocala Star-Banner Co. v. Damron*, 401 U.S. 295 (1971); *Time Inc. v. Pape*, 401 U.S. 279 (1971); *Rosenbloom v. Metromedia, Inc.*, 403 U.S. 29 (1971).

21. See *Gertz v. Robert Welch, Inc.*, 418 U.S. 323 (1974); *Old Dominion Branch No. 496, National Association of Letter-Carriers v. Austin*, 418 U.S. 264 (1974); *Time Inc. v. Firestone*, 424 U.S. 448 (1976); *Herbert v. Lando*, 441 U.S. 153 (1979); *Hutchinson v. Proxmire*, 443 U.S. 111 (1979); *Wolston v. Reader's Digest Association, Inc.*, 443 U.S. 157 (1979); *Keeton v. Hustler Magazine, Inc.*, 104 S.Ct. 1473 (1984); *Calder v. Jones*, 104 S.Ct. 1482 (1984); *Bose Corporation v. Consumers Union of United States, Inc.*, 104 S.Ct. 1979 (1984); *Dun & Bradstreet, Inc. v. Greenmoss Builders, Inc.*, 105 S.Ct. 2939 (1985).

22. *See FCC v. Pacifica Foundation*, 438 U.S. 726 (1978).

23. *See Brandywine-Main Line Radio Inc. v. FCC*, 473 F.2d 16 (D.C. Cir. 1972), *cert denied* 412 U.S. 922 (1973); *Trustees of The University of Pennsylvania*, 69 F.C.C.2d 1394, 44 R.R.2d 747 (1978); *Alabama Educational Television Commission*, 50 F.C.C. 2d 461, R.R.2d 539 (1975).

24. *See Office of Communication, United Church of Christ v. FCC*, 425 F.2d 543 (D.C. Cir. 1969); *Office of Communication, United Church of Christ v. FCC*, 359 F2d 994 (D.C. Cir. 1966).

25. The Libel Defense Resource Center reported that 80 libel verdicts in the 1980–1983 period averaged $2,174,633 each (*LDRC Bulletin* #9, Winter 1983–

1984, p. 28). It is generally believed that no libel verdict in the United States exceeded $1 million until *Frank v. Aware, Inc.*, 19 A.D. 464, 244 N.Y.S.2d 259 (1963) (verdict of $1,250,000. Reduced on remittitur to $550,000.)

26. A few jurisdictions recognized a qualified common law privilege to criticize public officials, *see,* for example, *Coleman v. MacLennan,* 78 Kan. 711, 98 P.2d 281 (1908), but most did not. *See New York Times v. Sullivan,* 376 U.S. 254, 280 n. 20. (1964).

27. *See New York Times v. Sullivan,* 376 U.S. at 270.

28. The newspapers with the largest circulation were the *New York Daily News,* the *Chicago Tribune,* and the *New York Mirror.*

29. Besides these, the only magazines of comparable circulation were *The Ladies Home Journal, Women's Home Companion,* and *McCall's* (*see Information Please Almanac* 1947, p. 809).

30. *See United States v. One Book Called "Ulysses,"* 5 F. Supp. 182 (S.D.N.Y. 1933), affd. 72 F.2d 705 (2d Cir. 1934).

31. *See,* for example, *Bigelow v. Virginia,* 421 U.S. 809 (1975); *Central Hudson Gas v. Public Service Commission,* 447 U.S. 557 (1980).

32. *Gertz v. Robert Welch, Inc.,* 418 U.S. 323 (1974).

33. *See Time Inc. v. Hill,* 385 U.S. 374 (1967); *Cantrell v. Forest City Pub. Co.,* 419 U.S. 245 (1974); *Cox Broadcasting Corp. v. Cohn,* 420 U.S. 469 (1975).

34. Blasi, *The Checking Value in First Amendment Theory,* AM. BAR F. RES. J. 521, 528 (1977).

35. *Abrams v. United States,* 250 U.S. 616, 629 (1919) (Holmes, J. dissenting).

36. Stewart, *Or of the Press,* 26 HASTINGS L.J. 631, 634 (1975).

37. P. Lahav, ed., PRESS LAW IN MODERN DEMOCRACIES. New York: Longman, 1985.

38. *Id.* at 199.

39. *Id.* at 234, 271–72.

40. *Id.* at 159.

41. *Id.* at 202.

42. *Id.* at 159.

43. *Id.* at 244, 293–94, 330.

44. *Id.* at 16–17.

45. *Id.* at 272–78.

46. For an excellent development of this argument, *see* Soifer, *Freedom of the Press in the United States,* in P. Lahav, *supra* note 37, at 79–117. *See also* Linde, *Courts and Censorship,* 66 MINN. L. REV. 171 (1981).

47. *See,* for example, *Associated Press v. United States,* 326 U.S. 1, 19–20 91945); *Pittsburgh Press Co. v. Pittsburgh Commission on Human Relations,* 413 U.S. 376, 381–83 (1973); *Houchins v. KQED, Inc.,* 438 U.S. 1, 8–9 (1978).

48. *See* M. Yudof, WHEN GOVERNMENT SPEAKS: POLITICS, LAW AND GOVERNMENT EXPRESSION IN AMERICA. Berkeley: University of California Press, 1982.

49. "[L]iberty of the press is as much the right of the lonely pamphleteer who uses carbon paper or a mimeograph just as much as of the large metropolitan publisher who utilizes the latest photocomposition methods" (*Branzburg v. Hayes,* 408 U.S. 665, 704 (1972)).

50. *See,* for example, Lange, *The Speech and Press Clauses,* 23 U.C.L.A. L. REV. 77, 100–107 (1975).

51. *See,* for example, Van Alstyne, *The Hazards of the Press Claiming a Preferred Position,* 28 HASTINGS L.J. 761 (1977).

52. *See Central Hudson Gas v. Public Service Commission,* 447 U.S. 557 (1980).

53. *Sharon v. Time Inc.,* No. 83 Civ. 4660 (S.D.N.Y. filed June, 1983).

54. *Green v. Alton Telegraph Printing Co.,* 107 Ill. App. 3d 755, 438 N.E.2d 203, 63 Ill. Dec. 465 (1982).

55. The amount of the settlement is reported in Abrams, *Why We Should Change the Libel Law,* THE NEW YORK TIMES MAGAZINE, Sept. 29, 1985, pp. 34, 90.

56. *See,* for example, Diamond, *"Time" After Sharon,* NEW YORK MAGAZINE, Feb. 11, 1985, pp. 27–28.

57. This estimate is given in Sanford, *Libel Suit, Countersuit,* WASHINGTON JOURNALISM REVIEW, June 1985, p. 16.

58. *See,* for example, Elliott, *"Time" Fights "Malice in Blunderland" Image,* AD-VERTISING AGE, Feb. 4, 1985, p. 3; Jones, *Libel Suits Show News Approaches of Papers, TV and Magazines Differ,* The New York Times, Jan. 31, 1985, p. 13.

59. *See* Lewis, *A Preferred Position for Journalism?,* 7 HOFSTRA L. REV. 595 (1979) (the author is a columnist for *The New York Times*); Royster, *Reflections on the Fourth Estate,* Wall Street Journal, Dec. 13, 1978, p. 24, col. 4; Silk, Leonard, *Is the Press More Equal?,* The New York Times, May 25, 1978, p. D2 col. 1; Editorial, *Bellotti and Beyond,* Wall Street Journal, May 5, 1978, p. 12 col. 1.

60. *See* Anderson, *Libel and Press Self-Censorship* 53 TEXAS L. REV. 422 (1975); Massing, *The Libel Chill: How Cold Is it out There?,* COLUM. J. REV. May/June 1985, p. 31.

61. *See Central Hudson Gas v. Public Service Commission,* 447 U.S. 557 (1980).

62. *Virginia State Bd. of Pharmacy v. Virginia Citizens Consumer Council,* 425 U.S. 748, 771–72 n. 24 (1976).

63. *See Burnett v. National Enquirer,* 144 Cal. App. 3d 991, 193 Cal Rptr. 296 (1983); *Calder v. Jones,* 104 S.Ct. 1482 (1984). The Hollywood community's en-thusiasm for Burnett's suit is described in R. Smolla, SUING THE PRESS New York: Oxford University Press, 1986, pp. 104–5.

64. *See,* for example, *Guccione v. Flynt,* 618 F. Supp. 164 (S.D.N.Y. 1985) (Guccione is publisher of *Penthouse;* Flynt is publisher of *Hustler*); *Keeton v. Hustler Magazine Inc.,* 104 U.S. 1473 (1984) (Keeton is an associate of Guccione).

65. According to one source, "60 Minutes" has generated at least 37 lawsuits. *See* D. Hewitt, MINUTE BY MINUTE. New York: Random House, 1985, p. 220.

66. 105 S.Ct. 2939 (1985).

67. 105 S.Ct. 15 2947 n. 8.

68. 105 S.Ct. 15 2947.

69. Compare *Red Lion Broadcasting Co. v. FCC,* 395 U.S. 367 (1969) with *Miami Herald Pub. Co. v. Tornillo,* 418 U.S. 241 (1974).

70. *See National Broadcasting Co. v. U.S.,* 319 U.S. 190 (1943).

71. As of 1982, there were 10,920 radio and television stations in the United States and 9,183 newspapers, of which only 1,740 were dailies. *Bureau of the Census, Statistical Abstract of the United States* 562, 564 (1984).

72. Among the most familiar examples of preferential treatment for the press are second-class mailing privileges, exemption from searches and antitrust laws,

confidential source protection, and special access to press galleries, news conferences, and disaster sites.

73. *See Behind Wave of Libel Suits Hitting Nation's Press*, U.S. NEWS & WORLD REPORT, Nov. 5, 1984, p. 53 (quoting Charles Battles, Jr., a media defense lawyer, and Jonathan Lubell, a plaintiff's lawyer).

74. *Dun & Bradstreet, Inc. v. Greenmoss Builders, Inc.*, 105 S.Ct. 2939, 2953 (1985) (White, J. concurring in the judgment); *Gertz v. Robert Welch Inc.*, 418 U.S. 323, 390–91 (1974) (White, J., dissenting).

75. *First Nat. Bank of Boston v. Bellotti*, 435 U.S. 765, 797 (Burger, C. J., concurring).

11

The Legal Model: An Editor's Comment

John R. Finnegan

The promise is exciting. Author David Anderson says he will show us how we can evaluate the balance that has been struck between legal accountability and freedom of the press in the United States. He suggests that we may be able to determine whether the media in this country are too free or too restricted. Unfortunately, he does not deliver on those promises. Nor does he answer a major question he raises, "How much legal accountability (for the press) is appropriate?" (Chapter 10).

He does not even come close. He suggests three ways one might consider measuring press freedom and legal accountability but each has flaws and, by his own admission, produces inconclusive results.

The flaws? One is that Anderson offers no theoretical framework for any of the three proposals. The first two—"historical evaluation" and "other societies"—are, as he says, comparative approaches and for the two to work one must accept Anderson's subjective view of press history both foreign and domestic. He fails to present sufficient evidence to justify the reader's acceptance of his assessments.

For example, in his historical evaluation of media freedom and accountability, he asserts that throughout the nineteenth and early twentieth centuries, the media were subject to "far more legal accountability" than today. I do not necessarily disagree with that position but I am uncomfortable with the leap he makes to conclude that

the freedom from accountability that the media enjoy today is not essential to a free society as we know it. The America we remember is largely a product of a value system in which freedom of expression was not exalted over other values to the extent it is today.

Indeed, one might go further and argue that the present extent of media freedom is inimical to the preservation of American political culture and institutions (Chapter 10).

Because Anderson does not explore in any depth the impact on the media of cultural, social, economic, and political developments in either the nineteenth or the early twentieth century, he arrives at such conclusions without adequate support. Indeed, it can be argued that value systems have fluctuated over the centuries and that there have been periods when freedom of expression, indeed, has been "exalted" over other values in American society.

The colonial press often made vicious personal attacks against their political opponents and government officials as did the party newspapers in the early nineteenth century. While there were libel actions launched against some individuals and newspapers in that period, much of that "free expression" not only was tolerated but accepted without legal action. Indeed, the aggressive journalism that developed prior to the Civil War led to name-calling that went far beyond any remarks that would be judged libel per se by today's standards. President Abraham Lincoln was hardly treated civilly by his opponents in or out of the media. He was the target of "continuous and unlicensed" criticism according to Edwin Emery in *The Press and America.*

And certainly, Eugene Debs, who led his American Railway Workers in the strike against the Pullman Company in 1894, and his enemies George Pullman, founder of the company, and James J. Hill, the St. Paul railroad tycoon, threw libelous charges and comments back and forth during that period without ending up filing libel actions. The newspapers of the 1890s—the period of "yellow journalism"—had little apparent concern for accuracy and fairness in their coverage and often used language and references in their editorial columns and news columns that today would end in major libel actions. Were libel actions used as frequently in that period or less frequently than they are today? And what about the relative verdicts? There is, perhaps, a worthwhile research project here that might give us some additional insights into this area of legal accountability.

There are a number of research models that could be used to trace the social and political development of the law in this area but Anderson does not take advantage of them. He does not explore the impact that the civil liberties mentality that developed in the early 1920s had on press freedom and legal accountability. Such an examination could help to explain the development of media law as we see it today. Anderson admits that his historical approach provides us with no answer as to whether the mix we have achieved in this country provides too much freedom, too little freedom, or just the right mix of freedom and accountability. So, why have we just gone through the entire exercise? He never says.

So much for historical comparisons. He also fails to make a distinction between legal accountability of the media and government restriction of the media. I see legal accountability as the public requiring the media to take responsibility for what they do and to accept penalties for adjudged wrongdoing. The media are accountable to the people, not to government. I do not see government restrictions and regulation, designed by government to protect itself, as part of the legal accountability issue. Anderson confuses the issues by combining them.

Was he more convincing with his second approach? Not much. Anderson admits that he is not a comparative law scholar or one who has personal knowledge of press law in West Germany, France, Sweden, Britain, and Israel. Nevertheless, he suggests that to maintain a free society in the United States, we need not cling "tenaciously" to our opposition to such things as prior restraint, seditious libel, or press licensing. He provides no evidence to prove that contention. Indeed, there are few similarities in the cultural, political, economic, and social development of those countries with the United States that would suggest our free society could survive loss of those doctrines.

He makes it sound as though the doctrine of seditious libel died in *New York Times v. Sullivan* in 1964. While it is true that Justice William Brennan declared the alien and sedition acts "null and void" in *Times v. Sullivan*, the fact is that the acts, although never repealed, lapsed in 1800, two years after adoption. Designed to curb "malicious and false statements published to defame officials," the sedition act of 1798 was misused in attempts to prohibit criticism of government and officials. Between 1800 and World War I, however, no similar attempt by government to control the press was made. A sedition law did not surface during the Civil War. As Emery notes, "the problem [of military censorship during the Civil War] was aggravated by the fact that the American press had become so prosperous, aggressive, and independent in the years preceding the war that it was sensitive to any form of restriction."[1]

The adoption of the Espionage Act of 1917 revived the sedition law approach. The Postmaster General of the United States was given life and death control over publications that used the mails for distribution. Socialist and German-American newspapers along with pacifist publications lost their mail privileges. Initially, publications barred from the mails were those who made "willful use of false reports or false statements with intent to interfere" with the operation of the war. That was broadened in the Sedition Act of 1918 to make it a crime to publish any "disloyal, profane, scurrilous or abusive language about the form of government of the United States or the Constitution or military or naval forces, flag or the uniform" or to use language intended to bring these ideas into "contempt, scorn, contumely or disrepute."

So, although the sedition law tool for government control of the press existed prior to 1964, it has been used only twice in our history and then for only very short periods in times of national crisis. The public has not been willing to trust the government with that kind of power over the media. Why? Those devices—prior restraint, sedition acts, and licensing—were used to assert the crown's sovereignty over the colonies. They were found to be totally incompatible with our new sense of sovereignty that resides in the people, not the crown or, in Britain's case today, the Parliament. Because he makes no effort to take into account the different political and social compacts made between the peoples of the United States, Great Britain, Sweden, France, and West Germany and their respective governments, Anderson is comparing apples and oranges.

The inclusion of Israel in the case further weakens his position. Israel is an anomaly. It is not a "free society" at all since it is on a war footing and views its handling of free speech and press as a national security issue.

Anderson's third approach—other speakers—is more analytical. He does get a bit closer to the theoretical framework in which to examine the issue. His discussion of the differential treatment of the media and examination of the political and legal issues involved is thorough and, therefore, much more convincing.

Still, I found myself unpleasantly surprised at his gratuitous generalization, "Local television news is frequently awful, but so are local newspapers, and in both cases the causes seem to have more to do with greed and lethargy than regulation" (Chapter 10). Of course, market share and affordability of talent would have nothing to do with the quality of local media. In any case, Anderson concludes that none of these methods of gauging the legal accountability of the press proves that there is too much or too little legal accountability for the media. Yet, he concludes, "It is useful to develop a method for evaluating the overall balance between media freedom and accountability." I wish he had. Obviously, the field still is wide open.

NOTE

1. Edwin Emery, *The Press and America*, 3d. ed. (Englewood Cliffs, N.J.: Prentice-Hall, 1972), 239.

12

A View from Abroad: The Experience of the Voluntary Press Council

Kenneth Morgan

When a foreigner speaks in America on anything as sensitive and political as media freedom and accountability, he should identify at the start the standpoint from which he views the problems being considered in order to set the stage on which the media operate in the country he knows best.

In America, there is the assumption that there should be channels for accountability of the media and that those channels must and should live within the confines of the First Amendment. Lest too much is taken for granted, it must be remembered that in Britain we do not even have anything to which we could make a First Amendment.

Britain is a country without a written constitution—a lack that probably conditions our attitude, for good or ill, to more things than we readily appreciate. It offers no formal guarantee of the freedom of the press, but since the abolition of press licensing and the newspaper stamp tax over a century and a quarter ago has been largely devoid of special press law. That is not to say that the press is wholly free: it is very far from that. Harold Evans described it as a half-free press. But it does mean that in contrast to the position in many Western European countries and in very sharp contrast to the position in many other parts of the world, newspapers are not licensed and journalists are not registered: neither, by law, enjoys much in the way of special privileges nor is exempt from the general statutory liabilities and responsibilities of the ordinary enterprise and the ordinary citizen.

At the same time, again in contrast to the position in much of Europe, Western Europe and all of Eastern Europe, neither newspapers nor journalists are loaded by law with special responsibilities. (Those who know the British law of defamation, of contempt, and Section Two of the Official Secrets Act, may feel that the general responsibilities to which all are subject are quite onerous enough.)

This is to complain. While allowing that national history and attitudes will shape what is the best or most acceptable recipe for different societies, generally, the less special press law a society has, the better.

It is against that background that Britain chose a voluntary press council to try to resolve the conflict between the society's belief in a free press and its demand for a responsible press.

Before the Second World War there was concern in Britain at the state of the press, its tendency toward concentration of ownership (less marked then than now), and the ethical standards of newspaper proprietors and journalists. There has long been an admirable adversarial relationship between politicians and the press. In the early 1930s Stanley Baldwin made the most celebrated criticism by a politician of a significant part of the British press. "Their methods are direct falsehood, misrepresentation, half-truths, the alteration of a speaker's meaning by putting sentences apart from the context, suppression and editorial criticism of speeches which are not reported in the paper. What the proprietorship of these papers is aiming at is power, but power without responsibility—the prerogative of the harlot through the ages."

And that was a conservative Prime Minister criticizing two conservative proprietors, Lord Rothermere and Lord Beaverbrook. One person who put somewhat similar strictures into the right perspective a half-century later was a former colleague of the writer, a distinguished editor and former member of the Press Council, Lord Jacobson. Opening a debate in the House of Lords on the state of the press, he warned, "Relations between politicians and the press have deteriorated, are deteriorating, . . . and should on no account be allowed to improve."

The spirit of the remark is right and applies ideally in most societies. The relationship between a country's press and its politicians should be distant and reserved rather than cosy and critical, even abrasive, on both sides rather than fawning or adulatory.

Baldwin's criticism had an echo in the more temperate but much wider concern about press standards and ethics that, soon after the end of the war, led Parliament to set up the first Royal Commission on the Press and that commission to recommend the establishment of a General Council of the Press to maintain professional standards and integrity.

The title had something of the ring of the General Medical Council (GMC), which exercised professional control over medicine, but an important difference was suggested. The GMC has a basis in statute: the Royal Commission proposed that the General Council of the Press should derive its authority from the press itself and not from the law.

It is significant that the recommendation should have been to set up a voluntary council rather than a statutory one. It was evidently going to be expected to rely on moral persuasion rather than the force of law and the right to impose sanctions. There are some signs that the same liberal view might be taken by a Royal Commission reviewing the role of the press today, although much the same view was taken by the third Royal Commission on the Press as recently as 1977.

At that earlier state (1949), however, despite the absence of a First Amendment, Britain stood very firm in her liberal and libertarian tradition that the contents of newspapers, while a proper subject of public concern, were an inappropriate one for determination by positive law. It recalls a view of the more general application than to press ethics alone. At the time of the First World War an English judge and former Liberal Member of Parliament, Lord Moulton, described another country:

The infinite variety of circumstances surrounding the individual and rightly influencing his action make it impossible to subject him in all things to rules rigidly prescribed and duly enforced. Thus there is wisely left the intermediate domain which, so far as positive law is concerned, is a land of freedom of action, but in which the individual should feel that he is not wholly free. This country which lies between law and free choice I always think of as the domain...of doing that which you should do, although you are not obliged to do it. I do not wish to call it duty, for that is too narrow to describe it, nor would I call it morals for the same reason. It might include both, but it extends beyond them. It covers all cases of right doing where there is no one to make you do it but yourself.[1]

That are, the domain as Lord Moulton put it of "obedience to the unenforceable," came to be the border territory that a voluntary press council has to police and in which it has to satisfy the public. In that duty it tests issues and judges conduct by ethics, not by law.

The recommending of a voluntary press council was the first modern formal attempt to resolve the conflict between a press that was free and a press that was expected to be responsible—between a press that could say what it liked, but was expected to say what it ought. It was a formal recognition that a privately owned press owed a duty to its readers and those it wrote about as well as to its writers and those who owned it. It was the formal rejection in Britain of the definition of a private enterprise press given by W. P. Hamilton of the *Wall Street Journal:* "A newspaper is private enterprise owing nothing whatever to the public, which grants it no franchise. It is therefore affected with no public interest. It is emphatically the property of the owner, who is selling a manufactured product at his own risk."[2]

Since then the consensus was developed, identified by the third Royal Commission, that the press should neither be subject to state control nor left entirely to the unregulated forces of the market.

The British Press Council was born of that consensus: the first of a new wave of voluntary, nonstatutory press councils of which it is generally regarded as the father—although one should not forget the existence of a couple of elderly grandparents, alive and well and still living in Scandinavia—the Norwegian Press Council and the Swedish Press Council founded in 1912 and 1916 respectively under other titles. In Britain, although the Royal Commission reported in 1949, the Press Council was not founded until 1953, voluntary but after a nudge from Parliament.

The commission recommended that it should include members from the press proprietors', editors', and journalists' organizations and some representing the lay public. In the early days, only one press organization supported the introduction of lay members—the National Union of Journalists. There were long negotiations between the bodies concerned and one must say no great enthusiasm was shown, particularly by the publishers' organizations to establish a watchdog over their industry. By 1952, agreement had still not been reached about the appropriate shape for a voluntary council—or even formally whether to have one. A Private Member's bill to create a statutory press council was debated in the House of Commons. It failed, but it attracted more support—90 votes—than anyone had thought likely.

The government of Mr. Clement Attlee—a consistently underrated, deceptively mild-mannered, soft-spoken man—let it be known discreetly that if the newspaper industry found insuperable difficulty in setting up a voluntary press council, Parliament and government might be prepared to help it.

There was immediately among newspaper proprietors a change of heart and a spirit of enthusiam such as has rarely been seen since the experience of an earlier publicist, Saul of Tarsus on the Road to Damascus. The difficulties in reaching agreement, genuine and serious as they were, were overcome, and the British Press Council was in business.

It was not then the council dreamed of by the first Royal Commission, nor the council we have today. It had no public members but consisted of 25 publishers, editors, and journalists. Its chairman was not an independent from outside, but one of the 25 elected by his colleagues. Those who understand English institutions will not be surprised that the first chairman to be chosen was the then principal proprietor of *The Times*. Since 1953, the council's scope, its profile and its workload have changed markedly but its objectives, set out in its constitution, have been constant:

• To preserve the established freedom of the British press.

• To maintain the character of the British press in accordance with the highest professional and commercial standards.

- To consider complaints about the conduct of the press or the conduct of persons and organisations towards the press; to deal with these complaints in whatever manner might seem practical and appropriate and record resultant action.

- To keep under review developments likely to restrict the supply of information of public interest and importance.

- To report publicly on developments that may tend towards greater concentration or monopoly in the press (including changes in ownership, control and growth of press undertakings) and to publish statistical information relating thereto.[3]

In large measure and sometimes in detail these objects have been adopted by other countries where press councils have been founded on the British model. It is the first three objects that have led to the council being likened to a watchdog with two heads barking in opposite directions: one to give warning *to* the press when its freedom is in danger, the other barking *at* the press when it abuses that freedom.

There have been two fundamental revisions of the council since its foundation. The first was 10 years on, in 1963, when on the advice of a second Royal Commission public members were introduced, at first very tentatively in the proportion of 5 public to 20 press—a safe working majority by any political standard. At the same time, much more wholeheartedly, the council accepted the Royal Commission's recommendation to appoint an independent chairman unconnected with the press. We have now had five, all lawyers although that is not a constitutional requirement. The first was Lord Devlin, from the highest tier of the British judiciary, a Lord of Appeal. The present chairman is Sir Zelman Cowen QC, head of an Oxford college, an Australian, and former governor general of Australia.

It took 25 years to get the proportions of press and public membership right. By 1978, on the advice of the third Royal Commission on the Press, the balance was evened—18 press members and 18 public members, with an independent, voting, chairman to just tip it to the public or nonpress side. In fact, the early political concern among journalists and publishers about, first, the existence and, then, the growth of a lay element on the council has proved misplaced.

It has never divided on any issue on party lines with the public members voting one way and the press members the other. It has remained true that, as in many other professions, the practitioners generally prove harsher critics of incompetence or unethical behavior by their colleagues than the laity. On the motes and beams principle, it may be said, too, that newspaper proprietors or their managers are pretty swift to mark and condemn what they see as unethical or unfair practices by their commercial competitors.

There is no problem in choosing press members: they are appointed by their own organizations—publishers, editors, and journalists, in agreed proportions, although it is a matter of regret to the council, and especially to me, that the National Union of Journalists has currently withdrawn from the council's activities. Its four seats have been left vacant at the request of the Trades Union Congress, which has recommended the union to return.

It is much more difficult to devise machinery for selecting 18 members of the public to represent 55 million. Originally, the selection of lay members was by the council itself. Now there is an open nomination procedure. Nominations for the six or so seats that become vacant each year are invited publicly by newspaper and radio announcements from any organization or individual who cares to make them. Men and women may volunteer for consideration if they have no one to nominate them. The only qualification is that they must have no connection with the press. The selection is then made by a small, separate Appointments Commission, two men and two women, chaired by an Oxford social historian, Lord Briggs, formerly professor Asa Briggs.

One index of the impact a voluntary press council is making is the readiness of the public to serve on it—they work hard; their expenses are paid, but there is no fee or honorarium. In 1978, when the nomination procedure was first used, the commission had to select 10 new members from 44 nominations. Two years ago there were 7 places and 1,095 nominations. Last year with some judicious pruning the list was 670 candidates for 6 seats.

It is significant and important that neither government nor Parliament plays any part in the nomination or appointment of the press or public members of the council. As indicated earlier, press councils tend to be shaped by countries' traditions, attitudes, and experiences. So it is in this respect.

Somewhat surprisingly, India had inherited a substantial code of press law from its days of the British Raj. The Indian Press Council, which has significant similarities to our own, is in fact a child of statute rather than simply voluntary association. One of the consequential differences is that a proportion of its public members are nominated by Parliament to represent the parties. The situation is rather similar in Portugal where although the Conselho de Imprensa was, in its phrase, "inspired by Great Britain's Press Council," its members include "four citizens with acknowledged merits elected by the Assembly of the Republic."[4]

In Britain the only time a government minister ever made a nomination of a possible public member—which was in the minister's private capacity—his nominee was not appointed! There has been a marked change in the profile of public members appointed since they were introduced in the sixties. From being, as critics charged, middle-age, middle-class, and male—the critics might, as in other countries, have added white—members are now chosen to be representative of different age, sex, and ethnic groups; different social, educational, and occupational fields, and from different parts of the United Kingdom. They include a former assistant commissioner of the City of London police, a Methodist minister, a professor and surgeon, a trading standards officer, a postman, a boilermaker, and a mountaineering school leader; an Asian, and an Afro-Caribbean; and 12 men and 6 women.

They and the press members each serve on one or more of the council's four committees: a General Purposes Committee, which deals mainly with the press freedom side of the council's work (for example, calls for the repeal of parts of the Official Secrets Act and for the introduction of a Freedom of Information Act, the review of contempt of court legislation, and the continuing argument about protection of confidential sources) and three complaints committees that, like the council itself, each meet at least once every month.

Each complaints committee has an equal number of press and public members. The mix, and that they should mix, is important. One of the most encouraging judgments I have heard on the council's conduct came in 1985 when, by coincidence, the Executive Secretaries of the Australian Press Council (founded on the British model in 1976) and the British Columbian Press Council (founded in 1983 after the spur of the Canadian Kent Commission) were in London at the same time and attended one of our complaints committee meetings. Both said the point that struck them most forcibly was that it was impossible to tell which were public and which were press members by the comments they made or the questions they asked the witnesses.

To produce consistency of judgment or "sentencing policy," the chairman of the council presides at meetings of all committees, and the meetings are attended by both vice chairmen (both of them press members elected by the whole council) and by the director. The principal job of the complaints committees is to consider the evidence about each complaint—usually written but in a growing number of cases given orally as well—and to recommend an adjudication to the full Press Council.

Any person may complain to the council about the content or conduct of any newspaper or magazine, paid for or free, that is available to the general public. In contrast to the position in other European countries, Sweden or West Germany, for example, a complainant need not have locus or be affected in any way by the matter about which he complains. In Britain itself, complaints to the Broadcasting Complaints Commission may only be laid by persons directly affected by the matter about which they complain. Our restricted right of the public at large to complain is important and highly desirable in the interests of protecting general press standards, but it does bring problems in its train—especially when a third party complains about a newspaper intrusion into someone else's privacy.

Although the council judges complaints on the basis of ethics not law there is inevitably an overlap with the law in some cases. Where a complainant alleges a criminal offence by a newspaper or journalist, the Press Council must step back, advising him that if he makes that allegation he must go to the police. The council cannot usurp the criminal courts.

Such cases are rare. More commonly a complaint may be laid about conduct for which the complainant could seek redress in the civil courts. Defamation, a lucrative and expensive branch of English law, is the obvious example. By one route, the courts, a complainant may hope to recover substantial damages but must risk large sums in costs. By the other route, the Press Council, he can hope only to clear his name, put the record straight publicly, and see the newspaper rebuked or censured—but he can do that at virtually no cost.

There is a danger that an aggrieved reader may seek both remedies, using the cheap route to enhance his chances of obtaining the financial benefit of the other. To avoid this, where it looks likely that a libel action might also be mounted, the council requires a complainant to sign a waiver of legal action before his complaint can proceed. The waiver system has been the subject of much criticism and appraisal. The arguments are finely balanced. Who shall stand between a free-born Englishman and his right to sue in the Queen's courts and what editor in his right mind is going to disclose information to the Press Council that may be used in a libel action against him? But the council and its director have found that the practical need for a waiver prevails. It is sought only in a minority of cases where the council or, in practice, its director thinks a libel action is a lively possibility. If a complainant refuses to comply we tell him to go and do his suing first, returning with any outstanding ethical issues to the Press Council after the legal carcass of the case has been picked.

By statute, the Broadcasting Complaints Commission is spared this problem. It is barred from dealing with any complaint for which the complainant could seek a remedy in the courts.

There was a good example of the occasional conjunction of the criminal law and recourse to the Press Council in preference to the civil law three years ago around a notorious spy trial, *The Queen v. Geoffrey Prime*. Prime, a civil servant, was jailed for 38 years for espionage. After his trial, he complained from prison to the Press Council about the publication of a background story in the *News of the World* about his links with a pedophile organization and the fear that he might have blackmailed prominent people in the United States and the United Kingdom. His complaint failed.

At the same time the attorney general, Sir Michael Havers, chose to use the Press Council rather than the civil law to fight *his* complaint against *The Sun* for its follow-up story to the Prime trial. Sir Michael denied its report that U.S. spy masters were convinced he had held back evidence of Prime's links with a pedophile organization to save embarrassing British security chiefs when he prosecuted the spy at the Old Bailey. The allegation was clearly a grave and damaging one that the attorney general could have pursued by a libel action in the civil courts. He chose not to do that but to sign a waiver and continue before the Press Council. His complaint was upheld—the Press Council ruling that the paper's claim should have been substantiated or withdrawn.

The complaints committees' meetings—like the council's own—are in private. At oral hearings editors, journalists, and complainants may bring a friend or colleague to advise and assist them, but they may not be accompanied by a lawyer. The parties attend together, each gives evidence and may be questioned by the other, and each may cross-examine the other's witnesses. Parties and witnesses are also questioned by the committee.

There is in this respect a marked difference between the Press Council's procedure and that of the Broadcasting Complaints Commission in Britain. There, too, each of the parties may give evidence to the commission but they are never present in the same room at the same time. It is a curious difference, and it is difficult to understand how the commission arrives at truth by that means in cases where there is a conflict of evidence. Perhaps its procedure owes something to those adopted in industrial conciliation in Britain while ours owes its pattern to the courts.

The Broadcasting Complaints Commission was set up as a statutory body in 1980 to deal with complaints against the BBC and the commercial radio and television companies. Its power of punishment, like the Press Council's, is limited to publication of an adjudication, but its members—there are five or six—unlike the Press Council's are appointed by the home secretary.

The BCC's brief is much more restricted than the Press Council's: to complaints of unjust or unfair treatment in sound or television and of infringement of privacy in programs or to obtain material for them.

The broad heads of the council's remit are inaccuracy, the right to publish, objections to comment, matters of taste (including particularly nowadays the treatment of race), selection of news, privacy, checkbook journalism, methods of news gathering (including the use of subterfuge), some issues affecting advertisements, the conduct of newspaper competitions, and the treatment of letters to the editor. The adjudication that a complaints committee recommends to the Press Council takes the form of a reasoned judgment upholding or rejecting the complaint.

When it has been adopted by the Press Council, perhaps after amendment or reconsideration, the adjudication is released generally to the press for publication in all save a rare minority of exceptional cases, usually those involving personal privacy or perhaps a child. The council gets good general publicity for its adjudications in the serious national press, the regional press, and by broadcasting. Very importantly from our point of view, the weekly professional journal for journalism publishes all adjudications in full, and the great majority of them are carried very fully on the wire service of the Press Association, which goes into virtually all British daily newspaper offices.

There is, however, a particular obligation on the editor of any newspaper or magazine that is the subject of a critical adjudication to publish that adjudication word for word in its own columns. It is a moral obligation, not a legal one, but it is almost universally observed. There have been only 11 occasions in 32 years when a newspaper or magazine found to be at fault has failed to honor the obligation, and in almost all those cases the publication concerned was a fringe journal rather than one of the general body of the British commercial national or regional press.

If a paper fails to publish a critical adjudication, the Press Council issues a second adjudication condemning it again for its original fault but condemning it more harshly for not honoring an obligation that the press in general accepts. As a rule, other journals than the defaulter prove happy to publish adjudications of this kind about their competitor and to publish them prominently!

There is a difference here between the British approach and those of press councils in some other countries. In India the press council, broadly similar to Britain's but backed by statute, may obtain an order from the courts requiring a newspaper to publish its adverse adjudication. For years, the present director though this might be the one legal backup worth having. He remained doubtful, however, of the wisdom of throwing even so narrow a plank bridge over the gulf that separates the land of moral obligation from that of legal enforcement, because of the difficulty of determining which mean and which measures might come crowding across the plank behind one. He concluded that he need not have worried. Last year he learned from Justice Grover, the chairman of the Indian Press Council, that it, too, relies effectively on moral persuasion and obligation. The power of its court order is illusory, for it is an order without means of enforcement. The fact that without our having power to seek such orders, offending newspapers do publish British Press Council adjudications in full is important, because that sanction of publicity is the only sanction the council has.

From time to time and from widely differing quarters, including the extreme right and the extreme left but not only from them, this point has been one of criticism. Should not the Press Council have stronger powers, should it not be given sharper teeth? It has never sought those powers or the sharpening of its teeth. Indeed, it is not easy to see how a voluntary nonstatutory council that stands, as it were, outside the country's legal system and outside the control of Parliament could properly be given the sort of penal powers that people envisage when they talk of stronger sanctions or sharper teeth. Apart from this practical point, there is another that is both practical and philosophical. If one could overcome the problem of arming a voluntary body with penal sanctions, what should those sanctions be?

There are really only three possibilities. They are discussed in ascending order of severity. The first is the power to fine. It is almost impossible to envisage a tariff of fines that could be imposed on the huge variety of papers—national dailies to giveaway locals, serious scientific periodicals to teenage pop magazines—with which the Press Council deals for the widely differing offences it has to try that would prove both a fair and an effective deterrent. In any event to impose a financial penalty could well substitute a mere commercial calculation for what ought to be an issue of professional or ethical standards.

It is true that there are press councils that, by agreement, impose fines. This does not much advance the argument, because of the nature and purpose of those fines. The Swedish Press Council imposes them on an ascending scale determined by the number of complaints upheld against a particular paper in a year. The Swedes are a highly practical people. They make no claim that the fines are a particularly appropriate or effective deterrent, but regard them as a useful revenue-raising device for the council: fair, on the basis that those whose conduct causes its most work should contribute toward its costs.

After fines, the next alternative in an attempt to impose responsibility or punish irresponsibility is the licensing and registration sanction. It is common enough: the requirement that newspapers should be licensed or journalists registered, and the power, therefore, to remove the license and suspend publication of a paper or to strike from the register and bar a journalist from practicing his profession as a punishment for irresponsibility.

There are many countries, East and West, left and right, where licensing and registration apply. The latest formally to propose putting them in the hands of a press council for disciplinary purposes was South Africa where this was recommended by the Steyn Commission in 1981. It proved too draconian even for them. One might prefer to live in a society where no one—not even a press council—has the power to bar a newspaper from appearing or a journalist from writing.

Finally, of course, the third and most severe sanction is to send the occasional editor to prison for the same reason the British once shot one of our own admirals, *pour encourager les autres.* There are more than enough people doing that throughout the world without Britain joining in.

One is driven back to the conclusion that the most appropriate and acceptable safeguard against the evils of publicity by a free press is publicity itself, and that, therefore, the sanction that the British Press Council now has—publication of a critical adjudication and particularly self-publication of it by the newspaper at fault—is the right sanction. Accepting this means, in practice, recognizing that part of the price of preserving a free press while cherishing a responsible press is the toleration of some measure of irresponsibility. However, there is a limit to the measure of irresponsibility a public—or a parliament—will stand.

The caseload of complaints to the British Press Council has increased markedly in recent years. It now runs at about 1,400 a year, and more than 10 percent of these warrant formal, full adjudication. In the two years 1980 and 1981, a total of 126 cases were adjudicated. In 1985 alone, 139 full adjudications were issued.

There are three reasons for the increases in these figures. One is that the consumer movement is still with us. Readers, quite properly, expect more say over the product they are offered than they once did. They expect the right to reply to, to comment on, and to criticize the newspapers they are given. The second reason is that the Press Council itself— like some in other countries—has a higher profile than it did in its early days. Its service is better known—although not yet well enough—and even criticism of its works in the council's favor by bringing it to the attention of the public.

When considering the interaction of press freedom and press responsibility, it is the third reason for the rise in complaints to the Press Council that is worrying: standards of newspapers ethics, and in some respects even standards of editorial competence, are indeed lower than they were and provoke, properly, more complaints.

Despite the long tradition in Britain of noninterference with the press by special law, a real fall in standards of press behavior and in the quality of much newspaper content have also made more real the danger that Parliament backed by public concern will take statutory powers to enforce responsibility on the press rather than leave it to the self-control of journalists, editors, and owners in partnership with the public. In this respect, the British press does well to beware the absence of a First Amendment.

There is a striking example. The danger in Britain has been closer since the Press Council published a major report following its inquiry into press conduct in the *Sutcliffe* case—the Yorkshire Ripper case—a notorious and horrific crime story, which involved the murder of 13 women. This was one of those occasions when the Press Council initiated its own inquiry, although it had also had complaints from the public about some aspects of the affair. At the end of a very detailed and far-reaching enquiry in a 200-page report, it condemned the conduct of many newspapers in three principal respects. Parliament and the public echoed the condemnation.

The three areas of criticism were of the way in which newspapers (as well as some broadcasting organizations, although they are not within the Press Council's ambit) disregarded in their reporting the prejudice to a fair trial for the man subsequently convicted of murder, the way in which some newspapers sought to buy up the stories of people involved in the case or related to, or associated with, the murderer (a form of checkbook journalism that was condemned as the payment of "blood money"), and the harassment by some journalists of people caught up in the tragedy, including the wife of the murderer and the mother of one of the victims.

Serious though they were, these three ethical failings were compounded and exceeded by a fourth: the way in which some newspapers and their editors were found by the Press Council to have dissembled and deceived in attempts to avoid its censure. It is this last piece of irresponsibility that posed a possible threat to continuing press freedom.

In its report, the Press Council warned that unless newspapers demonstrated, as many had not done in the *Sutcliffe* case, an intention to act with responsibility and self-control in matters such as pretrial prejudice, checkbook journalism, and harassment a much greater legislative control of the day-to-day conduct and content of the press than Britain had known for 200 years was likely to follow.

It was not an idle warning. In the debate in the House of Lords on the Press Council report, the Home Office minister, Lord Elton, said the government hoped that a voluntary Press Council might work cooperatively and effectively with the newspaper industry to ensure a free and responsible press without call for coercive powers. He ended, however, by repeating the caution:

We cannot, however, rule out the possibility of statutory controls in this field if serious public dissatisfaction with the conduct of newspapers persists and if that concern is not adequately met by the present arrangements. There are, as I have said, substantial difficulties of definition and enforcement. But no one should assume that those could not be overcome if the case was strong enough. There is pressure to do so and the strong opinions expressed today make it all the harder to resist them. That consideration must emphasize to the press itself the importance of complying with the Press Council's guidelines.[5]

After its condemnation of harassment, the unacceptable and unjustifiable pressures of journalists anxious to interview or photograph people or to bid for their stories, the Press Council's then chairman Sir Patrick Neill QC, wrote of a clear case for the press to put its own house in order. He said, "Editors and all employed in the procurement of news ought to exercise their intelligence and humanity to recognise situations in which it was wrong to pursue stricken individuals with questions which they had already refused to answer."

This was not to advocate that the press should cease to be vigilant to exposed crime, malpractice, and incompetence. It was an exhortation to temper zeal with discrimination and sensitivity. He added, "I do not myself believe that either public opinion or Parliament will indefinitely allow such scandals to be repeated and defenceless individuals to be thus persecuted without anything being done to remedy this situation."

At the same time the council emphasized, as we have done since, the need for the press to demonstrate not just its acceptance of, but its vigorous editorial and moral support—and financial support—for a voluntary press council. "Financial support," because we chose to draw our financial backing from the industry itself. No doubt by one means or another a British government could, like others, have been brought to sustain the Press Council from public funds. Our view so far has been that it would be wrong to risk the council's demonstrable independence of government by being beholden to it for our funds—although that would certainly have solved some practical problems we have had to face and may still face now. We chose instead to face the problem of being dependent on our constituent bodies—owners, editors, and journalists—for our income.

There is danger clearly that while our independence of government is demonstrable, the public may feel that our independence of the newspaper industry is not. It is a fine choice of evils one has to make, and in my view our search for alternative, acceptable sources of finance must continue.

In the meantime while it is tolerable to be dependent on the press organizations collectively for finance, it would be undesirable to accept direct contributions from separate publishers or publishing groups. The danger would be too great of individual publishers deciding to "contract out" and of the council coming to adjudicate only on the papers or publishers in membership instead of on the press at large.

Other choices have had to be made along the way. One was whether to rely as some press councils and many journalists' unions do on a general code of press conduct to offer guidance on ethics and responsibility. From time to time our press council has been urged to adopt and publish such a code but it has chosen not to do so. A difficulty about codes is their rigidity. I recall one conclusion of an Anglo-American discussion of journalistic responsibility at the Ditchley Foundation 10 years ago:

[T]he exercise of [press and broadcasting] responsibility, while based to some extent on consciousness of the political, cultural, and ethical heritage and traditions of a given society, must constantly be reviewed and updated in the light of current popular and politically representative reaction. Times change, and a society may come not only to accept, but actually to want, the public presentation of issues in a form it would previously have found distasteful or irrelevant.[6]

It may be more difficult to accept and implement that flexibility if you have bound yourself to a rigid code.

But apart from the obvious problem, another difficulty about codes for journalists is that they tend to be of two types. The first is of, say 10, 12, or 20 general principles after the manner of the Ten Commandments from which no one could reasonably dissent. Thus, truth is to be preferred to falsehood; beauty to ugliness; motherhood is, on the whole, a good thing; and so on. The snag is that given these general, unexceptionable precepts that are not in question, each case still needs to be approached on its own set of facts and merits, and both the editor and the complainant are likely to claim that the commandment or code is on their side.

The second type of code is very detailed indeed, running into hundreds of clauses and prescribing in great detail what may or may not be done and what may or may not be published. The very detail tends to create a Tom Tiddler's ground in which fine debating points and points of order may result in the ethically guilty going free or the ethically innocent falling foul.

Instead of adopting a formal code, therefore, the British Press Council has chosen to rely on building up case law, rather in the way that the English common law itself is built up of precedents established in the decisions of the courts. The council does, however, from time to time issue declarations of principle by way of advice to editors. These have concerned themselves with peculiarly difficult problems of newspaper ethics: the privacy of the individual (for Britain has no law about privacy), as in the *Sutcliffe* case; the propriety of buying up the memoirs of criminals and of paying witnesses for the right to publish their stories; and most recently, the professional conduct of financial journalists.

All the council's adjudications are set out in full in its annual reports, and last year it published *Principles for the Press*, which is an indexed digest of all its decisions in adjudications and statements from 1953 to 1984 and is, of course, to be updated each year.

You must forgive us for having concentrated on the development, the experiences, and the problems of the British Press Council. The reason is that it is the subject we know best, the justification: that it was the prototype on which most press councils have been modeled. They vary enormously from New Zealand's with 4 members to Israel's with 80. In a few, in India, for example, there is a formal link with government or Parliament. In some countries, Australia and the United Kingdom itself, for instance, it required a nudge from the executive or the legislature to get a voluntary council started. In one case, Sweden, a voluntary council coexists with a national ombudsman who acts in effect both as a court of first instance for complaints against the press and as prosecutor of those complaints that go forward to the council. In other countries, including Britain, a Press Council is now seeing the import from North America of the other kind of ombudsman, internal newspaper ombudsmen, not as an alternative to a press council but as coexistents.

A voluntary system of invigilation or self-control will always have shortcomings. You can, as part of Europe once did, *make* the trains run on time by taking state powers to do so, but newspapers are not railroads.

It was Prime Minister Clement Attlee in 1952 who gave British publishers, editors, and journalists the necessary nudge to get a voluntary press council going. There is a story that 11 years later on his birthday he was asked by a reporter "How does it feel to be 80, Lord Attlee?" After reflection, he took his pipe from his mouth and replied, "Considering the alternative, pretty good." The most modest thing you can say with certainty about voluntary press councils as an attempt to harmonize press freedom and press responsibility is that, considering the alternatives, they seem pretty good.

NOTES

1. Speech by John Fletcher Moulton, Lord Moulton, Lord of Appeal in Ordinary, in *Freedom and Restraint in Broadcasting*, Queen's Lecture by Sir Michael Swann FRS, chairman of the British Broadcasting Corporation, Berlin, May 29, 1975.

2. Quoted in Leon V. Sigal, *Reporters and Officials*. Lexington, Mass.: D. C. Heath 1973, p. 88.

3. The Press Council, Articles of Constitution. Printed in *The Press and the People*, annual reports of The Press Council, 1953–1988.

4. Constitution of Conselho de Imprensa, Portugal. Assembly of the Republic of Portugal, Law No. 31, 1978.

5. Lord Elton, Minister of State, Home Office. Official Report, House of Lords debates, July 20, 1983, col. 1190.

6. *Responsibilities of Communications Media*, Ditchley Paper No. 27, p. 13, Ditchley Foundation, January 1970.

REFERENCES

Jones, J. Clement. *Mass Media Codes of Ethics and Councils*. Paris: UNESCO, 1980.

Levy, H. Phillip. *The Press Council/History, Procedure and Cases*. London: Macmillan, 1967.

Mead, G. Roper. *The Press Council, A Media Guide*. Brennan Publication, 1978.

Morgan, Kenneth. *Press Conduct in the Sutcliffe Case*. The Press Council, 1983.

Paul, Noel S. *Principles for the Press, A Digest of Press Council Decisions, 1953–1984*. London: The Press Council, 1985.

The Press and the People. (annual reports of the Press Council 1954–1984) Nos. 1 to 31. London: The Press Council.

Privacy, Press and People. London: The Press Council, 1971.

(First) Royal Commission on the Press, 1947–1949. London: His Majesty's Stationery Office, 1949.

(Third) Royal Commission on the Press, Final Report. London: Her Majesty's Stationery Office, 1977.

Statutory Regulation and Self-Regulation of the Press, Mass Media File No. 2. Strasbourg: Council of Europe, 1982.

13

FREEDOM AND ACCOUNTABILITY: A SEARCH FOR SOLUTIONS

William A. Henry III

The critical question for every political system, certainly every democracy, is, Who shall govern the governors? In democracies, the answer is supposed to be clear-cut: the people. The essential element of democracy is frequent and meaningful review of the actions of government and, in modern industrial society, of the great private forces chartered and regulated by government. To help sustain this process, the United States has evolved two increasingly powerful institutions, the courts and the press. Acting in the former case by fiat and in the latter case by exposure and concomitant pressure, these two institutions assist the people in holding the mighty accountable.

The similarities and differences between the press and the courts are rich and complex and far beyond the scope of this paper. But there are two parallels of prime relevance to the subject of this inquiry, i.e., the regulation and self-regulation of the press. The first key likeness is that neither judges nor journalists have any material means of enforcing their findings, but must depend instead on the attention and esteem of the public. The courts command no armies, unleash no myrmidons, unless one counts a handful of federal marshals who are far from crack fighting troops. What makes court rulings inviolable is the expectation of the public—and the consequent agreement by litigants—that the courts shall be the final arbiter of social order. Similarly, the press has no power to subpoena, let alone indict or convict. Freedom of information rules grant at most a marginally greater access to data for journalists than for all other citizens. No public official, and certainly no private one, is legally obliged to grant interviews or hold press conferences. The press obtains its information because it claims to act on behalf of the populace as a whole, and the general public has come to endorse this notion of journalists as a kind of auxiliary representative government. Information dispensed by the press in turn has power only when the public responds, usually to the revelation of scandal, abuse, corruption, or injustice. The press succeeds because it echoes, rather than shapes or distorts, public opinion and values. Attacks on the freedom of the press—especially the use of journalists to spread "disinformation," a polite terms for lies—tend to be regarded, in the long run at least, as attacks on the public's right to a free marketplace of ideas and, hence, on democracy itself.

The second vital similarity between the courts and the press is that the legitimacy of their power is frequently challenged, particularly by government and major private institutions. Attorney General Edwin Meese brought on a fire storm of protest, but also won salvos of support, when he argued just before the 1986 general elections that the authority of a Supreme Court ruling is considerably less sanctified than some explicit provision of the Constitution. Some of Meese's deputies privately accused him of encouraging civil disobedience. His defenders replied that he was merely stating an indisputable point of law: that on matters about which the Constitution is not precise, judicial interpretation may shift over time. In any case he was sending a message that controversial Court decisions need not be obeyed as eternal but can be waited out in quiet resistance and the hope that the makeup of the Court, or of its judges' minds, will change. He also, intentionally, buttressed the argument that power ought to continue to reside in the hands of those who have it, barring noteworthy abuse, and the related idea that majority will, as expressed through the legislature and in other ways, should generally prevail over minority rights. Shorthand for this doctrine is "judicial restraint," a form of voluntary self-regulation of a nominally unregulated body.

The rights and powers of the press have been the subject of a comparable debate, much of it again initiated by conservative spokespeople and by the government. Despite the absolutist language of the First Amendment, what might seem like constitutional guarantees are often diluted to suit the temper of the times. Freedom of the press has frequently (although not very consistently) been restricted, especially in cases involving national security; criminal justice and the rights of the accused; and privacy, obscenity, and defamation. Not content with this success, some disgruntled critics have urged formal legal limitation of the First Amendment, while others have concentrated on attacking the press's legitimacy and reputation for fairness in an attempt to diminish its public following.

Viewed in this context of a larger political struggle, undertaken on behalf of government and allied private institutions and related to assaults against the courts, the current and frequent calls for regulation or self-regulation of the press may seem beneath serious debate. But widespread dissatisfaction with the press is well documented, and much of the protest is cogent and discerning. Even blameless news men and women join the fray out of embarrassment at the bad manners and professional misconduct of others or from simple discomfort at the swift rise in impact of their craft. The more temperate outside critics, along with not a few senior journalists, have in recent years preached an equivalent of judicial restraint, a self-regulation of journalism, individual by individual, institution by institution, perhaps by the trade as a whole, as a necessary corrective to power and a tactical pre-emptive strike against market erosion, legal onslaught, or, in the worst case, imposed restraints.

The purpose of this paper is not to evaulate the extent or validity of complaints against the press, a subject on which the Gannett Center and this author have been heard before, nor to argue the true and proper meaning of the First Amendment. We shall take it as axiomatic that the press, like any other *de jure* or de facto governing body in a democracy, ought to be subject to some sort of checks and balances, but that the means of applying them is open to discussion. The discussion below will be directed at assessing the basic avenues of regulation and self-regulation as to their efficacy, dependability, and lack of undesired secondary consequences. Most of the quoted material and a good deal of the thinking, derive from the Gannett Center conference on media freedom and accountability, held at the Center's offices on the Columbia University campus on April 4, 1986. This paper is not, however, a strict summary of that conference, nor should its participants be held responsible for the analysis herein.

BASIC ISSUES

The most common complaint about the daily newspaper, according to publishers, is that it smears ink on readers' hands. That shortcoming is beyond the scope of consideration here. Arbitrarily, so are objections to advertising, e.g., that it is too sexy or inadequately screened for honesty or manipulative of children. Similarly, although television entertainment programming is aired by the same companies that own the news networks, its alleged failings of taste and propriety are likewise outside the discussion. Nor can this paper closely address questions of minority representation and access, save in editorial decision making. These and similar complaints may be matters for self-review within the media industry, but they are not really complaints about the press, i.e., they are not purely journalistic in nature and cannot be judged by the same political and constitutional criteria. The First Amendment rights of an advertiser to misrepresent his product, for example, are plainly less defensible than the First Amendment rights of an editor to give short shrift to a political candidate whose philosophy displeases him.

The primary journalistic sins alleged by critics of the press are as follows: (1) violation of national security; (2) endangering the governability of the country by bringing to light programs or policy decisions better left private—e.g., prematurely exposing the Abscam operation or the Reagan administration's attempt to barter arms for hostages; (3) violating the privacy of individuals; (4) violating the privacy of corporations and institutions—e.g., by publishing internal memos or other documents; (5) damaging the reputation of an individual, either through falsehood or through truths that might best have been left unsaid—e.g., revealing a prominent citizen's juvenile criminal record or homosexual life-style; (6) damaging the reputation of an institution, again either through falsehood or through overemphasis on minor misbehavior rather than constructive contributions; (7) partisanship in domestic politics (sometimes a demonstrable excess, more often a vague charge amounting to an inadequacy of partisanship on the side of whoever is making the complaint); and (8) partisanship for or against a foreign nation or figure who may incur no direct loss but who may rely on a favorable image in bargaining with the U.S. government—e.g., *Time* magazine's alleged mistreatment of Ariel Sharon. In addition to these measurable categories there is a prevalent but murky charge of unfairness, a matter that—as a Supreme Court justice said of obscenity—is difficult to define but relatively easy to recognize. Unfair coverage rarely results in anything actionable (although it is an implicit issue in many libel suits and frequently leads to jury verdicts that are reversed); still, it is a growing item for attention, indeed perhaps the premier concern in the process of self-regulation. These purported misdeeds are the main impetus for calls to regulate the press. In judging the various models for press control, one primary concern will be the speed and effectiveness with which these things can be redressed.

Fundamentally, there can be only two kinds of control of the American press: regulation, imposed by government, and self-regulation, imposed by the owners of each individual journalistic institution. But each category embraces a number of options discussed in varying detail in individual sections below. Government regulation presently takes four basic forms: (1) legislation either restricting or, as in shield laws, enhancing the status of the press; (2) court rulings defining the scope of the First Amendment; (3) direct government licensure including a review of performance and content, a standard that the United States applies to radio and television station owners and that other nations apply to newspapers and even individual reporters; and (4) litigation, primarily for libel, in which the courts may indirectly shape future coverage of individuals or institutions by imposing economic sanctions for unacceptable prior coverage.

Self-regulation also involves a variety of activities, some conducted within an institution, some within the press as a community, some operating almost subliminally. Internal self-regulation may involve (1) adoption of an ethics code (particularly crucial in broadcasting, a form that does not readily lend itself to a number of the other techniques cited below); (2) appointment of an ombudsman; (3) publication of critical letters and op-ed page articles; (4) holding in-house seminars to discuss professional standards; and (5) having top editors meet with readers either in open forums or in sessions with organized protest groups. Examples of self-regulation within the journalism community as a whole include (1) the reportage and analysis of the nation's handful of press critics, who report acutely on overarching issues but rarely comment in much detail on the behavior of their own employers; (2) the research, judgment and sometime censure issued by press councils, most of which derive their funds from publishing or broadcast companies but which usually include a substantial number of nonjournalist citizens among their panelists; (3) widely disseminated codes of behavior, of the kinds adopted by the Associated Press and Sigma Delta Chi; and (4) conferences and studies devoted to journalism issues, of the kind held by the American Society of Newspaper Editors, the Foundation for American Communications, and other groups, including the meeting that helped give rise to this paper.

Although all of these mechanisms appear to be directed toward similar ends, their popularity varies erratically; a great fan of one device may be implacably opposed to another. The *Washington Post's* Executive Editor Benjamin Bradlee, for example, tends to take a combative "you, too, buddy" posture toward all challengers and openly baits conservatives who accuse his newspaper of blatant liberalism. Yet the paper has had a succession of ombudsmen, and when *Post* reporter Janet Cooke was forced to return a Pulitzer Prize she won for a fictitious "news" feature, Bradlee ensured total staff cooperation with the then ombudsman Bill Green, who produced an exhaustively condemnatory piece detailing how the *Post's* normal self-regulatory machinery had failed. *Time* magazine has published press criticism lambasting other news organizations since its very first issue. Yet the parent company refused to help save the National News Council in its dying days on the stated grounds that any review of a news organization's performance ought to be self-imposed. CBS has repeatedly fought for access to government documents on the basis that they were compellingly in the public interest. Yet during the libel case brought by General William Westmoreland, which involved vital matters of federal conduct during the Vietnam War, CBS officials aggressively (and ultimately unsuccessfully) resisted releasing their own in-house study of the documentary in question, even after having distributed a synopsis of its contents to the press.

As these examples suggest, whatever confluence there may be among the press on matters of ethical principle, there is mostly confusion and contradiction on how to put these principles into practice. The chief area of agreement seems to be a preference for self-regulation rather than government intervention—but then, that is in broad outline the preference stated by doctors, lawyers, car dealers, and undertakers about how to deal with miscreance or malpractice in their own trades. And little wonder, no one welcomes a loss of control over his circumstances of work. Nonetheless this paper will consider first the merits and demerits of various kinds of government regulation before proceeding to the means for self-policing.

LEGISLATION

Most journalists tend to believe there are virtually no legal restrictions on the press aside from libel. The actual situation is rather more complicated. Statutory controls on the press fall into three basic categories. The first is classification: defining some information as, say, "classified" or "top secret," so that the mere possession of it is a crime. The second is what the courts call "prior restraint": imposing rules governing what can be published and thereby blocking information from reaching the public. The third is prosecution: acting after the fact of publication to allege that doing so was a crime against society—as distinct from libel, in which an individual alleges personal harm.

The first two techniques are used primarily in national security cases and occasionally in variant forms in the criminal justice system. They amount to suppressing information and thus contravene the underlying American principle, shared by liberals and conservatives, of a marketplace of ideas. The rationale for such restrictive behavior is that the marketplace of ideas tends to confer oblique, even intangible long-range benefits, whereas in some cases the dissemination of sensitive information results in a clear and present danger. As a practical matter, government officials have had relatively little success pursuing either mechanism. The Reagan administration succeeded for a while in suppressing some unwelcome foreign policy stories by invoking the espionage laws governing classified material. It seems unlikely, however, that courts would have been willing to apply those laws to American mass media. Moreover, subsequent revelations that the Reagan administration had pursued apparently extralegal operations in Iran and Nicaragua vitiated the credibility of the White House's patriotic claims to secrecy. Prior restraint by government order has been a discredited technique since the Nixon administration, when the White House failed to win court orders pro-hibiting in advance the sequential publication of the *Pentagon Papers*. Some critics of the press would like to restore these devices to effective use—for at least as long as conservatives remain in power—but to do so would probably require an unachievable constitutional amendment.

Prosecution is a far more readily available device, not only for dealing with national security and the secrecy of the criminal justice system but also for discouraging pornography. Legislation is largely useless, though, in addressing the single biggest group of complaints about the press, those involving alleged mistreatment of individuals. Most jurisdictions have laws about defamation and invasion of privacy, but getting a pros-ecutor to take on a single person's case as a matter of state concern is very difficult, especially when the alternative avenue of libel litigation remains available.

Prosecution is largely a holdover from times before the press enjoyed its venerated late twentieth-century position as a bulwark against gov-ernment enormity. In an earlier America, and in other countries today (among them are France, West Germany, and even, to a lesser extent, Britain), the mere fact of insulting a government official or other prom-inent citizen might be grounds for prosecution; truth has not always been an adequate defense. Even today, nearly every jurisdiction has on its books laws vague enough to allow a publicity-seeking prosecutor to act against practically any journal for some offending story. Such action can gain a prosecutor publicity, attract to his camp others disaffected from the news organization he sues, and harass an unfriendly press— via both the nuisance value of the suit and the legal costs of defending against it. Virtually the only prosecutions against publications that are likely to succeed, however, are those against peddlers of smut and sa-domasochism; even with them it is difficult to meet the customary court standard of proof that they contravene established community values. In the end, although many prominent legal scholars, including the two newest appointees to Supreme Court positions, Justices Anthony Ken-nedy and Antonin Scalia, have urged further restrictions of the excesses of the press, no one in such a position has argued that legislation is the fitting and effective means.

An equal uncertainty besets the use of legislation to enhance the po-sition of the press, primarily through "shield" laws that protect journalists from having to name their sources. Such laws serve both reporters and their sources—whistle blowers in government or informants in private criminal activity—and are theoretically applicable to both criminal and civil cases. The constitutionality of such laws is not clear, however, and a great many judges—thinking, understandably enough, from the stand-point of protecting their own institutions—regard shield laws as an im-permissible obstruction to defendants seeking to assemble their own best case. The judges' argument is especially compelling in libel cases; indeed, in some jurisdictions, refusing to cite sources results in an automatic finding that there are no such sources, that, in other words, the story was made up outright and thus is all but indefensible.

Although such judicial treatment may seem harsh, even extortionate, many nations (and many veteran American journalists) reject the idea of privileged treatment for news organizations. In his Gannett Center remarks, Kenneth Morgan, director of Britain's Press Council, contended, "generally, the less special press law a society has, the better" (Chapter 12).

JUDICIAL RULINGS AND LIBEL

A scholar of press freedom who was writing, say, a dozen years ago would probably have attributed the then high status of U.S. journalism partly to the conventionally cited instances of press enterprise, Vietnam and Watergate, but more to the Earl Warren and Warren Burger eras of the U.S. Supreme Court, and especially to the *New York Times vs. Sullivan* libel ruling of 1964. Although court decisions have been important in defining the rights and duties of journalists from the beginning of the nation, arguably no judicial decision in U.S. history has so forcefully addressed, and endorsed, the role of the press in keeping government honest and, therefore, the broad latitude the press must enjoy to continue doing its job. Indeed, in all likelihood nothing so vital to the press has taken place since the passage of the First Amendment itself. As Professor David Anderson of the University of Texas Law School noted in his paper for the Gannett Center conference:

Not until 1925 did the Court recognize the First Amendment as a limitation on the states' power to hold the press accountable. No act of Congress was ever held to violate the First Amendment until 1965. In 1919, Justice Oliver Wendell Holmes's belief that citizens could not be punished for criticizing the government was a dissenting opinion. Until 1964, libelous statements were excluded from any constitutional protection, and until 1931 local authorities could shut down a newspaper they considered malicious, scandalous, and defamatory (Chapter 10).

Sullivan and some subsequent cases established the key notion that a public official (later, any so-called public figure, whether or not in government office) cannot claim to have been libeled merely because of unfair, even erroneous, discussion of his public activities. To win, such a person must establish "malice," the essence of which is not simple ill will but willful falsity or reckless disregard of the truth.

The *Sullivan* decision resulted in several years of open season on officeholders and, as its scope expanded, on anyone who was voluntarily involved in public controversy. Even some journalists who initially hailed the decisions as freeing the press to do its job later characterized it as a malign influence; they blamed it for a perceived increase in aggression and a concomitant decline in precise pursuit of fact. The Supreme Court apparently agreed and has seemed to backpedal on some subsequent libel decisions. Probably the most important instance was a footnote to a decision, written by Chief Justice Warren Burger, that discouraged a common post-*Sullivan* judicial practice of dismissing *pro forma* virtually all libel cases brought by public figures. Burger seemed to suggest that plaintiffs should be entitled to adduce facts and have their day in court. The result, whether intended or not, has been that libel trials are frequently dual in nature: the official proceedings concern the legal grounds for libel and frequently afford the plaintiff essentially no hope of recovery; the unofficial proceedings (on occasion, as in the *CBS-Westmoreland* and *Time-Sharon* cases, conducted with elaborate public relations fanfare) address the facts of the disputed coverage and attempt to persuade the court of public opinion that the piece in question was or was not unfair. Although this use of the courts is, strictly speaking, extralegal, some students of the press think that it serves the public good. Renata Adler, after researching a book on the *Sharon* and *Westmoreland* cases, more or less validated the notion. Representative Charles Schumer, Democrat from New York, and other political figures have pondered the value of having courts issue declaratory judgments about the truth or falsity of stories, thereby sidestepping the issue of damages. This provision, even though it would foreclose monetary gain, might well appeal to libel plaintiffs, most of whom have difficulty proving that even the most embarrassing or unjust story caused them actual financial harm.

The other major post-*Sullivan* swing of the pendulum was a Supreme Court finding that, in order to prove legal malice, plaintiffs are entitled to inquire into media defendants' "state of mind" when undertaking a piece. On the surface this is reasonable enough; in practice, it has led to extensive and intrusive deposition, exposing to public scrutiny the private conversations, notebooks, videotapes and audiotapes, and other personal files of editorial practitioners—allowing plaintiffs not only to make their cases but to avenge themselves by embarrassing their tormentors. Taken together, these judicial findings have actively encouraged targets of tough media coverage to use the courts for purposes of harassment or retaliation. On occasion, judges appear to have encouraged this abuse. In the *Sharon* case, for example, the trial judge—who had close ties to Israel, including civic duties and an apartment there—deferred until after the trial a decision on the most crucial question in the case: whether Sharon had any standing to sue in U.S. courts. In the end, the answer was that he did not. But in the meantime Sharon was allowed to use the trial process, at considerable expense to the U.S. taxpayer, to attempt to redeem his own political career through an attack on the credibility of *Time* (the principal employer, it must be noted, of the writer of this article).

Other libel cases have produced conflicting and troublesome results about the degree to which opinion is inviolate, especially when expressed as a hyperbolic equivalent of fact. A trial court case found it libelous for a restaurant reviewer to describe a Chinese chef's pancakes, sarcastically, as being as thick as a finger. Another case resulted in a judgment against a consumer electronics reviewer who said that a speaker's sound wandered around the room when he should have more precisely said that it wandered along a wall. A pair of syndicated political columnists, attacking a college professor on ideological grounds, were described by a federal trial judge as obliged to prove every assertion made, including some that appeared to be mere inferences, not factual statements. When such cases reach the appellate level, the antipress rulings typically are reversed, commonly on the reasoning that the general value of free speech outweighs any individual's claim to be judged—if judged at all— on the narrowest grounds. Indeed, libel cases in general tend to be won by the plaintiffs in trial courts but overwhelmingly reversed, on behalf of media defendants, on appeal. This is especially true with million-dollar-plus verdicts. The real penalty for being sued is the cost of legal defense, a consideration that often impels media defendants, or their insurers, to settle out of court even when eventual victory seems certain. And when libel charges are brought against small, crusading publications, such as the dairy industry's *Milk Weed* or *The Alton* (Illinois) *Telegraph*, the validity of the claim may be irrelevant: in the former instance, the financial burden of defense brought the publication to the brink of bankruptcy; in the latter, the disproportion between a court's libel award and the company's total value actually did put the newspaper into bankruptcy court and resulted in a punitive settlement of a case that the newspaper might well have got reversed on appeal.

Horrendous as these cases sound to journalists, there is a sense in which the cost and nuisance value of libel suits may serve the public interest, by discouraging publications from sloppiness and imbalance when covering public figures and by impelling reporters and editors to heed the complaints of news subjects. Studies have suggested that the single biggest impetus causing plaintiffs to sue for libel was their finding lesser avenues closed—specifically, being unable to get sympathetic or even open-minded hearings of their complaints from officials at the offending news organizations. This argument, however, has its shortcomings. Libel suits are lodged, if anything, more frequently against the nation's most eminent newspapers, because they aggressively seek and uncover news, than against the I-was-kidnapped-by-aliens tabloids. And there may be what the courts call a "chilling effect" on coverage. Few if any important news organizations will admit that their own enterprise has been constrained by fear of libel suits, but they all readily suggest that some other organizations have reacted by cutting back. This conversation may simply reflect competitive fervor. Equally, it may be that the news organizations that deny self-censorship have in fact imposed it and are admitting so in the guise of accusing others. Certainly media lawyers at companies that have endured protracted, well-publicized suits report that editors and reporters who in the past feistily resisted proposed prepublication changes now are much more ready to retreat at the first raising of a consultative attorney's eyebrow.

LICENSING

Licensing as a means of regulating journalistic institutions and individual practitioners is simply a dead letter in American debate. Even the Reagan administration, which was not noted for affection toward the press, had fiercely opposed the licensing of journalists by governments in the course of international diplomatic debates. This posture reflected a virtually universal feeling among the nation's opinion leaders, and seemingly the citizenry as a whole, that a credentialed press is the equivalent of no press at all. Similarly, there is simply no significant backing for the licensure of publications, except in the oblique sense of refusing to regard obscenity as falling under the rubric of press freedoms. This outlook is not universally shared even among our democratic allies. As Professor Anderson noted at the Gannett conference, countries as diverse as Sweden and Israel require publishers to obtain a license from the government. Israel's military censors, moreover, aggressively use the threat of shutting down a newspaper to enforce their bans on publishing sensitive information. Says Professor Anderson, "When the Israeli government designates particular subjects as secret, the press must submit articles on those subjects for prior review. Seditious libel is a crime punishable by termination of the newspaper, and truth is no defense (Chapter 10).

Where licensure remains a fact of life in the United States, although less and less, is in the broadcasting industry. As a matter of law, all television and radio stations operate as rent-free tenants of publicly owned airwave space; to retain their hold on their frequencies, these stations must go through some sort of regular renewal procedure. This renewal process by turns imposes and then disavows journalistic restraints on the station, endorses and then denies the notion that broadcasting is another form of the press and thereby eligible for First Amendment protection. Congress, the Federal Communications Commission (FCC), and the courts have contradicted each other, and often themselves, about how free the broadcast press can be.

Originally licensing arose because the number of radio and television frequencies was finite and, if not clearly allocated, electronic chaos would ensue—instead of receiving as many signals as there were programmers, as was the case in print, citizens who tuned in would hear only static. Perhaps because a former mining engineer, Herbert Hoover, oversaw the creation of the Federal Communications Commission, airspace was therefore treated as comparable to public land: exploitation rights to lumber, oil, or broadcasting could be leased for specified periods, but the underlying title remained in federal hands.

Over the years, rules evolved requiring stations to broadcast news, to program for specified demographic minorities, to offer equal time, if any at all, to competing political candidates and to provide comparable treatment to exponents of various points of view on controversial issues (the fairness doctrine). Courts specifically acknowledged that these rules compromised the First Amendment. Judge Skelly Wright said in a 1976 federal case, "The doctrine does, after all, involve the Government to a significant degree in policing the content of communication." Justice Burger has written:

A broadcaster has much in common with a newspaper publisher, but he is not in the same category in terms of public obligations imposed by law. A broadcaster seeks and is granted the free and exclusive use of a limited and valuable part of the public domain; when he accepts that franchise, it is burdened by enforceable public obligations. A newspaper can be operated at the whim or caprice of its owners; a broadcast station cannot.

Advocacy groups such as Action for Children's Television consequently pressed, sometimes successfully, for further programming requirements. These rules explicitly presupposed that civic virtue would run counter to commercial appeal.[1]

Gradually a commercial station's frequency came to be thought of as its principal asset, far outstripping the physical equipment, ongoing business, and goodwill. License renewal was automatic except for (and sometimes even in) egregious cases; nonrenewal came to be thought of as a huge economic penalty, far disproportionate to almost anything else administered by government-hearing officers or federal courts. According to remarks at the Gannett Center conference (Chapter 8) by Henry Geller, former White House telecommunications adviser, during one period some 2,400 complaints were brought before the FCC and only 94 were judged even to require the filing of a formal response. With FCC permission, station frequencies have been bought and sold, just as though they were the actual property of the station owners rather than the public, sometimes for hundreds of millions of dollars. Occasionally liberals would suggest that some sort of special tax should be imposed to recoup for the government some share of the capital gain on what was supposedly a public asset. Several times, public television itself specifically put forward such plans as a means of financing its own activities.

In contrast to all of this actual or proposed regulatory intervention, however, there appeared an even stronger wave of deregulatory enthusiasm, spurred by liberals mistrustful of price-fixing; conservatives opposed to government control; and, in the case of broadcasting, politically powerful networks and stations who longed to be free to do business as they pleased. The latter group repeatedly invoked the First Amendment, although journalism constituted a small fraction of the programming they aired; fiction of various sorts made up the bulk of it. By the middle 1970s, deregulation had captured the fancy of legislators and executive branch officials of both parties, and by the end of the second Reagan term the notion of public licensure of television stations was all but defunct. Some people continue to make a forceful case for government control of some sort, but given contemporary political realities it seems pointless to look to licensure to rectify the wrongs committed by broadcast or other journalists.

THE MARKETPLACE

Americans tend to believe in the myth of free choice in the marketplace as a paradigm for almost all social interaction. One traditional defense of press freedom, as mentioned above, is that it is part of a marketplace of ideas. And one commonplace claim of editors and publishers is that the sins of journalism can be redressed in the commercial marketplace. In the abstract, this is a seductive notion: poor performance will be recognized and reprimanded by enlightened consumers. But in reality, this model only rarely affords much potential for correction. The basic reason is a lack of competition. Disgruntled readers or advertisers may withdraw their custom from a local monopoly newspapers—which is the norm these days—but the sheer hunger for information, or the need to reach an audience, soon drives most of them back. A widespread boycott might be more effective. Yet in all but the unlikeliest cases, an individual or institution that is hard done by has little chance of persuading the public to adopt its case as its own, especially because the primary means of persuading said public is likely to be the very vehicle that has already offended. Moreover, the public constitutes not one audience but many, most of them self-selecting and frequently sharing a bias. If a publication serving a specialty audience attacks a perceived common enemy, the editor likely has little to fear from his readers, even if the attack is misinformed or patently unfair. As John C. Merrill, professor of jour-

nalism and philosophy at Louisiana State University, noted in his paper
for the Gannett conference:

The main problem is that in the real world the "people" seem to be largely
passive or unconcerned about the routine affairs of the media. Feedback of any
significant kind—when it comes from the people to the media at all—is episodic
and splintered. It offers little or no real guidance for media policies. The media,
we can say, are dependent, in a capitalistic society, on the marketplace for financial support but relatively unaffected, at least in the short term, so far as
professional and moral guidance is concerned (Chapter 2).

Some hard-liners believe that that is as it should be, urging that a
newspaper is affected with no public interest, that the owner is selling
a manufactured product at his own risk.

That risk is, of course, rather less great these days. Media properties
have become immensely profitable, much sought after in voluntary or
involuntary takeovers, and they enjoy the stable status of institutions.
Often their competitive instincts are spurred only by pride, not commercial necessity. Major mainstream publications, however jealous of
their prestige, have little to fear economically even from a story widely
adjudged inaccurate or unfair. Celebrated libel suits, such as Carol Burnett's against the *National Enquirer* or Ariel Sharon's against *Time*, are
reported by the news organizations involved to have had no measurable
long-term effect on circulation or advertising. Nor did *Newsweek* suffer
in any enduring way for its ballyhooing of the spurious Adolf Hitler
diaries. Probably the most conspicuous disproof of the marketplace theory of regulation is the largest newspaper based in New Hamsphire, the
Manchester Union Leader. Archconservative in outlook and truculent in
manner (even moderate Republicans such as President Gerald Ford
evoke front-page references on the order of "Jerry the Jerk"), the *Union
Leader* operates far outside the normal bounds of taste and decency, yet
it remains the premier organ of its state and, during presidential election
years, an influential factor in national politics. Its combination of malign
eccentricity and profit, although extreme, is far from unique. Major
newspapers from Indianapolis to Albuquerque to Santa Ana, California,
have been combative, if not spiteful, on the right; the blatanty liberal
Washington Post thrives in the nation's political capital, as does the almost
equally leftist *The New York Times* in the nation's commercial and cultural
capital. In some big cities, New York and Washington among them, a
newspaper that tilts toward one side is at least partially offset by a rival
biased the other way. But the balance is illusory. Most of the public reads
one daily newspaper, not several, and to the individuals or institutions
assailed by a newspaper, the absence of such a story in a rival—or even
an article in reply—is cold comfort. The main hope is to win a retraction

and apology from the offending publication itself, and perhaps to effect attitudinal change within the publication so that no such event can recur.

SELF-REGULATION

Tradition holds that the best press critic, ombudsman, code of ethics writer, and general keeper of the moral flame at any publication is its editor. This doctrine is most often intoned, needless to say, by editors themselves. Burton Benjamin, a longtime CBS News executive who conducted its in-house study of the Westmoreland documentary, invoked it at the Gannett Center conference: "There are ethics specialists in the newsrooms, and they are called editors. And I think that's where they belong. I would hate to see someone brought into any news room I ever worked and have told me, 'I'd like you to meet our new ethics specialist.' I wouldn't know whether he wanted me to go to confession or what." Some advocates of editors as chief moralists are simply reflecting in words what they do in actual practice. These editors by and large run publications that are activist enough to generate some complaints but decent enough to handle them maturely and humbly. Other editors, inevitably, are kidding themselves, in the fashion of chief executives of almost everything: they confuse any complaint about the institution they run with an attack on their personal integrity, and conversely, they tend to assume that if they are competent and virtuous, then their publication must be without blemish. Admittedly, the news business is, if no less arrogant, at least less insensitive than in the days when the standard response to a telephone call of complaint was to yell, "Nut on the line!" and then hang up. Editors, in their dual role as marketing directors of their publications, have come to recognize the public relations value of proffering at least the appearance of open-mindedness. Yet there is still a widespread residual impulse to regard anyone who claims to be aggrieved by the press as a crybaby and to answer complaints with rhetoric about press freedom instead of ruminations about press responsibility. That is the true context of all the seemingly endless conferences, symposia papers, and speeches about press self-regulation, which on the surface tend to bring out so much reasonable likemindedness that one wonders why they are necessary. Even the wisest news people find themselves advocating essentially contradictory values. *Los Angeles Times* publisher Thomas Johnson, for example, argued in 1984 that "the press must be its own policeman" but also that "we cannot insist on accountability from other powerful institutions in our society while simultaneously rejecting accountability for ourselves." Johnson might likely disagree, but most objective observers would argue that accountability to oneself can scarcely compare with accountability to voters or shareholders. Indeed, at base the argument for full First Amendment press freedom is an argument for unaccountability, for the Platonic notion that the truth in its ideal form will somehow emerge from an untrammeled press and that any kind of normative restraint will have unanticipated and dangerous consequences. As Professor Merrill of LSU put it at the Gannett conference, "In the freedom-accountability symbiosis the only logical accountability system or model is self-accountability, based primarily on a self-imposed foundation of ethics or morality," not economic pressure (Chapter 2).

The basic goals of self-regulatory systems within a publication are to ensure fair and honest reporting, to provide reconsideration of instances when reportage may have been dishonest or unfair, to provide a platform for divergent opinion or analysis from both prominent and ordinary citizens, and to open lines of communication between the editorship and the readership. As noted above, there are several means of working toward these goals, and few publications make use of all of them. Indeed, the ways in which any one of these devices is used can vary greatly from one news organization to another, and in some instances the device is used much more for the publisher's benefit than for the reader's.

The prime example of this last point is the most basic device, a promulgated (usually written) code of ethics. Such codes usually combine in one document two tangentially related concerns: standards and practices for the actual performance of one's job, such as whether it is legitimate to tape a conversation without the other party knowing, and proprieties about general conduct, such as fraternization with sources or invoking one's newspaper in a dispute with a recalcitrant credit card company. Dozens of newspapers have such codes, including most of the major metropolitan dailies. Leafing through them, one observes that many are silent on truly ticklish questions—whether a reporter may ever misrepresent his identity, whether it is legitimate to go under cover, whether a reporter may tolerate or even engage in criminal behavior in search of a story—but outspoken on the ownership's prerogatives. Almost all codes either forbid or regulate free-lance activity. They constrain political activity, even as a volunteer—not necessarily just for political writers who might have a genuine conflict of interest but also for others, simply because publicity about their involvement might inconvenience their employer. Many codes restrict or ban the use of material gathered on the job when writing for other publications, not to protect the rights of people interviewed, but to conserve the work product that management paid for. Codes of ethics routinely forbid accepting gifts from objects of news coverage but often provide for the gifts, and for such other items as reviewer's copies of books and records, to be distributed to charities of the management's choosing—even though charities are themselves frequent objects of news coverage. Similarly, reporters are often forbidden to use the newspaper's name, even to the extent of citing the fact of their employment, when engaging in outside employment, citizen involvement, or mere correspondence with tradesmen. But publishers and other executives routinely "represent" the newspaper in civic, business community, and cultural activities, and they often pressure the newsroom to provide (implicitly favorable) coverage to such groups.

Despite such widespread confusion and misuse, ethics codes serve several useful purposes. First, they attune reporters to the notion that there are ethical gray areas, that it is part of editors' jobs to adjudicate them, and that it is always wisest to check the rule book and, if still in doubt, ask someone in authority. Second, these rules provide an easy out in awkward situations—deflecting an offer of a free lunch or ski pass or whatever, not by condemning it as corrupting, but simply by saying that acceptance is not allowed. Third, the very fact of such rules, if properly publicized, can help reassure the public that news organizations are concerned with morality and honor.

The limit to the value of these rules is, as always, the good faith of the people following them. CBS News has a copious written code of ethics that answered, or could have, many of the questions of procedural ethics raised by the network's controversial documentary on General William Westmoreland. Indeed, investigator Benjamin asserted at the Gannett conference, "I can't think of anything significant that came out of the Westmoreland case that was not in the code." But the veteran producer who created the documentary either chose not to consult the rules or willfully defied them and remained unapologetic about the incident. As former CBS News President Van Gordon Sauter said, "Contrition is not a word in his vocabulary."[2]

Even when faithfully followed, ethics codes cannot, of course, anticipate all situations, nor do editorial managers want them to. Journalism is oriented toward personalities and situations, both abstractions, and the craft counts few moral absolutists but many situation ethicists among its ranks. Thus codes are frequently augmented, or supplanted, by in-house discussions, which may range from hypothetical cases to under-the-gun debates about how to deal with a specific problem. The former tend to be of little use, in part because busy and detail-oriented newspeople prefer not to spend time on matters not actually on the plate, in part because of that same tendency among news managers to weigh personalities and public temperament at least as much as general principles in making any decision. Group discussion of how to deal with a specific sensitive story, particulary one that unfolds over days or weeks, is far more often productive. But as a device for reassuring the public or bringing its concerns into debate, in-house talk has little in its favor: it cannot be seen to happen, it rarely involves much direct public input, it rarely results in any kind of public statement of policy, and it rarely leads to immediate, manifest changes in coverage.

Much more useful in public relations in the best sense is the "town meeting" mechanisms popularized by, among other places, the *Miami Herald.* One or more news executive makes himself available, either to existing community groups or to a free-for-all open to whoever comes, and explains why the news organization does what it does. This device has many advantages: it can alert editors to previously unperceived issues of coverage; it can lead managers to clarify, or for that matter reconsider, settled policy; and it can allay community fears, deflect outrage over controversial coverage, and in general win friends and influence people. But this device is also time consuming, emotionally charged, and too public for many editors' tastes. The open forum may also tend to attract extremists, even obsessives, whose opinions offer little insight into mainstream community concerns.

Editors generally prefer to deal with the community through the mailbox. Nearly all newspapers and journalistic magazines publish letters to the editor and an increasing number also open the op-ed page, or its equivalent, to one-shot expressions of opinion, generally solicited from acknowledged experts but occasionally received through the transom from ordinary citizens. In fact, some op-ed pieces begin life as letters too long for the letters column. Although the use of letters is virtually universal (one notable exception: *The New Yorker*), the specific intent in publishing them varies considerably. *Time* magazine, for example, has no other provision for correcting mistakes. Thus a disproportionate share of its letters set straight matters of fact; the mere publication of such a letter is construed by the editors (and in their belief, the readers) as an admission of error. At the *Boston Globe*, by contrast, as at increasing numbers of newspapers, pure error is dealt with in a prominently displayed daily correction box.[3] Thus, publication of an adversary letter at most newspapers does not necessarily mean that the writer was wrong—corrections take care of that—but only that there was another arguable point of view. The prevailing philosophy is that the reporter has his say in his original article and that therefore any disgruntled reader should have a fair chance at equal time, even if the reply letter omits some significant facts, takes a contorted view of others, and/or misstates the writer's original analysis. Only undisputed grievous error would disquality a letter. Most major publications receive many more letters than they can include; selection tends to be based on technical considerations, such as brevity and articulation, but most of all on being representative. This policy tends to cause publications that are already normative to become even more so. It generally excludes letters written from extreme points of view (zealous anticommunism and Biblical fundamentalism), dealing with uncommon passions (animal rights, fluoridation, and the like), or harping on much-discussed topics (abortion, feminism, and sexual liberty). Thus, even when the letters page provides access to people who disagree with the paper's editorial stance, the range of disagreement is often frustratingly limited for real dissenters. By contrast, smaller newspapers frequently publish most of the coherent and nonobscene letters they receive and occasionally rival the *London Times* of old for the odd diversity of its correspondence. Papers of any size, however, remain reluctant to publish direct attacks on their own coverage and in particular direct attacks on writers, except columnists, part of whose portfolio is to arouse controversy. Universal as the letters column is in print, it is a generally unused device in broadcasting, partly because air time is a much scarcer commodity than column inches are in a newspaper and partly because television stations have not been as successful as newspapers in finding a corporate sponsor (e.g., Mobil) to underwrite a letters page.

The most radical means of self-regulation—because it is the one device that provides for admission of misjudgment, including errors by senior editorial management—is the installation of ombudsmen. The term and the concept, as almost everyone must know by now, come from Sweden, which originated this notion that institutions need an in-house advocate for the disgruntled public outside. Although the ranks of American journalistic ombudsmen are thin—the total number is roughly three to four dozen, all from newspapers rather than newsmagazines or, as far as research indicates, television stations—there are virtually as many definitions of the job as there are tenants of it. Some ombudsmen are drawn from the ranks of reporters or editors, others come from entirely outside the news organization. Some have indefinite and presumptively long tenure, others are hired via nonrenewal contracts. Some report to the editor, some to the publisher. Some are free to research and write whatever they please. Most endure in-house bargaining, if not an outright veto-power from on high. Some write regularly, often to a fixed space, others take all the time and space they choose to pursue a problem. Some deal only with the behavior of the institution that employs them, others seek the context of how other news organizations have handled the same issues.

Some are mandated simply to represent the general public, with specific emphasis on aggrieved targets of coverage. Some consider themselves in-house press critics and feel free to take on a topic whether or not there has been a consequential complaint from outside. Some are glorified public relations counselors whose primary duty is to placate complainants rather than to serve as an avenging angel on their behalf. In general, the greater the ombudsman's detachment from the paper's chief editor, the greater his freedom and the more forceful his citizen advocacy. But the countervailing rule is that the closer the ombudsman is to the editor, the more likely it is that his recommendations will be put into effect. This divided mandate clearly reflects itself in the psyche of ombudsmen.

Clifford Christians reported at the Gannett conference about a study conducted through the Silha Center at the University of Minnesota that found: "Half of them think that in the final analysis, they're representatives of the newspaper, and the other half insist unswervingly that they're representatives of the public" (Chapter 4). Ironically, for all of this angst, ombudsmen may operate in something of a vacuum. One study of readers of the Louisville newspapers, which established the concept of a "reader representative" decades ago, indicated that 58 percent did not know the papers had an ombudsman.

INDUSTRY SELF-REGULATION

Like the self-regulation practiced within a news organization, the self-regulation within the news business as a whole ranges from general discussion to overt censure. It is the latter pole, of course, that arouses the most interest. Conferences and symposia help sensitize journalists to ethical issues. Industry-wide codes of ethics can define what is absolutely beyond the pale, but that may already be self-evident to most reporters and editors. Moreover, codes are difficult to enforce, especially among respecters of the First Amendment: the first act of the American Society of Newspaper Editors was to write a code of ethics, yet the organization promptly found itself spending five years debating whether to censure a member who had clearly violated the code by involving himself in the Teapot Dome scandal.

The two more impact-laden kinds of industry self-regulation are the judgments handed down by press critics and, especially, by news councils. Neither kind of operation has a particularly rich and vigorous heritage, to be sure. Although the newsweeklies are committed to press criticism (the section appeared in *Time*'s very first issue), their resources are limited, their sections run only about two-thirds of the time, many of the stories are largely reportorial rather than analytic, and the issues dealt with are almost always national or international. To the newsweeklies, it is news if another top-rank organization fouls up, but not, for the most part, if a regional daily does. Very few newspapers publish press criticism: notably, the *Los Angeles Times* and, less aggressively, *The New York Times, Washington Post,* and *Boston Globe* among a handful of others. Their stories are more often regional and occasionally unearth the small, but grievous, misdeeds of the local press. But much of the space is devoted to reviewing monthly magazine articles, which rarely form the cutting edge of journalism, and punches are often pulled. As former White House Counselor Lloyd Cutler noted at the Gannett Center conference,

"Every profession has a tendency not to speak ill of its brethren. I would think that one of the things the press could do best is to expose the weaknesses of its fellow members, as A. J. Liebling did so well. What has happened to the A. J. Lieblings? Where are they today?" Moreover, both the newsweeklies and most newspapers (the *Los Angeles Times* excepted) tend to do a timorous and incomplete job, or none at all, in reporting about themselves. Television and radio do very little press criticism, although when they do, it is mostly of high quality. The most consistent and copious coverage of all appears in press journals, which have notably included the award-winning *Chicago Journalism Review* and the *Columbia* (albeit too stuffy and too liberal) and *Washington* (albeit too glitzy and at times boosterish) *Journalism Reviews*.

The performance of news councils has been even spottier. The National News Council expired a few years ago of neglect by major news organizations, the same cause that limited its effectiveness during its life. Of the 50 states, only Minnesota has a long-standing, fully functional council. Alfred Balk, editorial director of *World Press Review*, noted at the Gannett conference that models for news councils have been put forward throughout the century.

[L]ocal press councils were advocated early in the 1930s by Chilton R. Bush, head of the Department of Communications at Stanford University. But only after World War II did interest perceptibly grow—with the Hutchins Commission report [a multiyear survey by leading intellectual lights, completed in 1947 and sponsored in part by Henry Luce, Balk explained] and other proposals. These included suggestions from Stanford and the University of Minnesota for a press-monitoring institute or council, from *Louisville Courier-Journal* and *Times* publisher Barry Bingham, Sr., for local press councils, and from media critic (later *Washington Post* ombudsman) Ben H. Bagdikian for university-based state councils.

With $40,000 from a Newspaper Guild fund bequeathed by former *Washington Daily News* editor Lowell Mellett, four local councils were established in 1967 in small western and midwestern communities. These closed shortly after funding ran out, and other small-town councils usually have been short-lived. Honolulu, to break an impasse in relations between the mayor and the press, birthed its council in 1970—the most significant local one to date (Chapter 6).

Britain's Press Council provides a model that many news executives would like to emulate. Founded in 1953, it has the following goals according to its charter:

To preserve the established freedom of the British Press; to maintain its character in accordance with the highest professional and commercial standards; to consider complaints about its conduct or the conduct of others towards it, and deal with these in a practical and appropriate manner; to keep under review developments likely to restrict the supply of information of public interest and importance; and to report publicly on developments towards greater concentration or monopoly in the press.[4]

Those goals seem relatively unexceptionable, and the council's record is remarkably constructive: it handles about 1,400 complaints a year and fully investigates and adjudicates about a tenth of them. The review board is made up of private citizens, both prominent and ordinary, and journalists. The proceedings tend to be civil, with occasional exceptions: one irate editor brought suit for libel against a police chief based entirely on the complaint the chief submitted to the the press council. Still, according to its director, Kenneth Morgan, in remarks at the Gannett conference, "[The council] has never divided on any issue on party lines with the public members voting one way and the press members the other (Chapter 12). But the Press Council enjoys two significant advantages that an American equivalent would be unlikely to obtain. First, the targets of the council's censure willingly publish the results of the proceeding in full, prominently displayed, with only 11 (most fringe journal) exceptions during the council's first 32 years—something that few U.S. publications, and probably no network news departments, would allow. Indeed, part of the reason the National News Council folded was that it failed to sustain a meaningfully broad dissemination of its findings. Second, complainants to the council are obliged to treat its proceedings as an alternative to libel litigation rather than a preliminary skirmish, and thus persuade news organizations to open their books and cooperate, whereas in the litigious United States a potential plaintiff would not (perhaps could not) sign away his rights, and therefore a potential defendant would likely resist all inquiries.

Even in Britain, this libel-suit waiver device does not fully protect publishers. As every editor who has read through the complaint mail knows, much of the most enraged invective comes not from the targets of coverage but from their adherents or even unauthorized admirers. As Kenneth Morgan observed at the conference,

You can immediately see the problem that arises where the individual making the complaint to us is not the individual who has apparently been defamed, but someone acting in what he believes is the public good. You can get a waiver from him, and much good may it do. He may have no cause of action anyway, and the editor may be forgiven for taking a fairly jaundiced view of the protection that's being offered (Chapter 12).

Nonetheless, the theory of a press council remains attractive. To the extent that it would substitute for libel suits, it would save news organizations substantial sums of money, especially for legal costs, and would also open the review process to many would-be plaintiffs who cannot afford to sue. To the extent that it would yield definitive judgments that a story was right or wrong, fair or unfair, it would provide the vindication (or retribution) that many libel defendants seek. To the extent that it exposed offending news organizations to the censure of their peers, it would tend to reinforce professional standards and discredit consistently shabby institutions.[5]

In practice, however, press councils face one huge obstacle. The real utility of such an organization is not in denouncing stories that are blatantly inaccurate or unfair, but in reviewing matters that are sprawling and complex (e.g., the Westmoreland-CBS brouhaha). To undertake such a task, the council must in effect report a story, which requires a massive expenditure of resources and, more important, a staff of seasoned journalists capable of retracing and assessing the steps taken by the original reporting team. The National News Council, in my personal experience, reviewed cases by sending out graduate students who may have been bright but who lacked the necessary experience and judgment to reach valid conclusions. Because the council's own vote was based on the facts presented and because there was scant opportunity for further study, the work of these untutored youth became the (highly questionable) basis of the council's findings. Obtaining a staff of sufficient stature for the task would almost certainly prove to lie beyond the financial resources of any imaginable news council.

CONCLUSIONS

Readers who make it to this point, without skipping, may well feel that no device for regulation or self-regulation is fully functional and that therefore journalists ought not to waste so much time (including the time spent reading this *tour d'horizon*) on this subject. In fact, however, there are heartening trends: the increased use of ombudsmen and the concomitant increase in the willingness of editors to listen to outsiders and to admit error, the rough and ready justice resulting from the admittedly costly use of the courts to make extralegal cases about accuracy and fairness, and the slow but steady rise in the amount and quality of press criticism. Even the devices that are not effectively serving the public needs are susceptible to amelioration. And of course the cumulative effect of a series of flawed or incomplete mechanisms can be considerably sounder than any one of its parts.

Beyond these modest observations, there are no cosmic plans to be put on offer: the devices that do not now exist, or that do not operate untrammeled, appear in the form they do because of the unwillingness of editors and publishers—and in some cases, readers—to subject themselves to further regulation or self-regulation of the press. The Gannett Center conference echoed the dozens of such conferences, informal or *ad hoc*, that this writer and most veteran journalists have attended: news-hounds are skeptics by nature, and it is much easier to get them to perceive the shortcomings in an idea than to arouse them to enthusiastic endorsement. Nor should there necessarily be some master design for improving the press. As Professor Anderson noted in his paper for the Gannett conference, "The mix of media freedom and accountability we have today is the product not of any grand plan, but of hundreds of rules fashioned at various times to resolve controversies of many different kinds (Chapter 10).

Nonetheless, the very process of journalists' applying (or submitting to) means of self-criticism can accomplish more than the devices themselves: by alerting editors, writers, and the institutions that employ them to the nature of concerns voiced by readers and by subjects of coverage, the initial inquiry becomes part of a pattern of sensitization. Journalists who have been forced to think about the impact of stories after the fact will find themselves asking pertinent questions about accuracy and fairness before the story is published, and thus before the often irreversible harm is done.

NOTES

1. After a time, Congress and various presidents also established a public, or educational, television system that would further serve the unserved minorities by operating outside commercial constraints. That scheme has significantly failed: in the absence of total public funding, the need for individual and corporate donations ultimately drove stations to seek the largest possible audiences, which in turn led them to provide programming increasingly comparable to that offered by commercial competitors. Indeed, much of the British programming purchased for public television was made for the commercial networks there. Public stations increasingly schedule old movies that were originally intended for commercial release, videotaped theater presentations that first ran on the commercial cable channel Showtime, and some new movies that are given both television and commercial theatrical distribution.

2. Van Gordon Sauter, private interview.

3. No corrective mechanism is more prominent these days than the combination of corrections and editor's notes featured in *The New York Times*. Norman Isaacs, former editor of the *Louisville Courier-Journal* and a vehement advocate of admissions of error, remarked at the Gannett Center conference: "It took years for *The New York Times* to get around to correcting its errors. It came to it belatedly. I must say that these days the corrections get down into trivia that boggle the mind. But I'm not about to complain because if you're going to do it, you should do it all the way.

4. The Press Council, Articles of Constitution. Printed in *The Press and the People*, annual reports of The Press Council, 1953–1988.

5. In explaining to a convention of the American Society of Newspaper Editors

why he generally declines to be interviewed, filmmaker Warren Beatty cited the sins of the *National Enquirer* and its ilk and faulted the better-behaved media for rallying behind the First Amendment instead of disavowing their ructious and raunchy rivals.

14

THREE VIEWS ON ACCOUNTABILITY

Theodore L. Glasser

No doubt the chapters in this book rest on a broadly liberal view of media accountability in that they each accept unquestioningly liberalism's three basic tenets: the efficacy of a constitutional state, the sanctity of private property, and the viability of a competitive market economy. Conspicuously but inevitably excluded from consideration, it follows, are approaches to accountability that either reject or transcend liberal ideals. Well outside of the scope of this book are systems of accountability that reject these Western tenets, for example, the debate over the New World Information Order in the report of UNESCO's MacBride Commission.[1] With the exception of the examples in this volume from the British Press Council, we have purposely confined ourselves to the American experience.

As the discussion and debate on these pages attest, accountability can mean many things. It can mean success in the marketplace or it can mean insulation from the marketplace. It can mean aspiring to professional ideals or it can mean abiding by standards of performance codified by the state. But if at times the options for accountability seem endless, most of the choices—and certainly the disputes of any intellectual consequence—can be collapsed into a very few basic issues concerning the always delicate balance between freedom and responsibility. In fact, two key questions seem to sum up the differences—as well as the difficulties—in defining accountability: (1) accountable *for what?* and (2) accountable *to whom?*

In their answers to these two questions and in their more general treatment of the relationship between freedom and responsibility, the contributors to this book align themselves with one of three broadly distinguishable schools of thought. John Merrill's defense of the marketplace and David Anderson's views on law and litigation converge on the importance of freedom of choice and individual liberty; both Merrill and Anderson honor the role of a "minimal state," and both view media accountability in terms of its capacity to protect—or at least not impair—the autonomy of individuals. Clifford Christians, in contrast, believes that journalists' visceral attachment to constitutional guarantees—their "fierce independence" and their absolutist views on autonomy—can only "preclude in the press a genuine appreciation of accountability"; what is needed, Christians argues, is a "generally accepted body of principles" that will provide not only journalists but the larger community with a morally rich vocabulary, the "soil from which accountability can grow" (Chapter 4). Henry Geller, Alfred Balk, and Kenneth Morgan offer a compromise position, an essentially republican system of accountability involving elected, selected, or appointed councils or commissions. Neither as extreme as Merrill and Anderson on the question of individual autonomy nor as extreme, in the other direction, as Christians in his call for a normative social ethics, Geller, Balk, and Morgan advance a "third-party" conception of accountability utilizing presumably independent arbiters of press performance.

HONORING FREEDOM OF CHOICE

For Merrill and Anderson, freedom and accountability are on opposite ends of a continuum; as Anderson puts it, accountability is the "converse of freedom"—to the extent that media are held accountable, their freedom is necessarily diminished. While neither Anderson nor Merrill doubt the need for some accountability, even at the expense of freedom, the only form of accountability they can fully reconcile with individual freedom is the accountability provided by an unregulated and unabused marketplace. To be sure, Merrill regards the marketplace as the "ultimate" opportunity for accountability and the one of the five models of accountability examined in this book "most compatible with the American dedication to both press freedom and press responsibility"; because the marketplace permits the maximization of individual as well as media autonomy, "it is the kind of accountability in harmony with the spirit of individualism, democracy, and freedom" (Chapter 2).

The American conception of democracy to which Merrill refers—and to which Anderson accedes—owes its intellectual debt to John Locke and what has been fairly termed the "liberal constitutionalist tradition" in modern democratic theory. Aided immeasurably by Adam Smith and other marketplace advocates, the Lockean tradition casts the individual in a survivalist role. It is the kind of democracy David Held describes as "protective" insofar as it limits the role of the state to that of the guardian of individual liberty and freedom of choice; emerging as it did in response to despotic monarchies and their claim to legitimacy, namely "divine support," protective democracies "sought to restrict the powers of the state and to define a uniquely private sphere independent of state action."[2] In other words, from Locke's perspective the state can protect individuals by safeguarding their liberty and thereby ensure their freedom of choice, but it cannot legitimately do what monarchs had done: prescribe a particular social and moral order.

What distinguishes protective democracies from other forms of self-government is the priority assigned to liberty and what this assignment portends for a conception of the "public interest." Reminiscent of John Milton's plea in *Areopagitica* for an end to licensed printing, advocates of a protective democracy argue that a coercive state can only undermine individual liberty and ultimately distance the press from the public and its interests. A press subject to the demands of the state not only compromises its own autonomy and freedom but can lose sight of the interests of its readers, listeners, and viewers; for it is only through free and unfettered competition in the marketplace that the public interest can express itself and make itself known to the press.

As Merrill states quite candidly, and as we might reasonably infer from Anderson, individual liberty is best managed by the "laws of nature"—or, as Adam Smith prefers, guided by the "invisible hand" of the marketplace. A protective state best serves the needs of its citizens by honoring their unimpeded choices; and these unimpeded choices, taken aggregately, constitute the public interest. Accordingly, and as proponents of media deregulation are now arguing, the public's interest *is* the public interest, and any effort by the state to contravene marketplace forces by imposing on the media its own sense of what the public wants or needs must be viewed as arbitrary, elitist, and altogether undemocratic.[3]

It is not difficult to discern in the marketplace argument, even as it is crudely sketched here, a basic presupposition about the reasonableness and rationality on the part of "free" individuals and utter disdain for a state that would want to regulate individuals and their relations with one another. Drawing as it does on Locke's view of human nature and political authority, it posits a society that develops its own moral order; the state preserves—but never amends and certainly never revises—that order by respecting individual differences and individual abilities.

But, significantly, if the state respects individual differences and individual abilities, then it cannot properly concern itself with equality if equality means "equality of outcome." In *Anarchy, State, and Utopia*, which follows closely the "respectable tradition of Locke," Robert Nozick illustrates the logic of "no presumption in favor of equality":

The major objection to speaking of everyone's having a right *to* various things such as equality of opportunity, life, and so on, and to enforcing this right, is that these "rights" require a substructure of things and materials and actions; and *other* people may have rights and entitlements over these. No one has a right to something whose realization requires certain uses of things and activities that other people have rights and entitlements over. Other people's rights and entitlements to *particular things,* (*that* pencil, *their* body, and so on) and how they choose to exercise these rights and entitlements fix the external environment of any given individual and the means that will be available to him. If his goal requires the use of means which others have rights over, he must enlist their voluntary cooperation. Even to *exercise* his right to determine how something he owns is to be used may require other means he must acquire a right to, for example, food to keep him alive; he must put together, with the cooperation of others, a feasible package.[4]

In short, the only conception of equality relevant to a protective democracy is equality of treatment by the state. And from this it follows that the public interest, like the marketplace itself, can never be more than a process, a means to some unknown end; for if the state can only guarantee individual liberty and freedom of choice, the public interest becomes a strictly private matter, a determination guided principally by self-interest.

If, as Anderson observes, the "media today are less accountable legally than they have been at any time in our history" (Chapter 10), that may be due to an increasingly powerful private sector and an increasingly appealing argument concerning the entitlement rights of those who own the media. Anderson's extensive review of media-related laws and litigation does not call into question the role of a protective or minimal state but rather provides example after example of the kind of protection the state can legitimately provide. To take the example of libel law, which Anderson reviews in some detail, when the media are punished for ruining someone's reputation by publishing false information, the state is merely protecting the plaintiff's right—the plaintiff's *entitlement*—to a "true" or "correct" reputation; even a minimal state, Nozick argues, must protect its citizens against "violence, theft, and fraud."

ESTABLISHING A MORAL CONSENSUS

Clifford Christians's search for a "conceptually adequate notion of accountability" begins with the acceptance of professional codes of ethics *if* codes carry with them some provision for enforcement. For that Christians recognizes is what John Dewey recognized many years ago: "Liability is the beginning of responsibility." And the goal of liability, Dewey reminds us, is not to "correct" the past but to direct the future; its aim is not to punish individuals for past deeds but to foster among individuals a "voluntary deliberate acknowledgment that deeds are our own, that their consequences come from us": individuals are *held* accountable for what they *have* done, to paraphrase Dewey, so that they may be responsive in what they are *going* to do.[5]

Current codes are unenforceable in part because they are conceptually confused and structurally flawed. At the very least, Christians argues, codes need to distinguish between "blameworthy" conduct and "praiseworthy" conduct, and it needs to be understood that failing to act in a praiseworthy manner does not mean that the conduct in question is necessarily blameworthy. Once refurbished, codes of ethics can at a minimum bring to the "culture of discourse among media practitioners" what Christians regards as a necessary, though hardly sufficient, condition of accountability: a "language of responsibility, duty and obligation."

But in the final analysis Christians assigns to codes of ethics—even enforceable codes—only a "penultimate status." Codes of ethics tend to be written *by* professionals and *for* professionals, and thus accountability tends to be largely an in-house matter. What Christians prefers is a broader conception of accountability, one that involves not only professionals but the "strangers" professionals serve. What Christians wants, therefore, is public accountability of the kind sociologist Alvin Gouldner describes: "To be 'accountable' means that one can be *constrained* to reveal *what* one has done and *why* one has done it; thus the action and the reason for it are open to a critique by strangers who have few inhibitions about demanding justification and reasonable grounds."[6] This enlarged sense of accountability not only involves the public in ways inimical to Merrill's marketplace model but fundamentally redefines the concept of the "public interest."

From Christians's perspective, the public interest means something more than merely the sum of individual interests; that is, the *public's* interest may not always be a reasonable measure of the *public* interest. And democracy itself means something more than simply a democratic form of government; a laissez-faire attitude on the part of the state may not be enough to extend the principles of democracy beyond government and into the day-to-day lives of ordinary citizens. What Christians rejects, then, is the minimalist disposition of a Locke or a Nozick. More to the point, he rejects what Benjamin Barber calls "thin" democracies "whose democratic values are prudential and thus provisional, optional, and conditional—means to exclusively individualistic and private ends."[7]

What Christians endorses is something akin to Rousseau's "general will"—as opposed to Locke's "will of all"—and a conception of the public interest as something shared and therefore common. Rather than being driven by personal and idiosyncratic preferences and desires, Christians's understanding of the public interest derives from a broadly social consensus of what the community needs to sustain itself and to establish and maintain the liberty of its citizens; it is a consensus built on what individuals would want if they thought of themselves not as private, separate, and autonomous but as citizens with a shared interest in the welfare of their community. Thus, in its broadest terms, the question is not, as Locke might put it: "What sort of society would rational, asocial, and purely self-interested individuals agree to?" Rather, as Rousseau might put it, the question is this: "What form of association would socially interdependent individuals agree to if they were interested in protecting their person and goods in being free?"[8]

When Christians challenges the "conventional wisdom that a free press can abide no governance except that self-imposed," and when he criticizes the media for their "fixation with negative freedom," he is not calling for the diminution of individual freedom. Instead, what Christians envisions is a kind of "direct" democracy in which liberty for individuals can be realized only where there exists equality among individuals (Chapter 4). Accordingly, a free press is not an individual goal but a common interest, and any effort to achieve it requires an equal capacity among individuals to participate in both its establishment and in securing its survival.

Christians's qualified support for codes of ethics and his plea for more "foundational work" brings to mind Robert Veatch's theory of medical ethics. Like Christians, Veatch laments "ethical positivism run amok in professional conceit," which inevitably develops among professionals when their codes of ethics treat professional obligation as nothing more than what the profession says it is. Christians is likely to agree with Veatch that the possibility that professional ethics "can be founded on custom or self-imposed standards without reference to any higher authority so stretches the meaning of the term *ethics* that one wonders whether it has not been simply misused."[9] And Christians is unlikely to find fault with Veatch's corrective: a truly moral profession "has had both its code of ethics and its authority to adjudicate ethical disputes accepted by the broader society."[10]

To transform pacts of mutual self-interest into a common framework for judging the morality of conduct, Veatch proposes a "triple-contract" theory of professional ethics. The first and broadest of the contracts between the profession and the community establishes basic moral principles—the content of ethics. The second contract articulates role-specific duties for the profession and, when necessary, role-specific privileges. And the third contract delineates the particular terms of particular relationships between members of the profession and the members of the larger community with whom they interact. Taken together, the three contracts provide a common ground for questioning and ultimately resolving ethical disputes among professionals and between professionals and the lay public.

Although Christians, like Veatch, wants to tap the "reservoir of value theory and informed ethical inquiry," both would be quick to add that what makes normative claims legitimate is not their appeal to a transcendant or universal truth but their acceptance among those who agree to live with and by them. Ethics is social, Christians and Veatch would agree; ethical claims can be justified only as they are grounded in moral facts, where "facts" are taken to be social phenomena and where the community is taken to be their source of epistemic authority.[11] A normative social ethics of the kind Christians proposes deals with questions of media accountability not by providing a blueprint for conduct but by offering a meaningful opportunity for a sustained, coherent, and unemotional discussion about the media and their service to the community.

ASSESSING MEDIA PERFORMANCE

There are, obviously, differences of considerable consequence between a council of volunteers that examines press performance and a government commission that regulates the press. Alfred Balk is quite correct in calling our attention to the American predilection for voluntary associations; it is telling that "the most famous twentieth-century group to study the U.S. press"—the Hutchins Commission—was initiated and largely funded not by the state but by *Time* magazine's Henry Luce (Chapter 6). In Britain, too, Kenneth Morgan points out, there exists a strong "liberal and libertarian tradition that the contents of newspapers, while a proper subject of public concern, were an inappropriate one for determination by positive law"; if the idea for a national press council required "a nudge from Parliament" in the form of a recommendation in 1949 from the first Royal Commission on the Press, the council itself was nonetheless a voluntary, not a statutory, creation (Chapter 12). Part of what distinguishes voluntary councils from government commissions, then, is that only the former can fully honor the importance of a *lack* of relationship between the press and the state. Morgan puts it deftly, "The relationship between a country's press and its politicians should be distant and reserved rather than cosy; and critical even abrasive, on both sides rather than fawning or adulatory."

While American and British liberalism requires a formal separation between the newspapers and the state, a somewhat different political logic applies to electronic journalism. Because, historically, the marketplace for broadcasting has been viewed as less accessible and therefore less competitive than the marketplace for newspapers, magazines, and other print media, owning a television or a radio station has been regarded as more of a privilege than an entitlement. As Henry Geller explains in his chapter on broadcast regulation, because the "airwaves are not inherently open to all," which translates into an "indisputable scarcity of broadcast stations," the state cannot only license broadcasters but can condition their licenses on the fulfillment of certain fiduciary responsibilities (Chapter 8).

The fiduciary model of accountability outlined by Geller underscores the importance of broadcasters operating within a "short-term public trustee scheme," a system of rules and regulations that requires stations to be responsive to the needs of their viewers or listeners *beyond* what the marketplace might demand. Of course, to what extent broadcasters should or must disregard the marketplace is the difficult and enduring question, for it has never been clear what Congress and the courts intended as the proper relationship between broadcasting and the realities of free enterprise. The legislative history of the Communications Act of 1934 suggests that Congress did not want broadcasters to be constrained by federally imposed programming priorities. And the Supreme Court seemed to agree when in 1940 it ruled that broadcasters are not common carriers: "Congress intended to leave competition in the business of broadcasting where it found it, to permit a licensee... to survive or succumb according to his ability to make his programs attractive to the public."[12] At the same time, however, Congress expects licensees to be responsive to the "public interest, convenience, and necessity," and the judiciary has cautioned broadcasters about their "enforceable public obligations."[13]

Perhaps the most controversial aspect of the regulation of American broadcasting has been the fairness doctrine[14] and its associated access rights. While it is true, as Benno Schmidt concludes in his excellent study of media access, that there "is no evidence that First Amendment tradition has ever reflected the idea of access as a constitutional right,"[15] Geller is prepared to argue that access *opportunities* are a fiduciary obligation; his is not a First Amendment argument per se but rather an argument he believes is compatible with constitutional guarantees.

To avoid "a deep intrusion into daily broadcast journalism," Geller argues that the Federal Communications Commission (FCC) should forego judging access or fairness claims on an issue-by-issue basis and instead judge whether, overall, "the licensee has acted consistently with its public trustee obligations." It is at the time of license renewal, Geller suggests, that the FCC can reasonably and appropriately judge a station's commitment to access and fairness. And to this he would add the burden of the standard of liability that has developed in libel law: a station could be found in violation of its public obligations only with a showing of bad faith—a "pattern of acting in reckless disregard" of access and fairness.

Press councils, in contrast, seldom deal with press performance "overall"; rather than assessing patterns of conduct, they ordinarily focus on the most egregious abuses of professional norms. Designed to treat issues of "social responsibility" reactively as opposed to proactively, press councils are typically called into action in response to—not in anticipation of—a breach of ethics. To take an extreme example, at the Minnesota News Council, which is the only remaining body of its kind in the 48 contiguous states, the council's members cannot themselves initiate a complaint against the press; their agenda is set entirely by the "acceptable" complaints brought to them by outsiders.

Part of the reason for a press council's reactive posture is its reluctance to act in ways the press might construe as contrary to the needs of an independent press. "All press councils," Claude-Jean Bertrand observes in his review of 32 press councils that have appeared around the world since World War II, "aim at preserving press freedom against direct and indirect threats of government intrusion. They all strive to help the press assume its social responsibility and thus obtain the support of public opinion in its fight for independence." Unlike the FCC, which struggles to define the "public interest, convenience, and necessity" even at the risk of contravening marketplace forces, press councils are generally unable to articulate a conception of the public interest that would call into question the media's freedom to compete in the marketplace; press councils, Bertrand concludes, are ill-equipped to "deal seriously with the economic threat to press freedom."[16]

That press councils provide a forum for complaints against the press and simultaneously claim to be defenders of press freedom is an irony not lost on media practitioners who understand press freedom to mean the absence of *any* coercion—no matter how benign or well-intentioned. Thus even if its stated objectives appear in decidedly pro-press terms, a press council cannot always count on the support and voluntary cooperation of the press itself. And without that support and cooperation, as the National News Council learned, there is little left to the legitimacy of a press council.

There are, then, differences of some substance between a voluntary association (e.g., a press council) whose aim is to hear complaints against the media and a state agency (e.g., the FCC) whose objective is to monitor the media in their effort to meet their fiduciary obligations. But there are similarities as well, not the least of which is a shared commitment to the viability of an essentially bureaucratic resolution of questions of media accountability: both models honor the importance of presumably detached, impartial, and independent panels whose members can fairly assess press performance.

If press councils are more inclined to deal with microlevel questions of media accountability, and if government commissions often move more in the direction of macrolevel questions, both operate on the assumption that the "natural" laws of the marketplace—even when those laws receive "artificial" support from legislators and jurists—cannot always and adequately deal with issues of media accountability. And although both models involve the public in their proceedings, neither voluntary associations nor state agencies extend to the public any meaningful opportunity for direct participation in their formulation of, and deliberations on, basic questions of philosophy and policy.

NOTES

1. For a worthwhile discussion of the MacBride report and its implications for American mass communication, see the symposium, "The Press, the U.S. and UNESCO," *Journal of Communication,* 31 (Autumn 1981): 102–187.

2. David Held, *Models of Democracy,* Stanford, Calif.: Stanford University Press, 1987, p. 41.

3. See, for example, Mark S. Fowler and Daniel L. Brenner, "A Marketplace Approach to Broadcast Regulation," *Texas Law Review,* 60 (Feb. 1982): 1–51. See also Edwin Diamond, Norman Sandler, and Milton Mueller, *Telecommunication in Crisis: The First Amendment, Technology, and Deregulation,* Washington, D.C.: Cato Institute, 1983.

4. Robert Nozick, *Anarchy, State, and Utopia,* New York: Basic Books, 1974, p. 238.

5. John Dewey, *Human Nature and Conduct,* New York: Modern Library, 1930, p. 315.

6. Alvin W. Gouldner, *The Dialectic of Ideology and Technology,* New York: Seabury Press, 1976, p. 102.

7. Benjamin Barber, *Strong Democracy,* Berkeley, Calif.: University of California Press, 1984, p. 4.

8. Joshua Cohen, "Reflections on Rousseau: Autonomy and Democracy," *Philosophy & Public Affairs,* 15 (Summer 1986): 284. See also Robert A. Nisbet, *The Quest for Community,* New York: Oxford University Press, 1953, pp. 140–175.

9. Robert M. Veatch, *A Theory of Medical Ethics,* New York: Basic Books, 1981, p. 92–94.

10. Ibid., p. 83.

11. For an extended discussion of knowledge—including ethical knowledge—as a human artifact wedded to the historical and cultural values of its community, see Richard Rorty, *Philosophy and the Mirror of Nature,* Princeton, N.J.: Princeton University Press, 1979.

12. *FCC v. Sanders Brothers Radio Station,* 309 U.S. 470,475 (1940).

13. *Office of Communication of United Church of Christ v. FCC* 359 F2d 994, 1003 (DC Cir., 1966).

14. Soon after Geller prepared his chapter, the FCC formally abandoned the fairness doctrine. However, the access questions dealt with by the doctrine are as much an issue today as they were before the doctrine's demise.

15. Benno C. Schmidt, Jr., *Freedom of the Press Vs. Public Access,* New York: Praeger, 1976, p. 240.

16. Claude-Jean Bertrand, "Press Councils around the World: Unraveling a Definitional Dilemma," *Journalism Quarterly,* 55 (Summer 1978): 241, 250.

Conclusion

Everette E. Dennis

In 1984 when the National News Council died, the prospects for media accountability in America seemed gloomy indeed. Critics complained that the media establishment, notably *The New York Times,* had killed the council and that thin-skinned journalists and broadcasters were not about to encourage any organized system of feedback. About the same time, public opinion polls were being interpreted by the same media leaders as a bad report card on confidence in the media. Thus the question, if not a press council, what? Some critics argued that libel suits might be the only effective way for people to talk back to the media, especially in a pro-business era marked by deregulation and a form of laissez-faire economics that was hostile to consumerism in all forms.

But the mass media are different than other businesses. To survive, they must, of course, be commercially successful, but they are also expected to defend the public interest. They are thus both profit-making enterprises and quasi-public interest organizations. How these priorities are sorted out depends on the owners of the media and their employees. Some have put money first. Henry Luce, for example, has been paraphrased as saying, "first the nickel, then the news." Other speak first of the free flow of information and freedom of expression and second of the necessity of advertising and other revenue producing activities.

In spite of riveting changes that have profoundly affected the news media in recent years, there is cause for cautious optimism when it comes to the glacial development of means to talking back. When we return to the models of media accountability introduced earlier in this book, the inventory is not unsatisfying for anyone who cares about an effective and responsive media system.

THE MARKETPLACE MODEL

Looking carefully at the marketplace, one can be optimistic. Far from being arrogant and uncaring, media organizations are engaging in considerable research, some of it for marketing purposes, some of it to take the temperature of public attitudes. Media people know more about their audiences than ever before and if they are smart, they will try to serve (and please) those audiences. They are doing so not by pandering to the lowest common denominator or the basest instinct, but by providing lively packages of news and information both in print and broadcasting that can, at the same time, survive in the market. There is more to the marketplace model than simple profit and loss statements. For example, media research (both that conducted by the industry and that carried out by universities), citizen organizations, and others will have a beneficial effect.

While much media research is quite self-serving, aimed at getting more readers or viewers for a given industry, network, or news organization, not all of it is. One example of exemplary "marketplace" research that has real benefit to the public is the Times Mirror organization's continuing series of studies that probe the public about their attitudes toward the media and their content. These are serious studies, conducted with scientific precision. Their results are available in reports and, more importantly, in ads placed in newspapers and magazines.

THE VOLUNTARY MODEL

To date most of the more visible voluntary efforts have failed. The press council died, having had little effect. And except for a few isolated instances, other such efforts have had little impact. Fair trial-free press committees, once healthy and strong, are flaccid now, due in part to the erosion of their voluntary efforts by the courts. A few of the action committees looking at media violence, children's television and other topics, continue to work quietly and with some effect. More ideological media critics and those representing special interests ranging from business to the arts also exist and are noticed.

Each year there are scores of national, regional and state conferences on media issues and problems, many of them made available on C-Span and in other forms. They range from sessions on coverage of elections to the role of victims of crime vis-à-vis the media. People interested in informing themselves about media issues are thus benefited, and many people who want to be personally involved in "feedback" participate in such sessions.

SELF-REGULATION MODEL

Self-regulation in broadcasting has fallen victim to deregulation, and some forms of self-regulation in the print media, for example, codes of ethics, have been strongly discouraged by lawyers who are fearful that such documentation will come back to haunt the media in the courtroom. Still, there is some cause for optimism. CBS commissioned a famed study, "The Benjamin Report," which stands as a model of what internal self-policing can do. Thirty or so newspapers have ombudsmen who work to help the public make their case and provide a lively feedback mechanism (this out of 1,750 newspapers) and there have been other efforts ranging from community coffee klatches to Philip Meyer's elegant proposal for an ethical audit, involving both the community and the news organization.

THE FIDUCIARY MODEL

Regulation was on hold during most of the 1980s. Broadcasters and cable operators were freed from many of the restrictions that keep them in line with a public interest standard. The FCC chairman during most of that period, Mark Fowler, openly said marketplace forces should supersede regulation. Rules affecting ownership, resale of broadcast properties, content control, advertising, and many others were virtually wiped off the books. There are many critics who doubt that this was good for the public and others who say that regulation will return one day, but those prospects were not likely at the end of the 1980s. State cable commissions and public utility commissions also provided few examples of good practice for cable operators. The fairness doctrine in broadcasting was similarly being challenged in an era of communication abundance. Regulation, of course, was based on a theory of scarcity and with scarcity no longer an issue, the role of regulation was severely restricted.

At the dawn of the Bush administration, the future of communication policy is naturally unclear. Some people, including several influential members of Congress, have urged a pullback from the laissez-faire approach of deregulation, while others urge an extension. One great test may come in the way that the FCC handles the HDTV (high definition television) issue, which involves a number of actors, with few speaking up for "the public interest."

THE JUDICIAL MODEL

Litigation continues to be one of the liveliest feedback mechanisms. Although it is an expensive and punitive way to critique the media, for many media plaintiffs it seemed the only effective means of capturing the attention of the media owners and managers. Libel suits abound, and communication law, covering topics ranging from privacy and copyright to advertising, was becoming a complex new field. No one, except perhaps a few lawyers, cheers these developments and there are many lessons for media people and the public in the flood of litigation. If nothing else, the high cost of libel should persuade many that means other than litigation are desirable ways to have a more accountable media.

Out of the extensive discussion of the libel dilemma in recent years have come a number of conferences, books, and proposals for reform. By late 1988, reports indicate that litigation involving the media is down, possibly temporarily, so the impetus for reform may be diminished. Nonetheless, the Washington Annenberg Program has drafted a proposal for libel reform that will no doubt engage lawyers, judges, media people, educators, and the public. It may be the first of many that will lead to change. Importantly, relaxing the libel laws can only be accomplished if there is evidence that other channels for accountability are open.

INTERNATIONAL CONSIDERATIONS

What, if anything, can we learn from the experience of people in other countries, other societies, who are also concerned about media freedom and accountability? Quite a good deal, I believe. The British Press Council still remains the best example in the world of accountability in action. It would likely not work in America, but inherent in its lessons is a common law of media ethics wherein the values expressed are not so distant from our own. Some of the means of accountability in other countries are essentially negative, such as press councils aimed at control and censorship. Always we are reminded of the genius of the First Amendment and of the special character of our media and our society.

Thus, the models presented here and the blood and guts of the activity that lives under their banners present a mixed picture of the relationship between the media and the public. It is, on balance, I believe, a slightly positive picture, but one that must be monitored and assessed regularly.

In a society where talk of "accountability" rankles those who style themselves First Amendment absolutists, the best answer for members of the public seeking redress of grievances against the media may come with the power of publicity. Media criticism whether practiced by writing elegant essays or by picketing a news organization does get attention. Few industries are as sensitive to criticism as the media, both institutionally and individually in terms of the reactions of editors, reporters, and broadcasters. These typically thin-skinned professionals do respond to criticism, sometimes defensively, but increasingly in a fashion where dispute-resolution can occur. Media people who understand that the value of the information they impart is tied to credibility don't really want to impair their relationship to the public.

If anything, though, this book and the essays contained herein ought to stimulate thinking among informed critics of the media as well as practitioners. All of us need to think more deeply about maximizing freedom of expression while allowing for feedback and response, however serious or trivial it may be.

BIBLIOGRAPHY

Abel, Elie, ed. *What's News: The Media in American Society.* San Francisco: Institute for Contemporary Studies, 1981.

Altheide, David L. *Creating Reality: How TV News Distorts Events.* Beverly Hill: Sage, 1976.

Altheide, David L. and Robert P. Snow. *Media Logic.* Beverly Hills: Sage, 1979.

Altheide, David L. *Media Power.* Beverly Hills: Sage, 1985.

Altschull, J. Herbert. *Agents of Power: The Role of the News Media in Human Affairs.* New York: Longman, 1984.

American Society of Newspaper Editors. *Newspaper Credibility: Building Reader Trust.* Washington, D.C.: American Society of Newspaper Editors, 1985.

Arno, Andrew and Wimal Dissanayake. *News Media in National and International Conflict.* Boulder: Westview Press, 1984.

Arterton, F. Christopher. *Media Politics: The News Strategies of Presidential Campaigns.* Lexington, Mass.: Lexington Books; D.C. Heath, 1984.

Bagdikian, Ben H. *Media Monopoly.* Boston: Beacon Press, 1983.

Ball-Rokeach, Sandra J., Milton Rokeach, and Joel W. Grube. *The Great American Values Test: Influencing Behavior and Belief through Television.* New York: Free Press, 1984.

Bennett, W. Lance. *News: The Politics of Illusion.* New York: Longman, 1983.

Berger, Arthur Asa. *Media Analysis Techniques.* Beverly Hills: Sage, 1982.

Bernstein, Carl and Bob Woodward. *All the President's Men.* New York: Warner Books, 1974.

Bogart, Leo. *Press and Public: Who Reads What, When, Where, and Why in American Newspapers.* Hillsdale, N.J.: Lawrence Erlbaum Associates, 1981.

Braley, Russ. *Bad News: The Foreign Policy of The New York Times.* Chicago: Regnery Gateway, 1984.

Brogan, Patrick. *Spiked: The Short Life and Death of the National News Council.* New York: Priority Press Publications, 1985.

Chamberlin, Bill F. and Charlene J. Brown. *First Amendment Reconsidered: New Perspectives on the Meaning of Freedom of Speech and Press.* New York: Longman, 1982.

Christians, Clifford G., Kim B. Rotzoll, and Mark Fackler. *Media Ethics: Cases and Moral Reasoning.* New York: Longman, 1987.

Collins, Richard, James Curran, Nicholas Garnham, Paddy Scannell, Philip Schlesinger, and Colin Sparks. *Media, Culture and Society: A Critical Reader.* London: Sage, 1986.

Dennis, Everette E. and John C. Merrill. *Basic Issues in Mass Communication: A Debate.* New York: Macmillan, 1984.

Elliott, Deni, ed. *Responsible Journalism.* Beverly Hills: Sage, 1986.

Gitlin, Todd. *The Whole World Is Watching: Mass Media in the Making and Unmaking of the New Left.* Berkeley: University of California Press, 1980.

Gitlin, Todd, ed. *Watching Television: A Pantheon Guide to Popular Culture.* New York: Pantheon Books, 1987.

Goldstein, Tom. *The News at Any Cost: How Journalists Compromise Their Ethics to Shape the News.* New York: Simon & Schuster, 1985.

Graber, Doris A. *Mass Media and American Politics.* Washington, D.C.: CQ Press, 1984.

Greenfield, Jeff. *The Real Campaign: How the Media Missed the Story of the 1980 Campaign.* New York: Summit Books, 1982.

Hallin, Daniel C. *The Uncensored War: The Media and Vietnam.* New York: Oxford University Press, 1986.

Hamilton, John Maxwell. *Main Street America and the Third World.* Cabin John, Md.: Seven Locks Press, 1986.

Hess, Stephen. *Government/Press Connection: Press Officers and Their Offices.* Washington, D.C.: Brookings Institution, 1984.

Hess, Stephen. *The Ultimate Insiders: U.S. Senators in the National Media.* Washington, D.C.: Brookings Institution, 1986.

Hulteng, John L. *Messenger's Motives: Ethical Problems of the News Media.* Englewood Cliffs, N.J.: Prentice Hall, 1985.

Isaacs, Norman E. *Untended Gates: The Mismanaged Press.* New York: Columbia University Press, 1986.

Kessler, Lauren and Duncan McDonald. *Uncovering the News: A Journalist's Search for Information.* Belmont, Calif.: Wadsworth, 1987.

Lambeth, Edmund B. *Committed Journalism: An Ethic for the Profession.* Bloomington: Indiana University Press, 1986.

Lashner, Marilyn A. *The Chilling Effect in TV News: Intimidation by the Nixon White House.* New York: Praeger, 1984.

Leonard, Thomas C. *The Power of the Press: The Birth of American Political Reporting.* New York: Oxford University Press, 1986.

Liebling, A. J. *The Press.* New York: Ballantine Books, 1961.

Linsky, Martin, Jonathon Moore, Wendy O'Donnell, and David Whitman. *How the Press Affects Federal Policymaking: Six Case Studies.* New York: W. W. Norton, 1986.

Lippmann, Walter. *Public Opinion.* New York: Free Press, 1965.

Lofton, John. *Justice and the Press.* Boston: Beacon Press, 1966.

Mayer, Martin. *Making News.* Garden City, N.Y.: Doubleday, 1987.

Merrill, John C. *The Imperative of Freedom: A Philosophy of Journalistic Autonomy.* New York: Hastings House, 1974.

Merrill, John C. and Ralph D. Barney. *Ethics and the Press: Readings in Mass Media Morality.* New York: Hastings House, 1975.

Merrill, John C. and S. Jack Odell. *Philosophy and Journalism.* New York: Longman, 1983.

Meyer, Philip. *Ethical Journalism: A Guide for Students, Practitioners and Consumers.* New York: Longman, 1987.

Nimmo, Dan and James E. Combs. *Nightly Horrors: Crisis Coverage by Television Network News.* Knoxville: University of Tennessee Press, 1985.

Parenti, Michael. *Inventing Reality: The Politics of the Mass Media.* New York: St. Martin's Press, 1986.

Rivers, William L. *The Adversaries: Politics and the Press.* Boston: Beacon Press, 1970.

Roshco, Bernard. *Newsmaking.* Chicago: University of Chicago Press, 1975.

Rowan, Ford. *Broadcast Fairness: Doctrine, Practice, Prospects: A Reappraisal of the Fairness Doctrine and Equal Time Rule.* New York: Longman, 1984.

Rubin, Bernard. *Questioning Media Ethics.* New York: Praeger, 1978.

Schiller, Dan. *Objectivity and the News: The Public and the Rise of Commercial Journalism.* Philadelphia: University of Pennsylvania Press, 1981.

Schmuhl, Robert, *Responsibilities of Journalism.* Notre Dame, Ind.: University of Notre Dame Press, 1984.

Schudson, Michael. *Discovering the News: A Social History of American Newspapers.* New York: Basic Books, 1978.

Smolla, Rodney A. *Suing the Press.* New York: Oxford University Press, 1986.

Tuchman, Gaye. *Making News: A Study in the Construction of Reality.* New York: Free Press, 1978.

Weaver, David H. and G. Cleveland Wilhoit. *American Journalist: A Portrait of U.S. News People and Their Work.* Bloomington: Indiana University Press, 1986.

INDEX

About the Editors and Contributors

DAVID A. ANDERSON is Rosenberg Centennial Professor of Law at the University of Texas at Austin. Past positions include Chief Counsel at the Texas Judicial Council (1972) and UPI bureau chief in Austin, Texas (1967–68). He has co-authored two books on the Texas Constitution and contributed numerous articles on libel law in such journals as *The Columbia Journalism Review* and *Trial Magazine*. Mr. Anderson is a former Senior Fellow at the Gannett Center for Media Studies.

ALFRED BALK is Editorial Consultant for the *World Press Review* where he has served in various editorial capacities since 1975. He served as editor of *The Columbia Journalism Review* (1969–73) and his books include *A Free and Responsive Press* and *The Free List*. Mr. Balk was a member of the executive council of the American Society of Magazine Editors (1977–83). He is currently a member of the Society of Professional Journalists/Sigma Delta Chi.

CLIFFORD CHRISTIANS, Ph.D., is a Research Professor of Communications at the University of Illinois-Urbana, where he is Director of the Institute of Communications Research and Head of the doctoral program in Communications. He has been a visiting scholar in Philosophical Ethics at Princeton and in Social Ethics at the University of Chicago. He is the author (with Kim Rotzoll and Mark Fackler) of *Media Ethics: Cases and Moral Reasoning* (1987).

RICHARD P. CUNNINGHAM was associate director of the National News Council from 1981 to 1984. Before going to the news council he was the first Reader's Representative, or ombudsman, at the *Minneapolis Tribune*. He was a newspaper journalist in Connecticut, Colorado, and Minnesota. Since the news council closed down in 1964 he has taught press ethics at New York University.

EVERETTE E. DENNIS is Executive Director of the Gannett Center for Media Studies at Columbia University and Editor-in-Chief of the *Gannett Center Journal*. He is author or editor of more than a dozen books including *The Cost of Libel, Reshaping the Media, Understanding Mass Communication*, and the *First Amendment*. He has also written more than 80 articles in professional journals, law reviews, and industry publications and is frequently quoted in the popular media about communication issues.

JOHN R. FINNEGAN is immediate past Senior Vice President and Assistant Publisher at the *St. Paul Pioneer Press and Dispatch* where he served in various capacities since 1951. He is the recipient of numerous awards, including the Award of Merit from the Minnesota Society of Professional Journalists/Sigma Delta Chi, for distinguished services in 1975 and again in 1985.

HENRY GELLER is currently the Director of Duke University's Washington Center for Public Policy Research. Mr. Geller served as Assistant Secretary for Communications and Information and Administrator in the U.S. Department of Commerce (1978–81). He was appointed Communications Fellow at the Aspen Institute Program on Communications and Society for 1975–77. Most of Mr. Geller's early career was spent at the Federal Communications Commission where he served as General Counsel (1964–70).

DONALD M. GILLMOR is Professor of journalism and mass communication and Director, Silha Center for the Study of Media Ethics and Law at the University of Minnesota, Minneapolis. He wrote or edited *Free Press and Trial, Mass Communication Law, Enduring Issues in Mass Communication* and *Justice Hugo Black and the First Amendment*. Gillmor has also written numerous book chapters and articles published in *Journalism Quarterly, Journal of Media Law and Practice, Media Information Australia, Current History,* and law reviews.

THEODORE L. GLASSER is an Associate Professor of journalism and mass communication and Associate Director of the Silha Center for the Study of Media Ethics and Law at the University of Minnesota. His articles have appeared in a variety of academic and professional publications, including *Journalism Quarterly, Journal of Broadcasting & Electronic*

Media, Journal of Communication, Critical Studies in Mass Communication, Communications and the Law, Policy Sciences, Nieman Reports, and *The Quill.*

WILLIAM A. HENRY III has been associate editor at *Time* since 1981. He has written for *Time* as press critic (1982–85) and continues to write as theater critic. The winner of two Pulitzer Prices (one as drama judge in 1986–87, the other in 1980 for criticism), Mr. Henry has lectured at several universities including Harvard and MIT. His numerous publications include *Visions of America* (1985).

JOHN KAMP is director of the office of Public Affairs at the Federal Communications Commission in Washington, D.C., where he serves as the FCC's chief spokesman. He represents the Commission in numerous contexts, including speeches and panels at industry, intergovernment and academic functions, and has testified before Congress. Before joining the FCC in 1980, Kamp was on the faculty at the University of Tulsa.

LEWIS LAPHAM is Editor-in-Chief at *Harper's Magazine* where he has also served as editor (1975–81) and managing editor (1971–75). Mr. Lapham has written for *Life, Harper's Magazine* and the *Saturday Evening Post,* where he also served as editor (1963–67). The author of *Fortune's Child* (1980), Mr. Lapham is a member of the Council on Foreign Relations.

JOHN C. MERRILL is Professor at Louisiana State University's School of Journalism. He served as Director of LSU's School of Journalism from 1980–1983. The author of numerous books (*Global Journalism, Philosophy and Journalism,* among others), he recently co-authored *Basic Issues in Mass Communications* with Everette E. Dennis. Mr. Merrill has also been a reporter, columnist, feature and editorial writer for the Greenville (Miss.) *Delta Democrat Times,* Natchitoches (La.) *Times,* Shreveport (La.) *Times,* and the Bryan (Tx.) *Eagle.*

KENNETH MORGAN is Director of the British Press Council where he has served in various capacities since 1970, including Deputy Director and Conciliator. He has been on the executive committees of several organizations, among them the International Federation of Journalists (1970–78). Mr. Morgan is a trustee of Reuters as well as a member of the CRE Media Group and the C. of E. Press Panel. His book, *Press Conduct in the Sutcliffe Case,* appeared in 1983.

A. H. RASKIN served as Associate Director of the National News Council from 1978–1984. He was a member of *The New York Times* staff from 1931–1977 where he was labor columnist (1976–77) and assistant editor of the editorial page (1964–76). Mr. Raskin has held teaching positions at several universities, including Columbia University's Graduate School of Business and Stanford University, and has co-authored *A Life with Labor* (1977). The recipient of many awards, Mr. Raskin was awarded the George Polk Memorial award twice (1953, 1964).